D0680816

MURDER ON FILE

the world's
most notorious killers

Richard and Molly Whittington-Egan

Neil Wilson Publishing Ltd.
Glasgow
www.nwp.co.uk

Neil Wilson Publishing Ltd
303 The Pentagon Centre
36 Washington Street
GLASGOW
G3 8AZ

Tel: 0141-221-1117
Fax: 0141-221-5363
E-mail: info@nwp.co.uk
www.nwp.co.uk

A catalogue record for this book is available from the British Library.

ISBN 1-903238-91-9
Typeset in Enigma
Printed and bound in Poland

Contents

Celebrity killers ix
Acknowledgements xii

Adams, Dr John Bodkin 1
Allitt, Beverley 3
Armstrong, Major Herbert Rowse 5

Bamber, Jeremy 6
Barber, Susan 8
Barfield, Velma 10
Bartlett, Adelaide 11
Berdella, Robert 12
Berkowitz, David 13
Bianchi, Kenneth & Buono, Angelo 14
Bible John 15
Bishop, Russell 17
Bittaker, Lawrence 19
Black Dahlia Murder 20
Black, Robert 21
Bogle-Chandler Murders 24
Borden, Lizzie 25
Bradfield, William & Smith, Dr Jay 26
Brady, Ian & Hindley, Myra 27
Bravo Mystery 29
Brudos, Jerome Henry 30
Bundy, Ted 31
Burke, William & Hare, William 32
Bywaters, Frederick & Thompson, Edith 33

Camb, James 34
Cannan, John 35
Carraher, Patrick 37
Chamberlain, Lindy 38
Chantrelle, Eugène Marie 39
Chapman, George 40
Charlton, Alan & Ali, Idris 41
Chikatilo, Andrei 43
Christie, John Reginald Halliday 45
Clark, Douglas 46
Cleveland Butcher 47
Copolino, Dr Carl 48
Corll, Dean 49
Corona, Juan 50
Cottingham, Richard 51
Cotton, Mary Ann 52
Cream, Dr Thomas Neill 53
Crippen, Dr Hawley Harvey 54

Dahmer, Jeffrey 55
DeSalvo, Albert 58
de Stempel, Baroness Susan 59
Donald, Jeannie 62
Dougal, Samuel Herbert 63
Downs, Diane 64
Duffy, John 65
Durrant, Theodore 67

Ellis, Ruth 68

Fahmy, Marie Marguerite 69
Fish, Albert 70
Flynn, Billy 71
Fox, Sidney 73
Fullam, Augusta & Clark, Henry 74

Gacy, John Wayne 75
Gallego, Gerald Armond 76
Gardiner, William 77
Gein, Theodore 78
George, Andrew 79
George, Barry 81
Glatman, Harvey 84
Glover, John 85

Haigh, John George 89
Hall, Archibald 90
Hanratty, James 91
Heath, Neville 92
Heidnik, Gary 93
Homan, Elbert 94
Hume, Donald 95
Huntley, Ian 96

Ireland, Colin 99

Jack the Ripper 102
Jack the Stripper 103
Jascalevich, Dr Mario 104
Jones, Arthur Albert 105

Kearney, Patrick 107
Kemper, Edmund 108
Kent, Constance 109
Kray, Ronald and Reginald 110
Kürten, Peter 112

Lake, Leonard & Ng, Charles	113
Lashley, David	114
Laurie, John	116
Lee, Jean	117
Light, Ronald	120
Long, Bobby Joe	121
Lucan, Lord	122
Lucas, Henry Lee	124
Lupo, Michele de Marco	125
MacDonald, Dr Jeffrey	127
Mackay, Patrick	128
Manson, Charles	129
Manuel, Peter	130
Maybrick, Florence Elizabeth	131
Merret, John Donald	132
Merrifield, Louisa	133
Milat, Ivan	134
M'Lachlan, Jessie	137
Morris, Raymond	138
Mudgett, Herman Webster	140
Mullin, Herbert William	141
Neilson, Donald	142
Nelson, Earle	143
Nilsen, Dennis	145
Pacciani, Pietro	146
Pageant Beauty Queen Murderer	149
Papin, Christine & Léa	152
Park, Gordon	153
Pitchfork, Colin	155
Pommerencke, Heinrich	157
Pritchard, Dr Edward William	160
Puente, Dorothea	161

Ramirez, Richard	164
Ridgway, Gary	165
Rifkin, Joel	168
Ruxton, Dr Buck	170
Sams, Michael	171
Schmid, Charles Howard	173
Shawcross, Arthur	174
Sheppard, Dr Samuel	177
Shipman, Dr Harold	178
Slater, Oscar	181
Smethurst, Dr Thomas	182
Smith, George Joseph	183
Smith, Madeleine	184
Speck, Richard	185
Starkweather, Charles & Fugate, Caril	186
Sutcliffe, Peter	187
Tanner, John	189
Thomas, Arthur	191
Wallace, William Herbert	193
Webster, Kate	194
West, Frederick & Rosemary	195
Wigginton, Tracey	197
Wilder, Christoper Bernard	199
Wimbledon Common Stabbing	200
Williams, Wayne	204
Woodfield, Randall	205
Wuornos, Aileen	206
Young, Graham	208
Index	209

Celebrity Killers

The concept of evil – long devalued, derided, and dismissed by psychiatrists and psychologists – seems to have undergone a measure of re-evaluation. The prolonged contemplation of certain varieties of serial killers and mass murderers has given pause to easy moral dismissal.

Dr Michael Welner, a forensic psychiatrist and professor at New York University, has observed that: 'People say evil is like pornography: they know it when they see it, but can debate whether or when it is harmful.' This, he maintains, 'is not true. We are finding widespread agreement about what is evil.'

The old order of murder has changed. The cosy domestic poisonings of Victorian and Edwardian England, the almost jaunty blood-letting with knife, gun, and blunt instrument, the tidier ligatures with rope, cord, and thin-biting wire, all these purposive acts, motivated by comprehensible, if not excusable, human passions of love and malice, greed and gain, profit and loss, have been overshadowed. Today, we have the gang wars, the drug-borne slaughtering, and the reigns of the terrifying silencers of the lambs, the random repeat killers, slaying total strangers for the sheer recreational love of killing. They are the Serial Killers.

The name was coined, so the story goes, in the 1970s, by FBI agent Robert K. Ressler, for the engagingly homely reason that such multiple murderers, killing in series as they do, brought back to him memories of the cliff-hanger film serials that he watched at the Saturday morning cinema in his home-town as a child.

But what exactly is a serial killer? How does he differ from a mass murderer? Is it simply a matter of semantics? Both, surely, are simply multicides? The determining diagnostic feature has to be the psychological motivation of the killer. The mass murderer kills numbers of people for any one, or any combination of, the classic motives – gain, revenge, elimination, jealousy, conviction, which is to say killing for an idea or ideal. The serial killer kills primarily for a compulsive sexual reason – often a

repulsive one – *Lustmord* – or out of pure love and lust for killing *per se*; although, of course, just to make things more complicated, incidental benefits might, accidentally as it were, accrue to be taken advantage of.

The serial killer is by no means a new, essentially 'modern' species of homicidal monster. It is just that, like the dinosaurs in Jurassic times, he has increased and multiplied to crescendo proportions since the 1980s. Serial murder is a growth industry. The up-and-coming thing. Years of rapt experimentation and innovation lie ahead.

The serial killer concept may be transatlantic, but one of the pioneer exponents of the mode was British – Jack the Ripper, back in 1888. Other home-bred produce includes Christie the Notting Hill Necrophile, Brady and Hindley the Moorland Infanticides, Peter Sutcliffe the Hammerman of the Yorkshire Ridings, and Dennis Nilsen the Cricklewood Scourge of the Gay. Undeniably though, it is America that has yielded the richest, thickest, and most variegated crop. Against this, however, must be weighed in the balance the fact that the most sophisticated, high-tech, state-of-the-art serial killer tracking down techniques are also American.

The foundation, in-depth, behavioural analysis study of the serial killer phenomenon was undertaken by a crack team of FBI specialists, the Behavioural Science Unit (BSU), at the FBI Academy, which stands, stoutly fenced and defended of access, in 600 acres of woodland at Quantico, in Virginia. It was the Quantico behaviourists who put together the typical profile of the serial killer. Most are solitary males, although some hunt in pairs – Bianchi and Buono, Lake and Ng; even mixed sex pairs, Brady and Hindley, Gallego and wife. Around ten per cent are doctors, dentists, or professional health workers of one sort or another. Almost a third turn out to have been mental patients or ex-convicts. They come from all walks of life and are frequently the products of broken, or severely brutal homes, where they have themselves been subjected to gross cruelty, sexual abuse, and in some cases prolonged and systematic torture, in deprived childhood. Quite often they have at some time in their lives sustained head injuries. Characteristically displayed early presignatory symptoms include bed-wetting (after the age of twelve), cruelty to animals, and mischievous fire-raising. They routinely graduate to thievery. Later, fear and distrust of women may be manifest. Part of the pattern, too, is alcohol, and, ever-increasingly nowadays, drugs, plus pornography, as buttresses for the serial killer's high dominance requirements, and short-cut escape routes into comfortable realms of fantasy. Serial killings are usually intraracial.

Returning to the scene of the crime is a not uncommon behavioural feature: sometimes for the practical purposes of necrophilia, or perhaps just to masturbate over the corpse. The clues left behind are little more than semen stains and pubic hairs. In some cases, though, semen has been recovered from the victim's vagina or rectum. Interestingly in this context, the British serial killer, John Francis Duffy, the Railway Rapist, whose sexual assaults escalated to murder in 1985-6, having perhaps heard of the then recent forensic advance afforded by DNA, or possibly aware that blood group identification could be made from sperm, stuffed burning paper handkerchief tissues into his victim's genitals in order to destroy sperm traces.

A development of the BSU was the National Center for the Analysis of Violent Crime (NCAVC), set up in 1984, in a huge, windowless, concrete bunker 60 feet below the Academy. America is so vast, not to say complex, with some 16,855 separate police, sheriff, and law enforcement agencies, that the transient, itinerant, or journeyman murderer poses a desperately difficult hunting prospect. A serial killer trolling for prey can cross any number of state lines and commit his crimes in any number of different jurisdictions, between which there may well be no communication, or, worse, the deliberate silence of jealous territorialism. Thus, the co-ordinating of geographically, and geopolitically, spread data is the vital function contribution by the NCAVC, where every murder committed in the United States is registered and analysed on computer, and whose central data pool is available to all law enforcement bodies. It is at once a clearing-house and a resource centre in the national fight against the menace of the footloose violent criminal, the spree slayer.

In the course of the last decade, major scientific advances have become available to help very materially in what used to be the near-hopeless search for the peripatetic serial killer. Blood grouping was one aid; the theory of 'interchange' patterns could be rewarding; DNA fingerprinting was the most dynamically positive discovery of all, and its techniques have steadily improved, and become more refined. Applied to 'cold cases', whose evidence has been preserved, as for example those of Hanratty, Colin Pitchfork, and Andrew George, convicted of the Hilda Murrell murder twenty-one years after the event, the results have been startling.

Meanwhile, the discussion about the nature of serial killing goes on. Professor Michael Stone, professor of psychiatry at Columbia University, has looked at a broad sampling of 500 British and American serial killers, and has found that while some were indubitable victims of mental illness, no such comfortable explanation could account for the aberrant behaviour in the cases of apparently perfectly sane individuals who had simply decided that they would enjoy killing. They had made a rational choice to enact their fantasies purely for pleasure. A determination of this kind, says Stone, defies psychiatric explication. 'Such people make a rational choice to commit terrible crimes over and over again. They are evil and we should be able to say that formally.' In this category he would include Ian Brady, John Wayne Gacy, Ted Bundy, Jeffrey Dahmer, and Frederick West.

Many of the cases which we describe in this book illustrate the fact that a large number of serial killers have characteristics in common, such as being a loner, experiencing difficulty with relationships, showing no remorse, only arrogance, and being possessed of an addiction to killing, which is repeated unless checked by outside intervention. When there is skill at blending in and continuing unchecked for many years, as in the worrying case of Dr Harold Shipman, who should have protected his patients from harm, then we should be very afraid, and very, very vigilant.

There seems to be no way yet devised to detect embryonic serial killers, nor to deter them once set on their course. It has been officially intimated that at any one time a score or so of serial killers walk among us on this right little, tight little island of ours. A chilling thought. The press constantly update the information about the continuing lives of contained notorious serial killers, held in prison or asylum, and we see their frightening faces glaring and staring at us, angry, sullen, unrepentant, swathed in vengeful musings. Sometimes experts interview them for hours on end, record every last detail of their childhood traumas, and assiduously tape their memories of how they felt as they committed their last crimes. And, especially in America, their brains are scanned for physical or physiological clues, before and after death. Indeed, the Killer Clown Gacy's bottled – or, rather, plastic-boxed – brain reposes 'amid her children's bicycles, hockey sticks and a chugging boiler', in the basement of pathologist Dr Helen Morrison's elegant three-storey home in Illinois.

Sometimes it looks as if there is going to be a breakthrough, some chemical imbalance, or interruption of the synapses, perhaps. But it all comes to nothing. Each serial killer thinks that he or she is unique, but he is really a robot, made of parts common to all, designed by man, or, perhaps, by a more devilish intelligence. The realisation in 2005 that our collateral ape ancestors sometimes fall upon another of their own kind with intent to kill is scarcely reassuring. The disturbing proportion of serial killers whose activities we have found it necessary here to record attests to the steady and perturbing upsurge of the robot.

Happily, though, they have not managed to burke entirely the old, gentle practitioners like Major Armstrong, Doctors Crippen, Cream, Pritchard, and Ruxton, Mesdames Bartlett, Bravo, Kent, Maybrick, and Smith, or such enduring partnerships as those of Messrs. Burke and Hare, and Bywaters and Thompson. Neither have the great enigmas, Oscar Slater and William Herbert Wallace been elbowed out by those who have, in some instances, elected for quantity rather than quality.

A word as to accuracy. In some cases the only reports available have proved worryingly conflicting, and we have, based on all the accessible information, estimated what seems to us objectively to be the most likely constellation of circumstances. This would apply to some out-of-the-way, and certain foreign, cases.

The international brotherhood of people who know about real-life crime carry within their heads, like so many Masonic signs, certain emblems of the Great Ones . . . the ' 'scuse fingers!' of the Armstrong case. The held big toe of the Bartlett case. The 'Hot water! Hot water!' of the Bravo case. The terrible breakfast of the Borden case. The cyclops eye of the Ruxton case. 'Qualtrough' the disembodied telephonic voice of the Wallace case. They will, perhaps, find also here among this latest cropping of criminous memorables, some new seductive *tesserae* to add to their personal mosaics.

RICHARD and MOLLY WHITTINGTON-EGAN

Acknowledgements

In the compilation of this book we have accumulated debts to many friends and fellow-workers. We wish to acknowledge and thank them.

Jonathan Goodman, veteran comrade-in-arms through many a print pitched battle.

Robin Odell and Donald Rumbelow, old friends and pioneer labourers in the killing fields of Jack the Ripper.

Paul Begg, Martin Fido, and Keith Skinner, young friends and leaders in the new wave of Ripper experts.

Also that determinedly debunking, Jack pursuivant, sole practitioner, the late Melvin Harris.

And, most especially, Stewart P. Evans, much-appreciated confrère and Ripperine consultant.

Nicholas Connell, ever ready, willing and able to help in the quest for out-of-the-way data, and Lisa Hinchliffe, who we found perpetually prepared to trouble shoot for us.

Across the water . . .

Albert Borowitz, who could always be relied upon for speedy resolution of any besetting problems of transatlantic malfeasance.

The late and sorely missed Clinton Krauss, of Vermont, rare book expert and rare friend.

Robert A. Flynn, of Portland, Maine, stalwart support and positive encyclopædist of all matters concerning the late Miss Lizbeth Borden, of Fall River.

We are sincerely grateful to an indispensable duo of Universal Providers of totally unobtainable books, The Elmers – Clifford and Marie – of Cheadle Hulme, and Paul Sheath, bookseller, of Malvern.

To another good friend, Wilfred Gregg, who continually, unfailingly, and uncomplainingly supplied from his unrivalled collection of world-wide criminous literature the elusive reference or fact that we sought, our most sincere gratitude.

To Stephanie Bilton we are deeply indebted for both her outstanding help in more recondite areas of research, and for her sterling work in providing many of the photographs which contribute so materially to the value of this volume.

Finally, we would thank Neil Wilson, our publisher, for friendship and sensitive help over the years.

RICHARD and MOLLY WHITTINGTON-EGAN

Dr John Bodkin Adams

The Passing Easer

TRIED AND ACQUITTED: Dr John Bodkin Adams.

ALLEGED VICTIM: Mrs Edith Alice Morrell (81).

LOCUS: 'Marden Ash', Beachy Head Road, Eastbourne.

DATE: November 13th 1950.

ALLEGED MEANS: Overdose of opiate drugs.

ALLEGED MOTIVE: Gain under the will.

CRIMEWATCH: On 18th March, 1957, there began at No. 1 Court, the Old Bailey, a classic trial, potentially capital, which was rich in expert medical evidence. Unfortunately, it was too late to be included in the *Notable British Trials* series. Before the event, as all present knew, there had been an investigation – some said a witch hunt – in Eastbourne.

Dr Bodkin Adams, born on January 21st, 1899, was seen by his detractors as a portly seaside Bluebeard, poisoning elderly, well-off patients in indecent haste for bequests under their wills. Sometimes, but not invariably, these alleged victims were lonely, without the counsel of relatives. Before the days of the NHS, it was normal, commonplace, for legacies to be made in favour of one's doctor, alongside solicitors, chauffeurs, gardeners. The more so if, as was often the practice of kind, silver-tongued Dr Adams, he had become a family friend.

Irish in origin, he found his niche in England more profitable. There was jealousy as he prospered. He worked hard, long hours, and served the poorer Panel patients willingly. Social climbing and avarice were less pleasing traits, but certainly became the leading medico of the gossiping, game-playing Eastbourne community. A lifelong bachelor, he had brought his mother and female cousin to share his villa, 'Kent Lodge'. He was religious, conducted Bible classes, attended meetings of the Plymouth Brethren, and was Joint Chairman of the YMCA. Collecting motor cars was a major hobby: if they rolled in via the testamentary route, so much the better.

He did attract a great many legacies, but his supporters advocated setting off the proportion of those sums, say £1000, against the larger total funds settled by the wills. They did add up though. He was not above acting as executor – which meant he knew what he would receive – nor shy of approaching a solicitor to facilitate a gift to himself, in order to alleviate the anxiety of the near-to-passing dear one. This behaviour was not illegal in itself nor was it reason to have him struck-off. There was talk, hearsay, and ghastly tales of malpractice, such as leaving a patient to die by wide-open windows, with all covering stripped off by the doctor's own podgy hands.

The police became convinced that mass-murder had been committed. But it was easier for a camel to pass through the eye of a bodkin than to convict Dr Adams. It was noted that he tended to administer heroic doses of the opiate drugs but he was not alone in this respect, and he held a diploma in anaesthetics, which indicated that he knew what he was doing – a double-edged sword.

Three dramatic exhumations proved fruitless. The decision was made to proceed on the indictment of murdering Mrs Edith Morrell, six years previously. There was no body to exhume: she had been cremated. Under the stress of police interest, Dr Adams became positively loquacious, not circumspect, and uttered some famous, ambiguous sayings: 'Easing the passing of a dying person is not all that wicked. She wanted to die – that cannot be murder. It is impossible to accuse a doctor.'

That, of course, was the crux of the trial, which is a kind of forerunner of the intense debate about 'mercy killing' which has seen other doctors in uncomfortable positions. When arrested, Dr Adams delivered himself of the worrying gem: 'I did not think you could prove it was murder – she was dying in any event.'

Challenged about his failure to declare his pecuniary interest on the request for cremation form, he replied sonorously, 'Oh! That was not done wickedly. God knows it was not. We always want cremations to go off smoothly for the dear relatives.' The words that the doctor unaccountably did challenge, most vehemently, through his counsel were spoken to his weeping receptionist as he was led away: 'I will see you in Heaven.'

The trial was a great disappointment to the Crown. Dr Adams was advised not to give evidence on his own behalf, which blunted the knives of cross-examination. It was a risk, but it worked. Adverse evidence from the nurses who had attended Mrs Morrell six years earlier was discredited when their old notebooks were produced and showed a wide discrepancy from records made at the bedside. Their discovery was most remarkable : the doctor thought that these were put away somewhere in his house, and his solicitor searched until 3 am before he found them at the back of a filing cabinet.

In the case of Mrs Morrell, doubt was cast on the necessity for such heavy medication in the treatment of arteriosclerosis and the after-effects of a severe stroke. The nurses reported no significant pain. Dr Adams said: 'Poor soul, she was in terrible agony.'

In fact, it appears that she had long been suffering from rheumatoid arthritis which was not brought in at the trial for some tactical reason and the morphine and heroin would have masked the pain. The celebrated devises of a Rolls Royce and a chest of silver turned out to be not as bruited. Mrs Morrell had removed Dr Adams from her will, as a punishment for his going away on holiday, and it was her son who restored the gifts.

Mr Justice Devlin found against the Prosecution: 'The case for the Defence seems to me to be manifestly a strong one.' The Jury took 46 minutes to acquit. A further indictment was not proceeded with. There had been some offences under the Drugs Act which the doctor admitted and the GMC struck him off for four years accordingly. Then he was restored to the Register, and resumed practice in Eastbourne. Forthwith, he sued 13 newspapers for libel and they settled out of court. When he died suddenly at the age of 84 after breaking his leg while clay pigeon shooting, his will amounted to £402,970 net, and he left a legacy to his own doctor.

PRIME SOURCES:
The Trial of Dr Adams. Sybille Bedford. Simon & Schuster, New York, 1959.
Where There's A Will. Rodney Hallworth & Mark Williams. Capston Press, Jersey, 1983.
Two Men Were Acquitted. Percy Hoskins. Secker & Warburg, London, 1984.
Easing the Passing. Patrick Devlin. Bodley Head, London, 1985.

Beverley Allitt

The Münchausen's Killer Nurse

MURDERER: Beverley Allitt.

VICTIMS: Liam Taylor (8 weeks). Timothy Hardwick (11 years).
Becky Grace Phillips (9 weeks). Claire Peck (15 months).
Also guilty of attempted murder of: Paul Crampton (5 months).
Katie Phillips (9 weeks). Bradley Gibson (5 years).
Also guilty of causing grievous bodily harm with intent to: Kayley Desmond (14 months). Henry
Chan (2 years); Patrick Elstone (7 weeks). Christopher King (9 months). Michael Davidson (7 years).
Christopher Peasgood (8 months).

LOCUS: Ward 4, Grantham and Kesteven Hospital, Lincolnshire.

DATES: February 23rd 1991 (Liam Taylor); March 5th 1991 (Timothy Hardwick); April 5th 1991 (Becky
Phillips); April 22nd 1991 (Claire Peck).

MEANS: Induced heart attack (Liam Taylor); Induced heart attack (Timothy Hardwick); Massive
injection of insulin (Becky Phillips); Massive injection of lignocaine (Claire Peck); Massive injection of
insulin (Paul Crampton); Induced Respiratory Arrest (Katie Phillips); Large injection of insulin
(Bradley Gibson).

MOTIVE: a morbid desire to attract attention to herself, regardless of the harm done, and to assert her
superior powers of nursing.

CRIMEWATCH: Beverley Allitt was a nurse who loved babies. Born on October 4th, 1968, she had, as far as anyone can tell, a perfectly happy, well-adjusted upbringing, with no deprivation or abuse. She may have had some problems about her sexual identity, and she kept complaining about her health as she matured, but she had a decent, loving fiancé, Steve Biggs. As he later explained, he had been the focus of violence – black eyes – and mental cruelty, inflicted on him by Beverley Allitt.

For six years she had, with hindsight, been exhibiting signs of severe mental disorder. She had attended casualty at Grantham about 40 times, while finding her nursing course difficult. The only known serious set-back in her life had been rejection by Boston's Pilgrim Hospital on the grounds that she did not have the necessary experience of caring for seriously ill babies. This rankled.

Grantham Hospital, however, was short-staffed, and glad to have her to nurse precisely those vulnerable babies. There she demonstrated her abilities, repeatedly running out of the cubicles shouting 'cardiac arrest!' and then helping heroically with the resuscitation. A number of desperately ill babies whom she had not killed out of hand were saved by being transferred to hospital in Nottingham. There was some permanent damage. Although the judge did not allow the diagnosis to be put to the jury, in case it prejudiced their decision, the theory was that Beverley Allitt was suffering from 'Münchausen's Syndrome by Proxy'.

Plain 'Münchausen's', named after Baron Münchausen, an eighteenth-century fantasist, had been recognised since the 1950s. Freud did not know about it. It is more common in men, and shows itself as false claims of illness, in order to gain attention, during which repeated visits to hospital are engineered. Well-observed signs and symptoms are manufactured by the faker, and he willingly submits to the most invasive surgery. He may even die, as it were accidentally: suicide is not the ultimate aim.

Some view the condition as a form of personality disorder. Others, and Freud would have agreed here, consider it to be an extreme variety of hysteria, where, after all, the gaining of attention is the point of the illness. Münchausen's is definitely not a madness, a psychosis, although it has been stated as such. It is no more an insanity than serial killing – under our present classification, that is.

Münchausen's By Proxy is a later identified variation, and so bizarre that people found it difficult to believe in its existence. This time, it seems to affect women – mothers especially – more than men. The strange performance impels sufferers to hurt and make ill, not themselves, but others, in order to reap attention and sympathy, perhaps, or praise, and usually in a hospital setting. Mothers were spotted on hidden cameras doing frightful things to their own children. It beggared belief. In the case of nurses, the scope and danger is only too apparent, with murder a definite possibility. This is not mercy killing.

One might wonder at the frenzied spree of Beverley Allitt's reign of terror, the sheer number of her victims, but there are comparable cases in America. There also seems to be an obsessive-compulsive aspect to the behaviour, which continues until capture. Here there is a parallel with serial killing.

When caught, Beverley Allitt displayed no remorse – a well-known feature of serial killers, but also showed to the public the utter smiling detachment of the most advanced hysterical patient. She pleaded Not Guilty at Nottingham Crown Court in 1993, and did not invoke the plea of Diminished Responsibility, which could, one supposes, have been argued around her Münchausen's By Proxy.

Convicted on May 17th, 1993, she was ordered to be detained at Rampton Special Hospital indefinitely.

PRIME SOURCES:
Angel of Death. John Askill & Martyn Sharpe. Michael O'Mara, London, 1993.
Murder on Ward Four. Nick Davies. Chatto & Windus/Random House, London, 1993.

Major Herbert Rowse Armstong

The Hay Poisoner

MURDERER: Major Herbert Rowse Armstrong.

VICTIM: Katharine Mary Armstrong (48): wife.

LOCUS: Mayfield, Cusop, Hay, Breconshire, Wales.

DATE: February 22nd, 1921.

MEANS: Slow poisoning with arsenic.

MOTIVE: Elimination of burdensome wife; amatory freedom; financial gain.

CRIMEWATCH: Born in Plymouth, May 13th, 1869. Went up to Cambridge. Qualified as a solicitor. Practised in Liverpool, Newton Abbot and, finally, Hay. Supporting the twin afflictions of doses of syphilis and a nagging wife, turned to salvarsan and arsenic as life-enhancers. Plagued also by dandelions, proclaiming his determination to be rid of pests, the Major went to war, openly, against the dandelions, and, secretly, against Mrs. Armstrong, armed with the 'magic bullets'. These foes vanquished, he then conducted a losing campaign against his rival solicitor, Oswald Martin, to whom at afternoon tea one day he handed an arsenic-loaded scone with the immortal words, "'scuse fingers!' These modest essays into self-betterment sadly misfired, with the result that the enterprising little man who strutted around Hay wearing riding boots, breeches, British warm and his wartime majority, became the only solicitor to be hanged — on May 31st, 1922 — for murder. And the dandelions of Cusop increased and multiplied. In 1995, Martin Beales, a solicitor practising in Hay from Armstrong's old office, and living in 'Mayfield', Armstrong's old home, published a spirited, and surprisingly persuasive, defence of his predecessor.

PRIME SOURCES:
Notable British Trial. Edited by Filson Young. William Hodge, Edinburgh, 1927.
Murder Revisited. John Rowland. John Long, London, 1961.
Exhumation of a Murder., Robin Odell. Harrap, London, 1975.
Dead Not Buried: Herbert Rowse Armstrong. Martin Beales. Robert Hale, London, 1995.

Jeremy Bamber

The White House Farm Massacre

MURDERER: Jeremy Bamber.

VICTIMS: Neville Bamber (61): adoptive father. June Bamber (61): adoptive mother. Sheila Caffell (27): adoptive sister. Daniel Caffell and Nicholas Caffell: her six-year-old twins.

LOCUS: White House Farm, Pages Lane, Tolleshunt D'Arcy, Essex.

DATE: August 7th, 1985.

MEANS: Shooting with a .22 Anschutz semi-automatic rifle.

MOTIVE: Gain: to inherit £400,000 family fortune.

CRIMEWATCH: A coldly planned massacre for cold cash. Jeremy Bamber (24) was to share a £400,000 estate with his adoptive sister, provided he worked on the family farm. But, unfortunately, he was not of an agricultural turn; sewing seed had a totally different meaning for him.

Born in 1961, he was the illegitimate child of a vicar's daughter. He had been adopted by the well-to-do Bamber farming family. Sent by them to a good boarding-school, he saw his despatch as rejection, and turned against his adoptive parents. In his twenties, his taste ran to Porsches rather than tractors, and free-spending sprees on the town rather than rural muck-spreading and reaping. To finance and fertilise the good life, he decided to accelerate and increase his inheritance by killing off the family, making it look as if his sister, who had suffered mental illness, had gone berserk with a gun, and then committed suicide. He was confirmed in this resolve when he heard that his mother was proposing to change the family will in favour of her twin grandsons. That did it. He determined upon immediate action.

At 3.36 a.m. on the morning of Monday, August 7th, 1985, Jeremy Bamber telephoned the Chelmsford police and told them that his father had just telephoned him from the farm saying, 'Please come over. Your sister's gone crazy, and she's got the gun.' Moments after a police car arrived at the gates of the 18th-century farmhouse, Bamber drove up and told them, 'My sister's a nutter. I think something terrible has happened. There are guns inside.'

Detectives arrived. They tried telephoning the farm, but the telephone was off the hook. It was four hours later that, armed officers having come to provide cover, the kitchen door was smashed down with a sledge-hammer, and the officers went in.

Everybody in the rambling old house was dead. It was a scene of chaos and horror, up-ended furniture and broken crockery everywhere. Neville Bamber lay dead in the kitchen, eight bullet wounds in his head and body. His wife, June, was lying on the floor in the doorway of her daughter, Sheila's, bedroom. She had been hit by nine bullets. On the bed lay Sheila, a former model, known as 'Bambi', beautiful even in death. A .22 rifle was lying across her body. Two bullets had entered her neck. And Sheila's twin boys lay where they had been sleeping in their beds – Daniel with five bullets in the back of his head, Nicholas with three.

The inquest, which was held at Braintree, brought in verdicts of murder and suicide. Neville and June Bamber were cremated on August 16th. Jeremy attended the funeral wearing a designer suit, a suitably tragic expression, and white make-up to give him a drawn look to emphasise his anguish. Then it was off to Amsterdam, first class all the way, for the 'grieving' Jeremy and his mistress, Julie Mugford.

But it was, a month later, Ms. Mugford who spilled the beans to the police. Jeremy, who, she said, strangled rats with his bare hands to test his resolve, had, with reference to his public display of grief at the funeral, chuckled, 'I should have been an actor'. He had also boasted to her that he had committed the perfect murder.

He had not.

It was the Bambers' nephew, David Boutflour, who, having made a search in the Bambers' gun cabinet, found there a silencer bearing traces of blood – Sheila's. The significance of this discovery was the ridiculousness of the implication that she could have shot herself twice through the neck, walked downstairs to return the silencer to the gun cabinet, and then walked back upstairs to lie down on her bed to die. Moreover, with the silencer attached, the gun would have been so long that she would not have been able to reach the trigger.

In December, 1986, at Chelmsford Crown Court, Jeremy Bamber was given five life sentences. Ever since his arrest, he vociferously proclaimed his entire innocence. After an earlier application to appeal was turned down, an appeal was subsequently heard in October, 2002. Bamber's legal representative, Mr. Michael Turner, Q.C., told the Court of Appeal that the original case against him had been so tainted by corruption and deceit that it could not be regarded as safe.

It was claimed that Bamber had been framed by police, whose investigation had been both corrupt and incompetent. They had deliberately withheld important evidence from his defence team, and the jury had been misled with regard to crucial DNA evidence.

Lord Justice Kay, who presided over the twelve-day appeal, said that advances in DNA technology since 1985 meant that the Criminal Cases Review Committee, which examines possible miscarriages of justice, had been right to refer the case to the Appeal Court. However, the blood evidence from the original trial still stood, and there was no new evidence that would influence a jury at trial. 'The more we examined the detail of the case, the more likely we thought it to be that the jury were right.' The verdict was ruled safe.

PRIME SOURCES:
SoleSurvivor: Children Who Murder Their Families. Elliott Leyton. Penguin Books, London, 1991.
Murder at White House Farm: The Story of Jeremy Bamber. Claire Powell. Headline, London, 1994.
Blood Relations: Jeremy Bamber and the White House Farm Murders. Roger Wilkes. Robinson, London, 1994.

Susan Barber

Paraquat Poison Pie

MURDERER: Susan Barber.

VICTIM: Michael Barber (35): husband.

LOCUS: 29 Osborne Road, Westcliff-on-Sea, Essex.

DATE: June 4th, 1981.

MEANS: Poison.

MOTIVE: Sexual.

CRIMEWATCH: Michael Barber (35), his wife Susan (29), and their three children – aged 8, 10, and 12 – lived in a modest, three-bedroomed, semi-detached, terrace house in Osborne Road, Westcliff-on-Sea. Barber worked as a warehouseman at nearby Rothman's cigarette factory. The couple had married in 1970. Compatible they were not.

From the very start highly-sexed Susan had been straying. She had left home twice, only to return for the sake of the children. She and her husband did not share many interests. Her idea of a good time was social drinking and parties. His, clearing off on a weekend fishing trip. And it was his unexpected early return, due to bad weather, from one such expedition that precipitated tragedy. He found his wife in bed with a young neighbour from four doors away, Richard Collins (25). Within days of her marriage, she had seduced Collins, then a 15-year-old schoolboy, and their affair had continued over the past ten years. A terrified Collins fled, nude, from the house, and Barber, in a fury, beat his wife up pretty badly.

On Thursday, June 4th, 1981, Michael Barber went in to work as usual. Shortly before lunch, he began to suffer from a blinding headache. After taking painkilling tablets given to him by the works' nurse, the headache eased, and he managed to complete his shift. Next day, he again had a headache, accompanied this time by stomach cramps and nausea. On Saturday, in addition to the persistence of the other symptoms, he was vomiting and complaining of difficulty in swallowing. The family's GP was

called in. He diagnosed a mild infection and prescribed an antibiotic.

By Monday, he was having trouble breathing, and his doctor, alarmed, sent him in by ambulance to Southend General Hospital, where he was admitted to the intensive care unit. Thoroughly puzzled, the doctors thought that he might be suffering from Goodpasture's syndrome, a disease which often starts with an upper respiratory tract infection, preceding the development of an acute inflammation of the kidney, that may lead to renal failure. When, on June 17th, he began to show signs of renal failure, he was rushed to Hammersmith Hospital, West London, which specialised in the treatment of kidney complaints. It was there that a junior doctor, who had had some experience of paraquat poisoning, suggested that blood and urine samples should be sent to the National Poisons Reference Centre for analysis. Barber's condition continued to deteriorate, and on June 27th, he died.

Professor David Evans, who carried out a post-mortem, thought that paraquat might have been the cause of death, but upon learning that there had been no intimation of its presence from the Poisons Centre, dismissed it. He did, however, remove the major organs of the body, and stored them in formalin. He also took tissue samples. A death certificate was duly issued – cause of death: cardiac arrest, renal failure, and bilateral pneumonia.

Michael Barber was cremated on July 3rd, 1981. Susan Barber shed no tears. So far as she was concerned, he had written his own death warrant that day he beat her black and blue. Filled with resentment, she had gone down to the garden shed where she knew there was a package of the poisonous weed-killer, paraquat, which her husband had filched from his previous employer, a firm of landscape gardeners. She had then cooked him his favourite dinner, steak pie, lacing the gravy with paraquat. Released by her husband's demise from the rôle of the unhappy housewife, she was immediately transformed into the merry widow, indulging in a binge of sex and alcohol. Under the call name 'Nympho', she advertised her sexual availability on citizen band radio, scandalising her nosy neighbours with the procession of aerial lovers beating a path to her home. She also managed to fritter away a very considerable portion of the £15,000 from the pension fund, plus £900 for the children, from her late husband's firm. Then, in October 1981, Nemesis struck.

Tissue submitted by Professor Evans was found to indicate the presence of a toxin, probably paraquat. It emerged that, due to some unidentifiable blunder somewhere along the line, the tests for paraquat poisoning ordered by the Hammersmith doctors had never been carried out.

On November 1st, 1982, Susan Barber stood trial at Chelmsford Crown Court, charged with murder and conspiring to murder. Richard Collins was charged with conspiracy. Both pleaded not guilty. Susan Barber said that she had given the paraquat to her husband with the intent only of making him ill: 'He had just beaten me up and I wanted to get away with my children. I thought if he was ill he wouldn't be able to come after me.'

The jury did not accept her explanation. Far from being a crime of passion committed in the heat of the moment, this was a crime of cold, cruel meditation. The trial judge, Mr. Justice Woolf, told her, 'I cannot think of a more evil way of disposing of a human being.' He then sentenced her to life imprisonment. Collins was given two years.

It was reported that, in July, 1983, Susan Barber was briefly allowed out of Holloway Prison in order to marry her call-signed 'Magic Man' of the air waves, 37-year old Rick Search.

PRIME SOURCES:
Hell Hath No Fury. Wensley Clarkson. Blake, London, 1991.
The Encyclopedia of Women Killers. Brian Lane. Headline, London, 1994.
Contemporary newspapers.

Velma Barfield

A Merciless Angel

MASS MURDERER

MURDERER: Velma (Margie) Barfield.

VICTIMS: Convicted of the murder of Stuart Taylor (56): fiancé.
Admitted in court, after conviction, during sentencing phase, to murder of: Lillie Bullard (64): her own mother. Dolly Edwards (85): Stuart Taylor's aunt and Velma Barfield's patient. John Henry Lee (81): husband of one of Velma Barfield's patients.

LOCUS: North Carolina.

DATES: December 30th, 1974 (Bullard). March 1st, 1977 (Edwards). June 4th, 1977 (Lee). February 3rd, 1978 (Taylor).

MEANS: Arsenic: ant poison (Lee and Taylor); rat poison (Bullard and Edwards).

MOTIVE: Curious. Money, according to due process of law, was at the root of it all. She killed mother to conceal the fact that she had borrowed $1,000 from a money-lender, who was pressing, having put up her mother's effects as collateral and used her social security card as identification. As for Stuart Taylor, she had forged his signature on three moderate cheques. No known motive for the other murders.

CRIMEWATCH: Velma Barfield was a nurse, thought of as an angel of mercy, and a grandmother. She overreached herself with her last victim, Stuart Taylor, who died, not at home, but in hospital, with no apparent cause of death. Arsenic was found in the liver. The body of Velma Barfield's second husband, Jennings Barfield, who had died in 1970, was also found, on exhumation, to contain arsenic, but that case was not proceeded with. John Henry Lee's invalid wife was still alive. Traces of arsenic were found in her living hair, but that case, too, was not proceeded with. A defence of insanity by reason of a 10-year dependence on Valium failed. In prison, she became a born-again Christian. Her last meal on Death Row was fried chicken livers, macaroni and cheese, collard greens, beans, bread, cake with peanut-butter icing and an iced drink. On November 2nd, 1984, aged 52, Velma Barfield, dressed in pink pyjamas, was executed in North Carolina's Central Prison, at Raleigh, by lethal injection of procuronium bromide, a muscle relaxant.

PRIME SOURCES:
Woman on Death Row. Velma Barfield. World Wide Publications, Minnesota, 1985.
Death Sentence. Jerry Bledsoe. Dutton, New York, 1998.
Contemporary newspapers.

Adelaide Bartlett

The Pimlico Mystery

ACCUSED: Adelaide Blanche Bartlett.

VICTIM: Thomas Edwin Bartlett (41): husband.

LOCUS: 85 Claverton Street, Pimlico, London.

DATE: January 1st, 1886.

MEANS: Chloroform by mouth.

MOTIVE: Elimination of unwanted husband.

CRIMEWATCH: Adelaide, certifiedly the daughter of Adolphe Collet de la Tremoille, Comte de Thouars d'Escury, allegedly the natural daughter of an undeclaring Englishman of great wealth and even greater consequence, born in Orleans on December 19th, 1855, married, under conditions, to say the least, bizarre, a humble, but aspiring, young grocer, Thomas Edwin Bartlett. The couple lived above the shop at Herne Hill, before transferring, via Merton Abbey, to Pimlico. Along the way they became entangled with a distinctly odd, 27-year-old Wesleyan cleric, the Reverend George Dyson, to whom Bartlett 'gave' his wife in the event of his demise, and who, impatient it seems, 'took' her prior to that sad occasion, in consequence whereof George and Adelaide found themselves in the dock. Her reverend companion, procurer of chloroform by appointment, having been pronounced an innocent, it still required all the forensic skill of Sir Edward Clarke to negotiate her acquittal. Whispers of Adelaide's noble birth confused the issue, as did the erroneous notion of liquid chloroform as an excruciatingly painful, impossibly difficult to administer, substance. Sir James Paget, Sergeant-Surgeon to the Queen, remarked that now that she had been found not guilty, Mrs. Bartlett 'should tell us in the interests of science how she did it.' Classic Victorian cosy domestic case.

PRIME SOURCES:
The Trial of Adelaide Bartlett for Murder. Edited by Edward Beal. Stevens & Haynes, London, 1886.
Notable British Trial. Edited by Sir John Hall. William Hodge, Edinburgh, 1927.
Did Adelaide Bartlett. . . ?: A Medical Opinion. Gordon Gwynn. Christopher Johnson, London, 1950.
Poison and Adelaide Bartlett. Yseult Bridges. Hutchinson, London, 1962.
Second edition, Macmillan, London, 1970.
The Pimlico Murder. Kate Clarke. Souvenir Press, London, 1990.

Robert Berdella

The Torture Man of Bob's Bizarre Bazaar

SERIAL KILLER

MURDERER: Robert Berdella.

VICTIMS: Larry Wayne Pearson (21). Gerald Howell (20). Robert Sheldon (18). Mark Wallace (20). Walter Ferris (20). Todd Stoops.

LOCUS: House on Charlotte Street, Hyde Park, Kansas City, Missouri.

DATES: 1984-7.

MEANS: Raped and tortured to death — hung upside down, electric shocks, suffocated with plastic bag.

MOTIVE: Homosexual sadistic slayings.

CRIMEWATCH: Berdella (born 1949), whose calling-card was, 'I rise from death. I kill death, and death kills me. Although I carry poison in my head the antidote can be found in my tail, which I bite with rage', owned Bob's Bizarre Bazaar, an occult curio shop. He was described by a neighbour as "an introverted, old hippie type from the sixties." On April 2nd, 1988, a woman who lived near Berdella found a naked youth, 23-year-old Christopher Bryson, shivering at her front-door. He was purple with welts and bruises, and he was wearing a dog's collar. After four days of torture, with Berdella injecting him in the throat, saying that the substance was a drain cleaner, Bryson had escaped by burning through his ropes with a book of matches. Police found some 200 Polaroid snapshots of rape, torture and death. Robert Sheldon's head was dug up from the garden. Larry Pearson's jawbone was also unearthed. The sadistic fantasies that haunted Berdella's mind and drove him to carry such brutalities into practice had been triggered by the 1965 sex-hostage film, The Collector, in which a young woman is captured and chained in a basement by an introverted lepidopterist. On August 3rd, 1988, Berdella pleaded guilty to the murder of Pearson and was sentenced to life imprisonment. On December 20th, 1988, he confessed to five more murders and was sentenced to five concurrent life terms. Succumbed to a heart attack, October 8th, 1992.

PRIME SOURCES:
Rites of Burial. Tom Jackman and Tony Cole. Virgin, London, 1995.
Contemporary newspapers.

David Berkowitz

Son of Sam

SERIAL KILLER

MURDERER: David Richard Berkowitz.

VICTIMS: Donna Lauria (18). Christine Freund (26). Virginia Voskerichian (19). Valentina Suriani (18). Alexander Esau (20). Stacy Moskowitz (20).

LOCUS: New York: Brooklyn, the Bronx, and Queens.

DATES: July 1976 - July 1977.

MEANS: Shooting by .44-calibre Bulldog revolver.

MOTIVE: No rational motive. Berkowitz preyed on courting couples in parked cars, impelled by 'demons' in his mind that commanded him to kill young women – to 'conquer' them because he could not seduce them.

CRIMEWATCH: A genuine case of insane killing – no question of feigned psychosis here – as evidenced by his post-capture writings, and by the state of his lair at 35 Pine Street, Yonkers, where grey blankets blocked out the windows and messages were scrawled on the walls. Berkowitz, born in 1953, loner, arsonist, security guard, was severely deluded and hallucinated vividly, tormented by 'demon dogs'. He had heard voices commanding him to kill. The orders were transmitted through a neighbour, Sam Carr's, dog, a labrador called Harvey. After a murder he felt flushed with power, and would go of to a café to celebrate with his favourite meal - hamburger followed by chocolate ice cream. He was caught through a traffic violation ticket. Glad that it was over, he pleaded guilty and was sentenced to 365 years' imprisonment.

PRIME SOURCES:
Son of Sam. George Carpozi Jr. Manor Books, New York, 1977.
Son of Sam. Lawrence D. Klausner. McGraw-Hill, New York, 1981.
Confessions of Son of Sam. David Abrahamsen. Columbia University Press, New York, 1985.
The Ultimate Evil. Maury Terry. Grafton Books, London, 1988.

Kenneth Bianchi & Angelo Buono
The Hillside Stranglers

SERIAL KILLERS

MURDERERS: Kenneth Alessio Bianchi and Angelo Buono.

VICTIMS: Elissa Teresa Kastin (21). Yolanda Washington (19) (Buono not convicted of this murder). Judith Lynn Miller (15). Kristina Weckler (20). Dolores Cepeda (12). Sonja Johnson (14). Jane Evelyn King (28). Lauren Rae Wagner (18). Kimberley Diane Martin (18). Cindy Lee Hudspeth (20). Committed by Bianchi only: Karen Mandic (22) and Diane Wilder (27).

LOCI: Buono's home: 703 East Colorado Street, Glendale, Los Angeles – first 10 murders except Yolanda Washington, who was killed in a car on the freeway. Catlows' House, Bayside Drive, Bellingham, Washington State – the last two murders.

DATES: October 1977 - February 1978 (first 10 murders). January 11th, 1979 (last two killings).

MEANS: Strangulation with a ligature.

MOTIVE: Sexual gratification: rape and torture.

CRIMEWATCH: Cousins by blood, accomplices in atrocity, Bianchi (26) and Buono (44) splayed nude bodies of girls on hillsides roughly concentric to Buono's house. Removed to Bellingham on an adventure of his own, Bianchi was easily arrested by association with Karen Mandic, and the list of convictions flowed from that point. A writer, Veronica Compton, who had asked Bianchi for help regarding a play that she was writing about a female serial killer, and through letters and visits to him revealed an obsession with torture and murder, agreed to a plan hatched by Bianchi. To prove that the Hillside Srangler was still at large, she was to drive to Bellingham, where Bianchi had committed his last two Strangler murders, strangle a woman and leave beside the body some of Bianchi's sperm, which had been smuggled out of prison in the finger of a rubber glove. The plan failed. Compton's selected victim proved too strong for her, and her would-be killer was arrested and sentenced to life imprisonment.

To escape the death penalty in Washington, Bianchi faked multiple personality, then entered into a plea-bargaining deal whereby he pleaded guilty and testified against Buono in California. Both sentenced to life imprisonment. Buono died of a heart attack on September 21st, 2002.

PRIME SOURCES:
The Hillside Strangler. Ted Schwarz. Doubleday, New York, 1981.
Two of a Kind. Darcy O'Brien. New American Library, New York, 1985

Bible John

True Identity Unknown

Serial Killer

Victims: Patricia Docker (25).Jemima ('Mima') McDonald (32). Helen Puttock (29).

Loci: Naked in the door recess of a back lane lock--up garage, Carmichael Lane, Battlefield, south side of Glasgow (Docker). Partly clothed in a bed recess in a derelict tenement at 23 Mackeith Street, Bridgeton, east end of Glasgow (McDonald). Fully clothed, lying against a back-court wall of 95 Earl Street, Scotstoun, west end of Glasgow (Puttock).

Dates: February 22nd-23rd, 1968 (Docker). August 16th-17th, 1969 (McDonald). October 30th-31st, 1969 (Puttock).

Means: Strangulation as with a belt or something strong, and face and head injuries caused by kicking and punching (Docker). Strangled with her own tights (McDonald). Strangled with one of her stockings. Bruising to the face. Clothes in disarray (Puttock).

Motive: Sexual gratification – one way or another.

Crimewatch: The unholy John collected his partners for the *danse macabre* that ended in back-street death, from the concrete *palais* known as the Barrowland Ballroom. The notion is that his intention was, if thwarted, rape. But there was no clear evidence of sexual assault; extraordinarily, all three victims were menstruating. Described by Helen Puttock's sister, Jeannie Williams, who met the man, as a handsome six-footer, age 25-35, with beautifully barbered, short-back-and-sides red hair, with a quotation from the Good Book ever ready on his tongue, he vanished like cigarette smoke.

For the first time in a Scottish murder hunt the Crown Office allowed the publication of an artist's impression of a man suspected of a serious crime. It was no use. The dancing psychopath has never been found. Hope surged in 1983. A man who returned after 10 years in Australia recognised Bible John as a friend he used to go to the dancing with at the Barrowland. Traced to a village near Amsterdam, the friend proved a remarkable look-alike, but there wasn't a scrap of evidence to tie him to the Glasgow dance of death killings.

Bible John was back in the headlines in January, 1996. One of the earliest suspects, in 1969, had been 31-year-old John Irvine McInnes, a former soldier in the Scots Guards. He had been picked up by the police, but not picked out by Helen Puttock's sister at an identity parade. She was indeed adamant that McInnes was not Bible John. Nevertheless, he continued to be officially regarded as a prime suspect.

Discharged from the army in July, 1959, he had worked as a furniture salesman in various stores around Lanarkshire and in Glasgow. In March, 1964, he had married Ella Russell, and she had borne him a daughter, Doreen, in 1964, and a son, Kenneth, in May 1968. But his wife and children had left him, and he was divorced in February, 1972.

He was known in the Lanarkshire town of Stonehouse as a bit of a loner, as well as a thief who had a police record. He was also known as a drinker, gambler, and womaniser, with a short temper, who never shied away from violence. And, indeed, he came to a violent end.

On April 29th-30th, 1980, at his mother's house – 26 Queen Street, Stonehouse – he took his own life, slicing into the brachial artery under his armpit, and bleeding to death. He was 41 years of age. All down the years, the police had continued to regard him as a likely Bible John, citing the department of coincidences: his strict upbringing by parents who belonged to the Plymouth Brethren sect, his sandy-reddish coloured hair, and the fact that he had definitely been at the Barrowland on the night of Helen Puttock's murder.

A small semen stain found on one of the brown nylon stockings worn by Helen Puttock, had, since the latter-day discovery of DNA, taken on a new importance, and the police were anxious to see if that stain contained McInnes' DNA. They succeeded in getting permission to exhume McInnes from his Stonehouse hillside grave. DNA samples had already been taken from McInnes' brother and sister, one of whose samples did match the DNA of the stocking stain.

However, the DNA recovered from John McInnes' uplifted corpse did not provide a satisfactory result, and on July 4th, 1996, the Lord Advocate issued a statement that forensic tests had failed to link McInnes with the semen stain. Tests conducted in connection with the bitemark which had been found on the victim were also inconclusive. So the mystery remains undisturbed, but to this day wry memories linger in the tough heart of Glasgow of the terrible coming of Bible John.

PRIME SOURCES:

Bible John. Charles N. Stoddart. Paul Harris Publishing, Edinburgh, 1980.

Bible John and Such Bad Company. George Forbes. Lang Syne Publishers, Glasgow, 1982.

Scotland's Unsolved Mysteries of the Twentieth Century. Richard Wilson. Robert Hale, London, 1989.

Blood on the Thistle: A Casebook of 20th Century Scottish Murder. Douglas Skelton. Mainstream Publishing, Edinburgh, 1992.

The Missing. Andrew O'Hagan. Picador, London, 1995.

Bible John: Hunt for a Killer. Alan Crow and Peter Samson. First Press Publishing, Glasgow, 1997.

Scottish Murder Stories. Molly Whittington-Egan. Neil Wilson, Glasgow, 1998.

Russell Bishop

The Babes in the Wood Mystery

ACCUSED: Russell Bishop.

VICTIM: Karen Jane Michelle Hadaway (9) and Nicola Elizabeth Christine Fellows (9).

LOCUS: Wild Park, Brighton.

DATE: October 9th, 1986.

MEANS: Manual strangulation.

MOTIVE: Sexual.

CRIMEWATCH: It became known as the Babes in the Wood murder mystery. Two little girls, Karen Hadaway and her friend, Nicola Fellows, left their homes – Nos 20 and 26 Newick Road, respectively – on the Moulsecomb Estate, on the outskirts of Brighton, Sussex, in the early evening of October 9th, 1986. They were seen buying chips at the 'chippy' on the local parade of shops in Park Road. They had last been glimpsed around 6.40 p.m. They had never returned home.

At 4.21 p.m. on Friday, October 10th, after a massive search by police and local residents, their dead bodies were found hidden in the dense undergrowth of a cave-like green den constructed by children in Wild Park, a nearby terrain of rugged downland which was a favourite play area for the neighbourhood youngsters. They were lying together, Karen with her right arm extended over Nicola, as if to protect her. 'Their eyes were open in mute supplication,' reports the casebook of Dr Iain West, the forensic pathologist who conducted the post-mortems. They had both been manually strangled and sexually assaulted.

Police suspected 20-year-old Russell Bishop, a mostly unemployed builder's labourer, part-time car mechanic, and sporadic petty thief, who had previously lived on the same estate as the murdered girls, and had known both them and their families. He was living now, with his partner, Jennie Johnson and their child, at 17 Stephen's Road, Hollingdean Estate. He was arrested on October 31st, 1986, and put up at Lewes Crown Court, charged with the double murder. The jury decided he was not guilty. Officially, the Babes in the Wood case remains unsolved. On the wink to a blind horse principle, the police announced, 'The investigation is closed. We are not looking for anyone else.' Three years went by. Then came the case of the Throttled Seven-Year-Old.

On February 4th, 1990, a couple, David and Susan Clifton, out walking at a beauty spot on the Sussex Downs known as the Devil's Dyke, saw with horror a small child, her clothing hanging in shreds about her, come stumbling towards them out of a bramble thicket of gorse bushes, to collapse sobbing in their arms. Her naked back was criss-crossed with scores of angry-looking scratches, her legs and feet oozed blood from the piercings of dozens of thorns, the whites of her eyes were copiously speckled with red spots of blood from ruptured blood vessels. Her throat bore the unmistakable marks of a man's hand around it.

The Seven-Year-Old had not died. But she was very lucky to be alive. Dr Iain West later explained: she had been throttled into unconsciousness by a deadly unarmed combat technique, known to SAS experts as 'The Sleeper'. It is a hold which compresses the carotid arteries and cuts off the oxygen supply to the brain.

The Seven-Year-Old (she was not named for legal reasons) had a terrible tale to tell. After Sunday lunch, at about half-past three, she had put on the roller-skate boots which she had had for Christmas, and gone out to play near her home, which was on the Whitehawk Estate, at

Brighton. Having popped briefly into a sweet shop, she had been skating homewards along the pavement of Haybourne Road when she spotted a parked red car with its boot open. As she drew level with it, a man jumped out of the car, seized her, warned, 'Scream and I'll kill you', bundled her into the boot, slammed it shut, and drove off with her at speed. When they reached the Devil's Dyke, the man opened the boot, gripped the little schoolgirl's throat, and squeezed hard. Within seconds, her struggling body went limp. He then carried her round to the back seat of the car, laid her on it, and sexually assaulted her. Certain that the child was dead, he dumped her naked corpse in a dense clump of brambles and thorns, climbed back into his car, and sped off.

The girl's description of her attacker fitted precisely that of Russell Bishop. What was more, he was the owner of a red Ford Cortina, such as she described. Forensic evidence made it plain that this time Bishop was unquestionably guilty. And so the jury found, as he stood once again in the dock at Lewes Crown Court, where, three years before, he had been absolved. This time he was sentenced to life imprisonment.

PRIME SOURCES:
A Question of Evidence: Who Killed the Babes in the Wood? Christopher Berry-Dee with Robin Odell. W.H. Allen, London, 1991.
Dr Iain West's Casebook. Chester Stern. Little, Brown, London, 1996.

Lawrence Bittaker

Killer By Numbers

SERIAL KILLER

MURDERER: Lawrence Sigmund (or Sigmond) Bittaker.

VICTIMS: Jacqueline Leah Lamp (13). Jackie Gilliam (15). Shirley Ledford (16). Lucinda Schaefer (16). Andrea Hall (18).

LOCUS: The suburbs of Los Angeles. Victims from Redondo Beach (Lamp, Gilliam), Sun Valley (Ledford), Torrance (Schaefer), Tujunga (Hall).

DATES: June to October, 1979.

MEANS: Strangling.

MOTIVE: Sex and torture.

CRIMEWATCH: Bittaker, a 40-year-old Burbank, California, machinist, teamed up with Roy Lewis Norris. The pair of sadists are said to have planned to kill one female victim of each teenage from 13 through to 19, inclusive, but were captured while still three victims short of completing their goal. Their method was to lure girl hitch-hikers into their van, nicknamed 'Murder Mac'. The girls would then be raped and tortured and mutilated, with pliers, an ice-pick and sledgehammer, before being strangled to death. They were charged on April 28th, 1980. Norris agreed to plead guilty to involvement in the murders on the understanding that the prosecutor would not ask for the death penalty. He received a sentence of 45 years to life. Bittaker, found guilty on February 17th, 1981, after California's first televised trial, was sentenced to death. He still awaits execution in San Quentin. He has nothing to kill now, except time. He enjoys a daily rubber of red-handed bridge with fellow murderers Randy Kraft, Douglas Clark and William Bonin. And he sells his finger-nail clippings to murder groupies.

PRIME SOURCE:
Contemporary newspapers.

The Black Dahlia Murder

MURDERER: Identity unknown.

VICTIM: Elizabeth Ann Short.

LOCUS: Vacant lot, South Norton Avenue, between 39th and Colisseum Streets, a block east of Crenshaw Boulevard, Los Angeles.

DATE: January 15th, 1947.

MEANS: Choked to death on her own blood.

MOTIVE: Sexual gratification – just possibly tinged with revenge.

CRIMEWATCH: Indulgence of sadistic frenzy. Body drained of every drop of blood. Cut in two. Subjected to some very fancy knife-work, including the letters 'BD' cut into the flesh of the thigh. Head battered. Face slashed almost beyond recognition. Mouth sliced at the edges from ear to ear to form a gruesome grin. Repeated cuts on thighs, arms, and breasts in both straight lines and circles. Scores of cigarette burns marking the flesh. Rope burns on the hands and feet.

Elizabeth Short, a Hollywood drifter with stardom dust in her eyes, was the ideal victim. Nicknamed the Black Dahlia because of her alluring trademark of seductive black clothing, she had a chequered history of juvenile delinquency, promiscuity, and alcoholism, and was, predictably, the product of a severely fractured home background. She became, in escaping thence, a footloose and fancy-free wandering sociopath, set fair to be attracted to the warmth of, and burned up by, the Klieg lights. There is some evidence that she was held captive by her torturer for the last week of her life. Despite floods of 'confessions' over the years, the identity of her captor and slayer – male or, it has been suggested, female, with involvement in a bisexual triangle – has remained impenetrable.

PRIME SOURCES:
Severed. John Gilmore. Zanja Press, Los Angeles, 1994.
Black Dahlia Avenger. Steve Hodel. Arcade Publishing, New York, 2003.
Contemporary newspapers.

Robert Black

The Rampaging Child Killer

SERIAL KILLER

MURDERER: Robert Black.

VICTIMS: Susan Claire Maxwell (11). Caroline Hogg (5). Sarah Jayne Harper (10).

LOCI: Coldstream, South Berwickshire. Portobello, Edinburgh. Morley, a suburb of Leeds.

DATES: July, 1982 - March, 1986.

MEANS: Probably suffocation. Most likely strangulation. Drowning.

MOTIVE: Sexual.

CRIMEWATCH: Robert Black was not a nice man. He had not been a nice child. But, then, his circumstances had not been very nice either. He was illegitimate. He had never known his father or his mother. He was born, on April 21st, 1947, at Falkirk Royal Infirmary, to Jessie Hunter Black, a 24-year-old Scottish factory worker. When he was just six months old she had handed him over for fostering to Mrs. Isabel 'Betty' Tulip, who lived in the Argyllshire village of Kinlochleven. He was rising eleven when she died.

From that point on, it was downhill all the way. Already, even at that tender age, he had begun to exhibit disturbing signs of sexual awareness and deviancy. He liked little girls, and took a delight in exposing himself to them. At school he proved, for a variety of reasons, unmanageable, and was packed off to the Red House Care Home, at Musselburgh. And there, over a period of three years, he was systematically abused by one of the staff. This is likely to have sexually exacerbated, rather than distressed, him.

Leaving behind him in Scotland a series of sexually oriented disasters, including an assault on a seven-year-old girl, whom he had lured into a derelict air raid shelter on the pretext of showing her a family of kittens who had made their home in there, he arrived in London, where he eventually rented an attic bed-sitter from two fellow Scots, Eddie and

Kathy Rayson, at 31 West Bank, Stamford Hill. He had also landed a job as a delivery van driver for the Hoxton based Poster Dispatch and Storage Company. This meant long-distance driving all over Britain, and gave him the opportunities he needed to indulge his fancy for little girls wearing white ankle socks. The first of these who had the misfortune to meet up with him was Susan Maxwell.

On Friday, July 30th, 1982, an afternoon of summer warmth and beautiful sunshine, Susan was returning home to Crammond Hill Farm, hard by the Northumbrian village of Cornhill. She had been playing tennis with her friend, Alison Raeburn, on the club courts of the border market town of Coldstream, on the Scottish side of the River Tweed. She was making her way towards Coldstream Bridge. Having just crossed over the bridge from the English side, was Robert Black, in his white Fiat van, and the sight of the slender, pretty girl in her tennis shorts and white ankle socks, swinging her tennis racquet and walking towards him, sent the old familiar urge pulsing its irresistible way through his body. He turned his van round and followed in her traces. Susan Maxwell never arrived home.

Thirteen days later – August 12th – her fully-clothed body was found 264 miles away, at Loxley, near Uttoxeter. She had been dumped in a wood close to a lay-by on the A518 Uttoxeter to Stafford road. The advanced state of putrefaction made it impossible to discern a cause of death, or to perceive if the child had been sexually assaulted. The police believed that she had been gagged with sticking plaster, tied up, and used sexually, before being suffocated. Identification was made by means of her clothing, fingerprints, and dental records.

It was July again – a year later, 1983. Sunny and gloriously warm; just like the day that Susan Maxwell vanished. Five-year-old Caroline Hogg lived in Portobello, the seaside resort three miles east of Edinburgh. That Friday, July 8th, the little girl had been to the birthday party of one of her friends. She was wearing her lilac and white gingham party frock and her best shoes. It was getting on for seven o'clock when Annette Hogg and her daughter arrived home to 25 Beach Lane. Caroline wanted to go out and play before going off to bed. Her mother said no. But she persuaded her stepfather, John Hogg, who said that she could play for five minutes, providing she stayed in the front garden.

But Caroline was tempted. There were the swings in the small park across the road, beside her school, the sands, and the mile-long promenade overlooking the Firth of Forth. Naughtily, foolishly, she wandered down Beach Lane to the promenade. And Robert Black was waiting. He took her hand in his. He led her to the little fairground. He treated her to a 15p. ride on the miniature double-decker bus on the carousel. She was seen there, holding the hand of a big, scruffy looking man with horn-rimmed, National Health style glasses. He was wearing a blue zip-up jacket and faded blue jeans. The pair were last glimpsed walking towards the car park.

The next time Caroline was seen, she was not recognisable. As in the case of Susan Maxwell, her body was too badly decomposed. On Monday, July 18th, 1983, her naked corpse was found in a ditch beside a lay-by, off the A444, near Twycross, in Leicestershire, 300 miles from Portobello, and just 24 miles from where Susan Maxwell had been found. She was identified by two hair bobbles, a silver locket, and her dental chart. It was impossible to say how she had died, or if she had been sexually interfered

with. It was now that the police decided that in all likelihood the murders of the two little girls were connected, and Hector Clark, Assistant Chief Constable of Northumbria, was appointed to head the ongoing investigation.

Three years went by. On the rainy evening of March 26th, 1986, 10-year-old Sarah Harper's mother sent her off to the corner shop, 200 yards from her home, at No.1 Brunswick Place, in the Leeds suburb of Morley, to buy a loaf and two packets of crisps. Robert Black had been making a delivery in the area, and was hovering. No one saw him take Sarah. No one saw Sarah – until, on the morning of April 19th, David Moult, walking his dog, Ben, along the bank of the River Trent, at Wilford, on the outskirts of Nottingham, saw her partially-clad body floating in the water. She had met her death by drowning, still alive when put into the water. She had brutal genital injuries. Both her vagina and anus had been seriously interfered with.

Yet again July. July 14th, 1990. That breathless afternoon David Herkes was mowing the grass in the front garden of his house in the village of Stow, near Galashiels, when he saw Mandy Wilson, his neighbour's six-year-old daughter, come walking out of her garden gate towards him. It was then that, out of the corner of his eye, he noticed a blue Ford transit van. Its driver, bald, middle-aged, with a beard, was cleaning the windscreen with a rag. Herkes bent down to clear a tangle of grass-cuttings. When he looked up, van, man, and child had vanished. Alarmed, he alerted the child's mother. She promptly telephoned the police. Mr. and Mrs. Wilson were standing in the street giving their daughter's description to a group of policemen, when suddenly they saw the blue van returning. The officers stopped the vehicle, dragged the driver out, and flung open the rear doors of the van. Inside, was a sleeping bag, zipped tightly shut. The officers tore it open, and there they found Mandy, almost suffocated.

The following August, after trial at Edinburgh, Black was jailed for life. While he was safely stowed away in Peterhead, detectives set to work warming up the cold cases of Maxwell, Hogg and Harper. They inched over every scrap of evidence that might connect

Black with the killings. They were under no illusions as to the man's character and capacity.

Convicted out of his own mouth, he had told them of how he had kept a toilet bag in the back of his van. In it, wrapped in an old sock, was a selection of implements which he used in a most peculiar way for sexual stimulation. When he needed to defecate, he would do so in the rear of the van, on a piece of newspaper. He would then insert one or other of these objects anally, while masturbating. He had taken Polaroid photographs of himself in the mirror, inserting various objects into his anus – a wine bottle, a telephone handset, and the leg of a table. They came up with a very persuasive file of facts. The Crown lawyers decided that, although the evidence was circumstantial, it was enough to convince a jury. And so it proved.

In April, 1993, at Newcastle Crown Court, Black was found guilty on ten counts, including the three murders. He was sentenced to life imprisonment on each of the charges, and Mr. Justice Macpherson recommended that he should serve at least 35 years on each of the three murder convictions. As he was being taken down from the dock, Black turned to the detectives whom he had hoodwinked for so long and said mockingly, 'Well done, boys!' It was a sentiment that was echoed, albeit on another plane, by everyone in the court.

Prime Sources:
Fear the Stranger. Former Deputy Chief Constable Hector Clark with David Johnston. Mainstream, Edinburgh & London, 1994.
The Murder of Childhood. Ray Wyre and Tim Tate. Penguin Books, London, 1995.
'Well Done, Boys'. Robert Church. Constable, London, 1996.

The Bogle-Chandler Murders

Victims Dr Bogle and Margaret Chandler

MURDERER: Identity unknown.

VICTIMS: Dr Gilbert Stanley Bogle (38). Margaret Olive Chandler (29): wife of Geoffrey Chandler.

LOCUS: Lane Cove River Park, Sydney, New South Wales.

DATE: January 1st, 1963.

MEANS: Unknown. Presumption: most likely some rare unidentifiable poison. A later suggestion: 'Japanese chocolate', yohimbine.

MOTIVE: Unknown. Possibly jealousy. Revenge?

CRIMEWATCH: Dr Bogle was one of the world's top-flight physicists. He was also an unfaithful husband and a faithless philanderer. Any search for a motive must probe the widish arena of his sexual athleticism. At the time of his untimely demise, Gib Bogle's latest playmate was his friend Geoff Chandler's wife, Margaret. Bogle's wife, Vivienne, found bothering profitless. Geoff, who had a thing of his own going was not too bothered. After a New Year's Eve party, Gib and Margaret drove out to a secluded lovers' lane, in Cove River Park. All unknowing, they had a rendezvous with death. When found, Bogle's face was deep purple; a little blood trickled from his nose and the corner of his mouth. Margaret lay, mockingly half-clad, under the flattened cardboard sheets of a mouldy beer carton. The corpses were scrutinised down to the tiniest split-atom by batteries of doctors. They could find absolutely no reason why they should be dead. Neither was there any clue to the killer. But Mrs. Margaret Fowler, Gib's late passionate friend, herself a physicist married to a chemical engineer, cannot perhaps be so lightly dismissed as Dr Gib dismissed her.

PRIME SOURCES:
The Bogle Mystery. Stafford Silk. Howitz Publications, Sydney, 1963.
So You Think I Did It. Geoffrey Chandler. Sun Books, Melbourne, 1969.

Lizzie Borden

The Fall River Axe Murders

ACCUSED: Lizzie Andrew Borden.

VICTIMS: Abby Durfee Gray Borden (63): stepmother.
Andrew Jackson Borden (70): father.

LOCUS: 92 (now No. 230) Second Street, Fall River,
Massachusetts.

DATE: August 4th, 1892.

MEANS: Bludgeoning with a hatchet.

MOTIVE: Believed to have been to protect her and her sister's inheritance – which she saw her father giving away. Some would postulate hatred of her stepmother and that Father had to be killed because he would have known Lizzie to have been the murderer.

CRIMEWATCH: It seems inconceivable that Lizzie Borden should have walked out of the New Bedford Courthouse with a Not Guilty verdict. And yet the perverseness of that New England jury has been perpetuated by posterity. At least two other serious candidates for the bloodstained laurels have been proposed: Lizzie's elder sister, Emma (42), and Bridget Sullivan (26), the Irish housemaid. And still the freshly-bloodied pretenders keep popping up, Old Uncle John Vinnicum and all. A terrible blow to the unsullied virtue of Miss Lizzie was struck on the September day, long after the trial, when she was alleged to have shoplifted two porcelain paintings from the stylish Tilden-Thurber store at Providence, Rhode Island. Neither did her relationship with actress Nance O'Neil, and its rumoured undertones of lesbianism, improve the spinster Borden image in the tight-lace Fall River community. Eyebrows were raised, too, when, in 1904, Emma, who all her life had watched over Lizzie like a little mother, and must have known her guilt, left the home they shared. The sisters were never to see each other again. Lizzie died, not having properly recovered from a gall-bladder operation, aged 68, on June 1st, 1927, at Maplecroft, 7 French Street, Fall River. It was 34 years after her acquittal.

PRIME SOURCES:
The Fall River Tragedy. Edwin H. Porter. Press of J. D. Munroe, Fall River, 1893. (Very scarce as Lizzie went round buying up and destroying all the copies she could lay her hands on.)
Trial of Lizzie Borden. Edmund Pearson. Doubleday, Doran, New York, 1937.
A Private Disgrace. Victoria Lincoln. G. P. Putnam's Sons, New York, 1967.
Goodbye Lizzie Borden. Robert Sullivan. Chatto & Windus, London, 1975.
Lizzie Borden: A Casebook of Family and Crime in the 1890s. Edited by Joyce G. Williams. J. Eric Smithburn, M. Jeanne Peterson, T.I.S. Publications, Bloomington, Indiana, 1980.
Lizzie Borden: The Legend, The Truth, The Final Chapter. Arnold R. Brown. Rutledge Hill Press, Nashville, Tennessee, 1991.
Forty Whacks: New Evidence in the Life and Legend of Lizzie Borden. David Kent. Yankee Books/St. Martin's Press, U.S.A., 1992
The Commonwealth of Massachusetts vs. Lizzie A. Borden: The Knowlton Papers 1892-1893. Michael Martins and Dennis A. Binnette. The Fall River Historical Society, Massachusetts, 1994.
Lizzie Borden Past & Present. Leonard Rebello. Al-Zach Press, Fall River, Massachusetts, 1999.
Lizzie Didn't Do It! William Masterton. Branden Publishing Company, Boston, 2000.

William Bradfield & Dr Jay Smith
The Main Line Murders

MURDERERS: William Sidney Bradfield and Dr Jay Charles Smith.

VICTIMS: Susan Reinert (*c.* 36). Karen Reinert (11): her daughter. Michael Reinert (10): her son. Also missing, since 1978, presumed dead (no criminal proceedings) are Jay Smith's troublesome daughter, Stephanie Smith Hunsberger, and her husband, Edward Hunsberger.

LOCUS: Not known. Susan Reinert's nude body, bruised and with chain marks, was found, on June 25th, 1979, in the boot of her Plymouth Horizon, in the car park of the Host Inn, Harrisburg, Pennsylvania. Karen and Michael were never found.

DATE: On June 22nd, 1979, in a hailstorm, the three victims hurried out of their house at 662 Woodcrest Avenue, Ardmore, Pennsylvania, and were never seen alive again.

MEANS: Susan Reinert died from a dose of morphine.

MOTIVE: Once smoke screen put up by Bradfield dispelled, more simple than it appeared. The 'Satanic rites' scenario, as mooted, was never a true runner, even if there was plenty of swinging sex going on in the upper reaches of Upper Merion High School. Despite his claims that he never sought to benefit, Bradfield stood to gain under Susan Reinert's will and life insurance policies of $730,000, and he *did* try to get those monies in. Her children had to be killed because they were eye-witnesses. Alternatively, they were part of the murder plan *ab initio* in case through the court, *they* stood to gain. Motive not so clear for Jay Smith. A share of the proceeds? Sadistic enjoyment? Repayment of Bradfield's alibi for him at his trial for robbery of a Sears, Roebuck store?

CRIMEWATCH: Although convictions were obtained, this case has never been fully fathomed. No confessions. No knowing how to apportion the guilt between the accomplices, or exactly when and where the killings took place. Nicknamed 'The Prince of Darkness', saturnine Dr Smith, Colonel in the US Army Reserve, behaved very strangely during his tenure as principal at Upper Merion, but his mental status was never at issue. Teacher Bill Bradfield, obsessed with Ezra Pound, denied romantic involvement with Susan Reinert, and offered a shaky alibi. In 1983, aged 50, he was convicted on three counts of conspiracy to commit first-degree murder, and sentenced to life imprisonment. Smith, aged 58, was convicted in 1986 on three counts of first-degree murder, and sentenced to die by the electric chair. Dr Jay Smith appealed and was granted a new trial, but the Pennsylvania Supreme Court later reversed itself and ordered his release because of prosecution misconduct in the original trial.

PRIME SOURCES:
Engaged to Murder. Loretta Schwartz-Nobel. Viking, New York, 1987.
Echoes in the Darkness. Joseph Wambaugh. William Morrow, New York, 1987.

Ian Brady & Myra Hindley
The Moors Murders

MURDERERS: Ian Brady and Myra Hindley.

VICTIMS: John Kilbride (12) – Hindley convicted here only as accessory after the fact. Lesley Ann Downey (10). Edward Evans (17). Also: Pauline Reade (16) –No conviction. Keith Bennet (12) --No conviction.

LOCI: Saddleworth Moor, Yorkshire (Kilbride, Reade, Bennett). 16 Wardle Brook Avenue, Hattersley, Manchester (Downey, Evans).

DATES: November 23rd, 1963 (Kilbride). December 26th, 1964 (Downey). October 6th-7th, 1965 (Evans). July 12th, 1963 (Reade).June 16th, 1964 (Bennett).

MEANS: According to Hindley's confession, Brady told her that he strangled the boy with a thin piece of string (Kilbride). According to Hindley's confession, Brady strangled the girl with a piece of string (Downey). Hacking with a hatchet and strangulation with an electric flex (Evans). The throat was cut (Reade). According to Hindley's confession, Brady told her that he strangled the boy with a piece of string (Bennett).

MOTIVE: Pleasure in killing. Power. Sadism. Sexual gratification, with actual sexual interference by Brady.

CRIMEWATCH: According to Hindley's confession to Detective Chief Superintendent Peter Topping in 1987, her rôle, as Brady's creature, was not to participate in the killings, but to abduct the victims. Thus, John Kilbride went 'like a little lamb to the slaughter.' In the cases of Reade and Bennett, the DPP decided against a new trial, although both Brady and Hindley had implicated themselves by their statements to Topping, and by helping the police, more than twenty years later, to search for the two graves on Saddleworth Moor. Pauline Reade's body was found on July 1st, 1987. Keith Bennett still lies hidden.

Brady has also confessed to five other murders, but the police have not been able to substantiate his claims: he 'bricked' a man on wasteland behind Piccadilly Railway Station, Manchester; he stabbed a man under the railway arches in the Calton area of Glasgow; he threw a woman into the canal near the Rembrandt public-house, Manchester; he shot and buried an 18-year-old youth on Saddleworth Moor; he shot a hiker at Loch Long, Scotland, and buried him.

Brady, born January 2nd, 1938, is said to be suffering from a paranoid psychosis. He is held at Park Lane Hospital, Liverpool. Hindley, born July 23rd, 1942, was at Cookham Wood Prison, Rochester, Kent.

Having spent 36 years – nearly two-thirds of her life – behind bars, Myra Hindley died, aged sixty, at 4.55 p.m. on Friday, November 15th, 2002. In 1998, she had been transferred from Durham Prison to Highpoint Prison, sited at a bleak former RAF base in Suffolk. For some time she had been in increasingly poor health, ingesting 24 different drugs – 42 pills – a day, for angina, asthma, bronchitis, depression, insomnia, irritable bowel syndrome, menopausal symptoms, osteoporosis, and an assortment of psychological problems, and raised cholesterol. Her weight had ballooned, and she had a 40-a-day cigarette habit. She had over the years proved a troublesome, manipulative prisoner, and had attracted a succession of lesbian lovers.

In January, 2000, she had a stroke in the left side of her brain. In October, 2002, she was admitted to hospital with 'unstable angina'. Returned to prison after treatment, she fell ill on November 10th, having caught a cold which left her short of breath. She was given antibiotics for a chest infection, but her condition deteriorated rapidly. She was reported to be struggling for breath, unable to gasp more than five words at a time, and, on November 12th, she was sent, under the name of Christine Charlton, into West Suffolk Hospital, at Bury St. Edmunds. She died there, in Room J on Ward G2, of, according to a post-mortem carried out by Dr Michael Heath, bronchial pneumonia, brought on by hypertension, and coronary heart disease. She was cremated at Cambridge City Crematorium, after a twenty-five-minute private service, which was held at 7.30 p.m.

Brady reacted to the news of his former lover's death with stony silence. He, who had for years been struggling against forced-feeding in an attempt to starve himself to a longed-for death, bitterly resented the fact that she had contrived to die before him. And Brady himself, the one-time clean-heeled, jackbooted young Nietzschean Nazi, was brilliantly limned in the Daily Mail, by the well-known author, Geoffrey Wansell, as 'a 64-year-old man huddled in an old overcoat, his skin yellowing like parchment, his once pencil-thin body bloated to almost 12 stone in weight, his hair grey and thinning, his claw-like hands refusing to touch any food or drink: a man willing his own death.' He sits in his hospital room absolutely still, 'only his tiny, dark eyes move, darting from side to side, when the male nurses come in . . . to force-feed him through a rubber tube that runs up his right nostril and down into his stomach.'

He had, at the beginning of the year 2000,

launched an action to stop the hospital force-feeding him. But the Court, at a hearing which was held in private, ruled that his mental condition was not such that he was in a position to decide his fate, and Mr. Justice Kay said that the hospital was entitled to force-feed him. In 2001, helped by the crime writer, Colin Wilson, who had been corresponding with him in prison for ten years, Brady produced a book, The Gates of Janus: Serial Killing and its Analysis By the 'Moors Murderer'. By 2002, Brady had for a quarter of a century been refusing to take any exercise in the open air. He remains the sullen eremite of Liverpool's Ashworth High Security Hospital.

PRIME SOURCES:

The Moor Murders. David Marchbanks. Leslie Frewin, London, 1966.

The Monsters of the Moors. John Deane Potter. Elek, London, 1966.

Satan's Children. Judge Gerald Sparrow. Odhams, London, 1966.

Beyond Belief. Emlyn Williams. Hamish Hamilton, London, 1967.

On Iniquity. Pamela Hansford Johnson. Macmillan, London, 1967.

The Trial of Ian Brady and Myra Hindley. Edited by Jonathan Goodman. David & Charles, Newton Abbot, 1973.

Devil's Disciples. Robert Wilson. Express Newspapers, London, 1986.

Brady and Hindley. Fred Harrison. Ashgrove Press, Bath, 1986.

Return to Hell. Robert Wilson. Javelin Books, London, 1988.

Myra Hindley. Jean Ritchie. Angus & Robertson, London, 1988.

For the Love of Lesley. Ann West. W. H. Allen, London, 1989.

Topping. Peter Topping. Angus & Robertson, London, 1989.

The Gates of Janus: Serial Killing and its Analysis By the 'Moors Murderer.' Ian Brady. Feral House, Los Angeles, 2001.

The Bravo Mystery

MURDERER: Unknown.

VICTIM: Charles Delauney Turner Bravo (30): husband.

LOCUS: The Priory, Bedford Hill Road (now Bedford Hill), Balham, London.

DATE: April 21st, 1876.

MEANS: Antimony (Tartar emetic).

MOTIVE: Elimination.

Florence Ricardo Bravo (suspect)

CRIMEWATCH: Charles Bravo, Barrister-at-Law, penny-pinching second husband of less than five months of wealthy Florence Ricardo (30), went upstairs to bed in their beautiful Strawberry Hill gothic home, The Priory, somewhere about a quarter past nine on the night of April 18th, 1876, rushed forth from his bedroom in his nightshirt shouting for hot water to drink, and three days after that was dead of antimony. Accident? Suicide? Murder? If the latter (and it almost certainly was), there were three popular suspects - the widow, the widow's companion-housekeeper, Mrs. Jane Cannon Cox (49), and the widow's erstwhile 'ancient lover', 68-year-old Dr James Manby Gully, wizard of the Malvern water cure. There was a 'trial by inquest', from which Mrs. Bravo and Mrs. Cox emerged as equal favourites so far as the public was concerned, but neither attracting the further interest or action of the law. Type specimen of a nineteenth-century *cause scandaleuse*, the Bravo affair has matured into one of the great, abiding Victorian murder mysteries. A tragic figure, Florence did not long survive Bravo, dying, like her first husband, Lieutenant Alexander Ricardo, of drink, at Coombe Lodge, Southsea, Hampshire, on September 17th, 1878.

PRIME SOURCES:
The Balham Mystery: or, The 'Bravo' Poisoning Case. Broadsheet issued in seven weekly parts, 1876.
The Bravo Case. F.J.P. Veale. The Merrymeade Publishing Co. Ltd, Brighton, 1950.
How Charles Bravo Died. Yseult Bridges. Jarrolds, London, 1956.
Suddenly at the Priory. John Williams. Heinemann, London, 1957.
Murder at the Priory. Bernard Taylor and Kate Clarke. Grafton Books, London, 1988.
Death at the Priory: Love, Sex and Murder in Victorian England. James Ruddick. Atlantic Books, London, 2001.

Jerome Henry Brudos

A Case of Necrophilia

SERIAL KILLER

MURDERER: Jerome Henry Brudos.

VICTIMS: Linda K Slawson (19). Jan Susan Whitney (23). Karen Elena Sprinker (19). Linda Dawn Salee (22).

LOCUS: 3123 Center Street, Salem, Oregon. Brudos' home.
In the basement there (Slawson).
In the garage workshop (Whitney, Sprinker, Salee).

DATES: January 26th, 1968 (Slawson). November 26th, 1968 (Whitney). March 27th, 1969 (Sprinker). April 23rd, 1969 (Salee).

MEANS: Strangulation.

MOTIVE: To be the man who had power over women. Expressing hatred of women, and reaping sexual gratification.

CRIMEWATCH: Brudos hated, and was disliked by, his mother, who repeatedly compared him disadvantageously with his brother. He early exhibited aberrant traits. First shoe fetishism. Graduated to female underwear fetishism, stealing from clothes-lines and enjoying dressing up in them. In 1956, aged 17, committed to Oregon State Mental Hospital, Salem, for beating up a girl. Joined US Army, March, 1959. Discharged on psychiatric grounds, October. A skilled electrician, married Darcie Metzler (17). Two children. Overbearing, though not unkind, husband, but his sexual psychopathy accelerating. Prior to 1968, had beaten, choked and raped, but never killed. Then murdered four women. Thought to have killed a fifth - Stephanie Vilcko (16) - but no firm proof. By now, full-blown, dangerous sexual psychopath, exhibiting sadism and necrophilia. Photographed victims before and after death. Cut breasts from Whitney and Sprinker to make paper-weights, and the left foot from Slawson, which he stored in the freezer, to try high-heeled shoes on it. Kept also Whitney's body hanging from the ceiling of his workshop and used it for intercourse after work. Sentenced to life in Oregon State Prison, 1969.

PRIME SOURCE:
Lust Kille. Andy Stack (Ann Rule). New American Library, New York, 1983.

Ted Bundy

The Campus Killer

SERIAL KILLER

MURDERER: Theodore Ted (Robert) Bundy.

VICTIMS: At least 23, possibly 40, girls; perhaps even more.

LOCI: Washington, Oregon, Utah, Colorado, Florida.

DATES: April 1st, 1974–September 2nd, 1978.

MEANS: Usually bludgeoning, also strangling.

MOTIVE: Sexual gratification: there was multiple perversion.

CRIMEWATCH: Unable to cope with his illegitimacy, voyeur, psychology graduate, law student, not such a genius as he imagined (IQ 124), Bundy was a personable, plausible chameleon, at home on campuses and expert at vanishing girls away. Happiest in a Volkswagen, he kept on the move, and twice he escaped from custody. His personality began to disintegrate. He entered the Chi Omega sorority house, Florida State University, Tallahassee, and moved from room to room laying about him with a cudgel. His final known victim, Kimberley Leach, was only twelve years old. In court in Miami in 1979, he enjoyed the glamour of defending himself. Bite marks on a body were powerfully evidential, and he was sent to Death Row. On January 24th, 1989, he was electrocuted, aged 42, at Florida State Prison.

PRIME SOURCES:
The Stranger Beside Me. Ann Rule. W. W. Norton, New York, 1980.
Bundy: The Deliberate Stranger. Richard W. Larsen. Prentice Hall, New Jersey, 1980.
The Phantom Prince: My Life With Ted Bundy. Elizabeth Kendall. Madrona, Seattle, 1981.
The Only Living Witness. Stephen G. Michaud and Hugh Aynesworth. Simon & Schuster, New York, 1983.
Ted Bundy: Conversations With a Killer. Stephen G. Michaud and Hugh Aynesworth. Signet Books, New York, 1989.

William Burke & William Hare

The Edinburgh Body Snatchers

MASS MURDERERS

MURDERERS: William Burke & William Hare.

VICTIMS: Certainly 16. Very likely 17. Possibly more.

LOCI: Known loci - Log's Lodgings, Tanner's Close, West Port, Edinburgh, and Gibbs Close, Canongate, Edinburgh.

DATE: 1828.

MEANS: Smothering or 'burking'.

MOTIVE: Simple, straightforward financial gain.

CRIMEWATCH: Wrongly styled body-snatchers. They murderously manufactured the goods they purveyed to the medical schools. Both men were Irish, though they practised in Scotland. Burke hanged January 28th, 1829. He was 36. Pieces of the rope sold at 2s.6d. per inch. Burke's skeleton and a pocket-book bound in his flayed skin are preserved in Edinburgh medical collections. Forget the old canard about Hare, who was around the same age as Burke at the time of the murders, ending up as a blind beggar on the north side of London's Oxford Street. Poetic Justice: Burke's cadaver was dissected by the medics, and his skeleton now stands, a monument to himself, in the anatomical museum at Edinburgh University.

PRIME SOURCES:

Trial of William Burke and Helen M'Dougal (With Supplement). John MacNee. Robert Buchanan, Edinburgh, 1829.

The Westport Murders. Anon. Thomas Ireland, Edinburgh, 1829.

The History of Burke and Hare. George MacGregor. Thomas D. Morison, Glasgow, 1884.

Notable British Trial. Edited by William Roughead. William Hodge, Einburgh, 1921.

Burke and Hare: The True Story. Hugh Douglas. Robert Hale, London, 1973

Burke and Hare: The Resurrection Men. Jacques Barzun. The Scarecrow Press, Metuchen, New Jersey, 1974.

Burke and Hare. Owen Dudley Edwards. Polygon Books, Edinburgh, 1980.

Frederick Bywaters
& Edith Thompson
The Stabbing of Percy Thompson

MURDERERS: Frederick Edward Francis Bywaters. Edith Jessie Thompson.

VICTIM: Percy Thompson (32): husband of Edith.

LOCUS: Belgrave Road, Ilford, Essex: along which the Thompsons were walking home to 41 Kensington Gardens shortly after midnight, returning from a visit to the theatre.

DATE: October 4th, 1922.

MEANS: Stabbing – by the hand of Bywaters..

MOTIVE: Elimination of husband for amatory ends.

CRIMEWATCH: The jury believed that Edith Thompson had incited her lover to murder her husband. Her love-letters, which Bywaters, a ship's writer, had preserved in a locked box on the SS *Morea*, made sinister reference to powdered glass and poison, although the post-mortem, conducted by Sir Bernard Spilsbury, proved negative on those matters. Both Edith Thompson (28) and Frederick Bywaters (20) were hanged at 9 a.m. on January 9th, 1923, she at Holloway Prison, he at Pentonville. It has been suggested that she might have been pregnant.

PRIME SOURCES:
Notable British Trial, edited by Filson Young, William Hodge, Edinburgh, 1923.
The Innocence of Edith Thompson, Lewis Broad, Hutchinson, London, 1952.
Bywaters and Mrs Thompson, Ernest Dudley, Odhams Press, London, 1953.
Criminal Justice, René Weis, Hamish Hamilton, London, 1988.

James Camb

The Porthole Murder

MURDERER: James Camb.

VICTIM: Eileen Isabella Ronnie 'Gay' Gibson (21).

LOCUS: Cabin 126, Union Castle liner *Durban Castle*.

DATE: October 18th, 1947.

MEANS: Probably strangulation.

MOTIVE: Can be only conjectural: e.g. concealment of rape, or plain sadistic murder, in a man who had previously attacked three women on shipboard.

CRIMEWATCH: Camb (31) admitted disposing of the body of the attractive young actress, to whose cabin he had paid a secret visit that night, by pushing it out through the porthole. His defence was that she had died of natural causes – a fit – during voluntary sexual intercourse with him, and that he had panicked. Scratches were found on his wrists. He was convicted of murder, sentenced to death, reprieved and sentenced to life imprisonment in 1948. Released on licence in 1959, he was in trouble in May, 1967, for indecent assault on an eight-year-old girl. He was put on probation for two years. But in May, 1971, found guilty of 'lewd, indecent and libidinous practices' towards three young girls, he was sent back to prison. Finally released in 1978, suffering with heart trouble. Died July 7th, 1979. He was then known as James Clarke.

PRIME SOURCES:
Notable British Trial. Edited by Geoffrey Clark. William Hodge, Edinburgh, 1949.
The Girl in the Stateroom. Charles Boswell and Lewis Thompson. Gold Medal Books, New York, 1951.
The Porthole Murder Case. Denis Herbstein. Hodder & Stoughton, London, 1991.

John Cannan

The Bristolian Lady-killer

MURDERER: John David Guise Cannan.

VICTIM: Shirley Anne Banks (29).

LOCUS:. Not known. Likely to have been either Bristol, or by Dead Woman's Ditch, in Great Wood, near Over Stowey, in the Quantock Hills of Somerset.

DATE: Murder committed between October 8th and 29th, 1987.

MEANS: Bludgeoning to death with a heavy stone.

MOTIVE: Sexual.

CRIMEWATCH: Thursday was late night opening for the shops in Bristol, and it was on Thursday, October 8th, 1987, that Shirley Anne Banks, only recently returned from honeymooning on the Isle of Capri, decided to drive down in her orange Mini Clubman saloon to the Broadmead Centre to buy a new dress at Debenhams. She was never seen again alive.

On Thursday, October 29th, 1987, precisely three weeks to the day since Mrs. Banks' disappearance, there came, at about five minutes to four o'clock in the afternoon, into a boutique named Ginger, at 20a Regent Street, Leamington Spa, a man wearing a crash helmet and brandishing a knife. He threatened the shop's 40-year-old owner, Carmel Cleary, and her manageress, Jane Child. His assumed intent was robbery. Mrs. Cleary ran out of the shop screaming, and, foiled, the intruder fled. After a chase through the streets, he was caught and arrested.

He was identified as John Cannan, of Flat 2, Foye House, Bridge Road, Leigh Woods, Bristol. His black BMW, found parked nearby, was searched. In it was found a replica .38 Smith and Wesson revolver, and his briefcase in which was the tax disc from Shirley Banks' car. In his garage at Foye House, repainted blue, and fitted with new registration plates, was the car itself.

Cannan (35), the product of a good home, was well educated and above average intelligence. Handsome and superficially charming in the brand image of his kind, he was a car salesman. He denied any knowledge of the vanished

Shirley Banks, and insisted that he had bought the car from a dealer. His record, however, belied the easy candour of his manner.

He had a history of committing acts of violence and of rape. He had been released on July 25th, 1986, after serving five of an eight-year sentence for the rape of a pregnant woman in Sutton Coldfield in 1981. And on October 6th, 1986, he had been questioned about the vicious rape of a woman motorist in Reading, but there had been insufficient evidence to charge him. A year later, on October 7th, 1987, he had attempted to kidnap Julia Pauline Holman, who was sitting in her car at Canon's Marsh car park. It was only her loud screams and the execution of a well directed kick that saved her as he tried to push his way into the car. Next day, Shirley Banks was not to be so fortunate.

On Easter Day, April 3rd, 1988, Jill Hooper was walking with her husband and children along a forest trail in a conifer plantation known as Great Wood, a little over a mile from the A39 Bridgwater to Minehead road, in Somerset, when she saw a naked female body lying face down in the water of Dead Woman's Ditch, so called because of a murder committed in that spot two centuries before.

Shirley Banks had been found.

She had been bludgeoned to death with, forensic pathologist Professor Bernard Knight thought, a heavy stone or rock. After six or seven months' exposure, the body was in a fairly advanced state of decomposition, and was identified by the work that had been done on the teeth. Oddly, by an act of God some might say, the only surviving skin on her hands was part of the palm of her left hand, and this, together with hand prints taken from objects in her home, was enough to prove that a thumbprint found in Cannan's luxury flat was definitely hers.

His trial opened at Exeter Crown Court on April 5th, 1989. The prosecution alleged that he had forced her, at knife or replica pistol point, to drive to his flat. She was kept prisoner there, and raped. Then, either her corpse, or, if she was still alive, she, was driven to the remote Somerset woodland, to be killed.

Slightly puzzling was the evidence of Mrs. Amelia Hart (69), who, in the early afternoon of October 9th, 1986, had seen someone being attacked in Leigh Woods, situated hard by the Foye House block of flats. She said that a man was punching something that she could not see, and she heard a youth or girl's voice shouting 'No, oh! No!' and a man saying 'I warned you what I would do. I warned you. I warned you,' followed by a blood-curdling scream.

On April 28th, 1989, Cannan was found guilty of the kidnap and murder of Shirley Banks, the attempted kidnap of Julia Holman, and also on counts of rape and buggery. Mr. Justice Drake gave him three life sentences, and added the recommendation that the period that he served in prison 'shall be the period of your life'.

This was surely a wise proviso, since it seems more than likely that Cannan was a serial killer in embryo. Indeed, his hand is suspected in two unsolved cases of 1986. He is known to have been in Bournemouth on May 3rd, 1986, the day that Sandra Court (27) was found floating in a water-filled ditch by Avon Causeway, Hurn, Christchurch. She had been strangled.

He was also suspected of being the 'Mr. Kipper' – Cannan had been nicknamed 'Kipper' because of his taste for wearing broad kipper-style ties – with whom the 25-year-old estate agent, Suzy Lamplugh, kept an appointment to view a house in Shorrolds Road, Fulham, West London, on July 28th, 1986. She has never been seen since.

PRIME SOURCE:
Ladykiller. Christopher Berry-Dee and Robin Odell. True Crime, Virgin Publishing, London, 1992.

Patrick Carraher

Stabber From the Gorbals

MURDERER: Patrick Carraher.

VICTIMS: James Sydney Emden Shaw (23). John Gordon, junior (39).

LOCI: Junction of Ballater and Thistle Streets in the Gorbals district of Glasgow (Shaw). In Taylor Street, near McAslin Street, in the Townhead district of Glasgow (Gordon).

DATE: August 14th, 1938 (Shaw). November 23rd, 1945 (Gordon).

MEANS: Stabbing.

MOTIVE: Relief of drunken aggression.

CRIMEWATCH: Twice tried for murder in Glasgow. Petty criminal denizen of the Gorbals. Product of the sub-world of McArthur and Long's *No Mean City*. A street brawler. Violent. More violent in drink. Fatal stabbing of the young soldier, Shaw, reduced to charge of culpable homicide (*Anglice:* manslaughter). Sentenced to three years' penal servitude. Defence based on psychopathy, alcoholism, 'persecution mania', and diminished responsibility (then available only in Scotland) failed and, for the murder of Gordon, he was hanged at Barlinnie Prison, Glasgow, on April 6th, 1946. Carraher was 39 years old.

PRIME SOURCE:
Notable British Trial. Edited by George Blake. William Hodge, Edinburgh, 1951.

Lindy Chamberlain

The Dingo Baby Case

ACCUSED: Alice Lynne (Lindy) Chamberlain. Pastor Michael Chamberlain: husband.

VICTIM: Azaria Chantel Loren: daughter, aged nine weeks.

LOCUS: Ayers Rock, Northern Territory, Central Australia.

DATE: August 17th, 1980.

MEANS: Suggested: cutting of neck with sharp instrument, such as small pair of scissors. Necessarily conjectural, based on bloodstain pattern on discovered garment, as body never found.

MOTIVE: Unknown. Prosecution unable to offer any. Mrs. Chamberlain's doctor negated explanation of post-natal depression.

CRIMEWATCH: Baby allegedly carried off from tent by wild dingo. Scientific evidence held to contradict this scenario. Bafflingly controversial case. February 2nd, 1986, Azaria's matinée jacket found. June 2nd, 1987, the Chamberlains' convictions quashed and they were acquitted. But argument still divides Australia.

PRIME SOURCES:

Azaria; Wednesday's Child. James Simmonds. TPNL Books, Melbourne, 1982.

The Dingo Baby Case. Richard Shears. Sphere Books, London, 1982.

Evil Angels. John Bryson. Viking, Penguin Books, Australia, 1985.

The Dingo Baby Case. Ken Crispin. Lion Publishing, Tring, England, 1987.

Innocence Regained. Norman H. Young. The Federation Press, Annandale, New South Wales, 1989.

Through My Eyes. Lindy Chamberlain. William Heinemann, Australia, 1990, London, 1991.

Eugène Marie Chantrelle
The Dominant Dominie

MURDERER: Eugène Marie Chantrelle.

VICTIM: Elizabeth Cullen Dyer or Chantrelle (25): wife.

LOCUS: 81a George Street, Edinburgh.

DATE: January 2nd, 1878.

MEANS: Poison. Probably opium. Administered on a piece of orange and/or in lemonade.

MOTIVE: Elimination, plus gain. Wife insured for £1,000.

CRIMEWATCH: Extremely nasty, luxuriantly hirsute venefic. A Frenchman. Born at Nantes in 1834. A gifted linguist, followed the profession of teacher in England, where he was jailed for nine months for 'an outrage of a very gross nature' upon one of his pupils. He repeated this free French sexual liberalism while, in 1867, teaching at Newington Academy, a private school in Edinburgh. Having seduced and impregnated her, he was constrained to marry his unfortunate 15-year-old pupil, Elizabeth Cullen Dyer. She bore him four sons. Brutal and dipsomaniacal, he treated the poor young woman shamefully for ten years – first at No. 95 and then No. 81a George Street, and on holiday at 17 Pitt Street, Portobello. He tried to blame her death on a leaking gas-pipe in the bedroom. His was the first non-public execution to take place in Scotland, being carried out by William Marwood within the Calton Jail, Edinburgh, on May 31st, 1878. He made no confession. Before burial, a plaster cast was made of his head for exhibition in the Phenology museum. Wife buried, grave T118, Grange Cemetery, Edinburgh.

PRIME SOURCE:
Notable Scottish Trial. Edited by A. Duncan Smith. William Hodge, Edinburgh, 1906.

George Chapman
aka Severin Klowsowski
The Borough Poisoner

MASS MURDERER

MURDERER: George Chapman, properly Severin Klosowski.

VICTIMS: Mary Isabella Spink (41): masquerading as 'wife'. Elizabeth Taylor (36): masquerading as 'wife'. Maud Eliza Marsh (19): masquerading as 'wife'.

LOCI: Prince of Wales Tavern, Bartholomew Square, Finsbury, London (Spink). Monument Tavern, Union Street, Borough, South-East London (Taylor). Crown public-house, Union Street, Borough, South-East London (Marsh).

DATES: December 25th, 1897 (Spink). February 13th, 1901 (Taylor). October 22nd, 1902 (Taylor).

MEANS: Antimony in all three cases.

MOTIVE: Desire for a change of quasi-matrimonial partner, with a clawing-in of any financial pickings on the way. An element of sadism may have been attached.

CRIMEWATCH: Parallel facts of timing and abode can be adduced to argue that Chapman was really Jack the Ripper under another hat, operating domestically after the East End streets had become too hot for his pleasures. Inspector Abberline it was who first raised this no longer fashionable hare, congratulating Chapman's arresting officer, Inspector Godley, 'You've got Jack the Ripper at last.' Chapman's exotic background was persuasive. In origin he was a Russian Pole, a *Feldscher* or barber-surgeon. Not a frank madman, but reckless, lively, libidinous, cunning cyclist with the police cycling club, photographer of his besotted victims. Born on December 14th, 1865. Hanged at Wandsworth on April 7th, 1903.

PRIME SOURCE:
Notable British Trial. Edited by H. L. Adam, William Hodge, Edinburgh, 1930.

Alan Charlton & Idris Ali

The Cardiff Corpse in a Carpet

Victim Karen Price (reconstructed from skull)

MURDERERS: Alan Charlton & Idris Ali.

VICTIM: Karen Wendy Price (15).

LOCUS: 29 Fitzhamon Embankment, Cardiff.

DATE: Probably during the week of 1st to 8th August, 1981.

MEANS: Probably strangulation.

MOTIVE: No rational motive. Probably a rage attack during heightened sexual activity, and possibly under the influence of drugs.

CRIMEWATCH: The skeleton in the carpet was discovered by four workmen who were digging a ditch in the rear garden of 29 Fitzhamon Embankment, a dingy area of Cardiff. It happened on December 7th, 1989, eight full years after the murder. The body lay only two and a half feet below the surface, but had not previously been disturbed in any way. It was face down. The roll of carpet was bound with black electric cable. The skull was covered by a white plastic bag, and a black dustbin bag shrouded the upper body. The wrists were bound behind the back, also with black cable.

The skeleton was found to be that of a young woman, about 15 years old and 5ft 4 in. tall. There were some fragments of surviving clothing, notably 'Karman Ghia' jeans and a grey 'Levi–Strauss' sweatshirt, made in America for the British market in December, 1980. This was a date marker. The cause of death was obscure.

A forensic odontologist, Dr David Whittaker, found that the teeth and their roots exhibited a pink discolouration, which is indicative of strangling. Extensive and exhaustive enquiries were made under three main heads: missing girls; previous residents at the old, run-down house; and imaginative scientific endeavours. Dr Zakaria Erzinçlioglu, a Cambridge University entomologist, took the dating of the burial as far back as 1984, by estimating the time-span of the 'coffin flies' found in the grave, and the

cycle of the colony of woodlice which had been existing on the fungus of the bones.

In order to determine the racial origin, the Natural History Museum compared the skull with a database of 2,500 others, and came up with the result that the girl was of European or Indian type. There were some fair hairs adhering to the scalp, and it was further suggested that she was of Mediterranean blood. Her teeth were quite prominent. Still the dead girl was unclaimed, the time-lapse against her. In the end, it was the technique of facial reconstruction which proved to be the most rewarding.

Medical artist, Richard Neave, of Manchester University, created a clay model of the dead girl's face, by means of taking casts and then building up the clay to the depth of pegs indicating standard depths of flesh. Shoulder-length hair completed the effect. The dummy eyes stared out, and the strange head, an eerie terracotta colour, turning on several planes, made a great impact on all who saw it on television.

Two social workers made separate calls to say that they recognised the girl as Karen Wendy Price, born on September 4th 1965, an absconder from Maes-Yr-Eglwys Assessment Centre, at Church Village, near Pontypridd. She had last been seen there on July 2nd, 1981. Her parents, a Cypriot father and a Spanish mother, had assumed that she had moved away and was living a new life. The centre had closed in 1984, and after two years the registers were closed. Genetic fingerprinting, using scrapings from the femur of the skeleton and blood samples from Karen Price's parents, showed that the chances were one in 10,000 that Karen Price was indeed the dead girl. However, extreme science was not the ultimate key to the mystery.

On January 15th, 1990, the 'Crimewatch' television programme featured a reconstruction of Karen Price's last known days of freedom, out on the town, and clearly at risk. That night, a young man who knew a great deal about her contacted the police through an intermediary. Idris Ali, aged 24, a convicted burglar, had seen 'Crimewatch' with three companions. They were mulling it over, and he could not resist telling them that he had been friendly with Karen. Indeed, they had been at Special School together. He asked Meic Corcoran to telephone the police with a message that 'There's a bloke in the house that knew Karen Price.'

At interview, Ali was scared and told differing stories, but a general picture emerged. He was 15 years old in the summer of 1981, on the loose in Cardiff, and when he came across runaway Karen, he managed to induce her to work as a prostitute. He was her teenage pimp. Two other under-age girls, Mandy and Jane, were involved.

One evening, by evil chance, they all met Alan Charlton, older at 21, a powerful, flashy 'bouncer', a weight-lifter with a violent past. He inveigled them to attend sex parties at his basement flat at 29 Fitzhamon Embankment –

the crucial address. There was money in it for the youngsters. The terminal, bad party exploded into a cataclysmic scene, when Charlton suddenly lost his temper. Only four people were present: Charlton, Ali, Karen, and Mandy. They were probably smoking cannabis. The two girls refused to strip and perform together for pornographic photographs. Charlton 'went berserk' and strangled Karen. There was some suggestion of 'necrophilia'.

Mandy, who was only 13, was a witness to the terrifying scene: she was traced and gave evidence for the Crown. Ali's part in the murder was unclear, and he claimed an element of duress exerted by the older, stronger man. Perhaps this was so, although duress is not, as was to be pointed out by the judge at the trial, a defence to murder. Both Ali and Charlton, acting in concert, buried the corpse some four days later, after it had been concealed in a cupboard.

Both men were put up for murder at Cardiff Crown Court on January 21st, 1991, and both were convicted. The Judge said that he was sure that Charlton had played the major rôle. The sentences were not identical: Alan Charlton was to serve imprisonment for life, but Idris Ali was treated as a 16-year-old, to be detained indefinitely, 'during Her Majesty's Pleasure.'

PRIME SOURCE:
Dead Giveaway: Murder Avenged From The Grave (Chapter 6). Donald Thomas. Michael O'Mara, London, 1993.

Andrei Chikatilo

The Russian Ripper

SERIAL KILLER

MURDERER: Andrei Romanovich Chikatilo.

VICTIMS: 52 young women, girls and boys, probably more.

LOCI: An area around Rostov on Don in Southern Russia, North East of the Black Sea. Usually outdoors, in the woods, once while on a business trip to Moscow.

DATES: December, 1978 – November, 1990.

MEANS: Stabbing, strangulation, bludgeoning, with mutilation.

MOTIVE: Sexual. Unable to sustain an erection, he found that overpowering a victim, witnessing the agony, hearing the screams and, above all, seeing the blood-flow, stimulated an orgasm, as he lay on the body in gross simulation of intercourse.

CRIMEWATCH: When the western world first saw the images of Chikatilo, grimacing, shaven-headed, in his iron cage in the courtroom, he seemed scarcely human, like a creature from the forest. The Russian culture at the time had denied that serial killers existed in their social régime, but they do occur, and are, in their characteristics, the same, with minor local variations, all across the globe.

Right up to his arrest, Chikatilo (born in 1936) presented himself as a neatly dressed graduate, dedicated comrade of the Communist Party, family man with two children, and grandchildren. Typically, his wife, Fayina, knew nothing of his crimes and he had convincing reasons for his brief absences from home, when he had to travel in the course of his job as a supplies clerk. Like any classic serial killer, he set off regularly on journeys of intent, using, in particular, the railway services.

He would prowl, polite and self-effacing, up and down trains until he found a young person who would get off at the next halt with him. Enticements such as chewing-gum were offered. Once, he had held more important posts as schoolteacher, having studied hard at Rostov University and obtained a degree in Russian Philology and literature, after law school at Moscow University had, to his deep chagrin, turned him down. Eventually, he had had to leave teaching, because of his record of gross sexual abuse of children in his charge.

He was a disappointed man in all respects, especially in his sex life. Once caught, he made no secret of his inability to sustain an erection, rather like our own Reggie 'No Dick' Halliday Christie. He did manage by some means to father two children. According to his own account, he first achieved full sexual satisfaction, and realised his destiny, when he saw the blood welling from his first murder victim, on December 22nd, 1978. Lena Zakotnova was only nine, and had been lured into his clandestine, sparsely furnished shack, to which he took prostitutes.

Did he, as he pushed himself even further into his sadistic crimes, actually practise cannibalism? He was widely thought to have done so, but the evidence is not clear. Certainly, he mutilated the bodies, and cut off body parts, especially tongues; sometimes genitalia were missing from the crime scene. What he did admit, was that he liked to chew the uterus: the texture excited him. Like the original Jack the Ripper, he delved for the womb. At first he slashed the eyes, believing in the old story that the retina's last picture was of the murderer, and that it could be recalled.

An important turning-point in the long-running case came early on, in 1984, when he was arrested and found to have a different blood group from the semen samples taken from victims. After that, whenever his name came up in the investigation, he was discounted. Too late, Japanese scientists discovered that one in a million men are 'paradoxical secretors', with their semen and blood of different types. This rare anomaly had protected Chikatilo and allowed his rampage to continue until his suspicious, predatory behaviour, accosting likely young targets, finally caused his arrest. It was very wrong that four young men of subnormal intellect had confessed to the crimes while in custody, and that one man, Aleksandr Kravchenko, who had a bad sexual record and had the misfortune to live on the same road as Chikatilo's sex shack, had already been executed for the murder of Lena Zakotnova.

Captured in 1990, Chikatilo caved in and co-operated. He seemed to enjoy taking the police officers to the scenes of his crimes, as in the case of our Moors Murderers. They provided him with a large dummy, so that he could demonstrate exactly what he had done to his victims. On trial, in Rostov in 1992, however, his behaviour became bizarre. He pulled his trousers down suddenly and shouted, 'Look at this useless thing! What could I do with that?'

As Judge Leonid Akuhzhanov droned out the charges over three days, some of the wailing relatives in court fainted, and so did two of the soldiers guarding the prisoner's iron cage. Chikatilo was executed by a shot in the head early in 1994: no set date is pronounced in Russian criminal law.

It was speculated that an early trauma might have unhinged Chikatilo's mind: his mother had told him, when he was five, that a cousin of his had been abducted and eaten during the famine of the 1930s, when cannibalism was widely rumoured. He did have an abnormal EEG, a slightly hydrocephalic skull, and unequal pupils, suggesting some pathological organic state, but he was almost certainly simulating insanity at his trial.

PRIME SOURCES:

The Red Ripper. Peter Conradi. BCA and Virgin Publishing, London, 1992.

The Killer Department. Robert Cullen. Orion, London, 1993.

Comrade Chikatilo. Mikhail Krivich and Ol'gert Ol'gin. Barricade Books, Fort Lee, New Jersey, 1993.

John Reginald Halliday Christie
The Rillington Place Strangler

SERIAL KILLER

MURDERER: John Reginald Halliday Christie.

VICTIMS: Ruth Margarete Christine Fuerst (21). Muriel Amelia Eady (32). Beryl Susanna Evans (20): fellow-tenant. (?) Geraldine Evans: Beryl's 13-month-old baby. (?) Ethel Christie (54): wife. Kathleen Maloney (26). Rita Nelson (24). Hectorina MacLennan (26).

LOCUS: 10 Rillington Place (later re-named Ruston Close), Notting Hill, London.

DATES: August 1943 (Fuerst). October 1944 (Eady). November 8th, 1949 (Evans). November 10th, 1949 (Geraldine Evans). December 14th, 1952 (Ethel Christie). January 1953 (Maloney). January 1953 (Nelson). March 6th, 1953 (MacLennan).

MEANS: Strangulation with a ligature.

MOTIVE: Generally, sexual gratification with necrophilia. In the case of Mrs. Christie, plain elimination. Baby Geraldine was killed because her motherless presence would have been incriminating.

CRIMEWATCH: Timothy John Evans was hanged at Pentonville on March 9th, 1950, for the murder of his daughter, Geraldine. He had confessed to killing both his wife and daughter, whose bodies were found in the washhouse, although he later retracted and blamed Christie. On March 24th, 1953, the bodies of Maloney, Nelson, and MacLennan were discovered in a papered-over alcove in the kitchen. Mrs. Christie's body was under the floorboards of the ground-floor front room. The skeletons of Fuerst and Eady were dug up from the garden. Christie confessed to the murder of Beryl Evans, but not to that of Geraldine. The apportionment of guilt is still hotly debated. Christie (born April 8th, 1898) was hanged at Pentonville on July 15th, 1953. On October 18th, 1966, Evans was granted a posthumous free pardon.

PRIME SOURCES:
Medical and Scientific Investigations in the Christie Case. Medical Publications Limited, London, 1953.

Horne Office Report: The Deaths of Mrs. Beryl Evans and Geraldine Evans, by J. Scott Henderson, Q.C. Her Majesty's Stationery Office, July 1953, Cmd. 8896.
Supplementary Report: The Case of Timothy John Evans, by Mr. J.Scott Henderson, Q.C. Her Majesty's Stationery Office, September 1953, Cmd. 8946.
The Man on Your Conscience? An Investigation of the Evans Murder Trial. Michael Eddowes. Cassell, London, 1955.
Notable British Trial. Edited by F. Tennyson Jesse. William Hodge, Edinburgh, 1957.
The Christie Case. Ronald Maxwell. R. S. Gray, London, nd.
The Two Stranglers of Rillington Place. Rupert Furneaux. Panther Books, London, 1961.
Ten Rillington Place. Ludovic Kennedy. Gollancz, London, 1961.
The Case of Timothy John Evans, Home Office Report of an Inquiry by The Hon. Mr. Justice Brabin. Her Majesty's Stationery Office, October 1966, Cmnd. 3101.

Douglas Clark
The Sunset Slayer

SERIAL KILLER

MURDERER: Douglas Daniel Clark.

VICTIMS: Marnette Comer (17). Gina Marano (15). Cynthia Chandler (16): Marano's step-sister, Exxie Wilson (20). KarenJones (24). Sixth unidentified young girl.

LOCI: A ravine near Sylmar, San Fernando Valley: mummified body found June 30th, 1980 (Comer). Along a Los Angeles highway exit road, two bodies found June 12th, 1980 (Marano, Chandler). Studio City - Burbank area of LA. In sedate Burbank neighbourhood, body found June 24th, 1980 (Jones). In an alley, headless body found, June 24th, 1980 (Wilson). Missing head found June 27th, in wooden box in the driveway of a Burbank resident's home. Saugus-Newhall area of LA. Body of a nude girl discovered March 2nd, 1981.

DATES: June 1st, 1980 (Comer). June 11th, 1980 (Marano, Chandler). June 24th, 1980 (Wilson, Jones). Date unknown (unidentified girl).

MEANS: Shooting with small-calibre gun.

MOTIVE: Enjoyment of perverse sexual practices, with attendant necrophilia.

CRIMEWATCH: Clark, a 34-year-old boilermaker, and his mistress, Carol Mary Bundy (37), a nurse, spent the summer of 1980 cruising Hollywood's Sunset Boulevard in his station wagon looking for young women – prostitutes, 'mysteries', runaways – to sate Clark's kinky appetite. His particular fancy was to shoot a girl through the head at the climax of fellatio. He would then strip her of her underwear, to be saved as a potent trophy, have intercourse with the corpse and, the ultimate refinement, carry away her severed head to be subsequently made-up like a Barbie doll by Bundy and used as an object of sexual gratification. On August 9th, 1980, the headless body of John Robert Murray (45), Bundy's former boyfriend, was found in his parked car a few streets from his Van Nuys home. He had been shot and stabbed many times. Bundy was arrested. Pursuing a tip-off, police arrested Clark – August 11th – charged him on six counts of murder and with aiding and abetting Bundy. He tried to blame all the killings on her and Jack Murray, declaring the couple were Ted Bundy copy-cat killers. Changing her plea of not guilty by reason of insanity to guilty, Bundy, mother of two, drew a 52 years to life sentence. Clark, condemned to the San Quentin gas chamber on March 16th, 1983, told the jury, 'I don't march to the same drummer as you do.' He is sill sitting on Death Row.

PRIME SOURCE:
The Sunset Murders, Louise Farr, Pocket Books, Simon & Schuster, New York, 1992.

The Cleveland Butcher

SERIAL KILLER

MURDERER: Identity unknown.

VICTIMS: Official body count: 12 victims. Speculatively: 13-40.
The official 12 are Edward Andrassy, Florence Sawdey Polillo,
Rose Wallace and 6 unknown men and 3 unknown women.

*Frank Dolezal – was he the
Cleveland butcher?*

LOCI: In and around Cleveland, Ohio. Kingsbury Run, Jackass Hill, at East 4th Street (Andrassy and
Body 2, unknown male). 2315 East 20th Street, alley behind (Polillo). Kingsbury Run, Woodland
Avenue and East 51st Street (Body 4, tattooed male). Big Creek, near Clinton Road, Brooklyn (Body
5, male). Kingsbury Run, stagnant pool below East 37th Street bridge (Body 6, male). Shore of Lake
Erie, beach at foot of East 156th Street (Body 7, female). Under east portion of Lorain-Carnegie Bridge
(Wallace). In Cuyahoga River at West 3rd Street and Erie Railroad (Body 9, male). In Cuyahoga River
near Superior Avenue (Body 10, female). Intersection of East 9th Street and Shore Drive (Body 11,
female, and Body 12, male).

DATES: September 23rd, 1935 (Andrassy and Body 2). January 26th, 1936 (Florence Polillo). June 5th,
1936 (Body 4, male). July 22nd, 1936 (Body 5, male). September 10th, 1936 (Body 6, male). February
23rd, 1937 (Body 7, female). June 5th, 1937 (Wallace). July 6th, 1937 (Body 9, male). April 8th, 1938
(Body 10, female) August 16th, 1938 (Body 11, female and Body 12, male).

MEANS: Decapitation. Retracted neck muscles indicate at, or immediately after, death.

MOTIVE: Probably sheer *Lustmord*. Sadistic pleasure with bizarrely variable sexual psychopathy. Three
of the males emasculated.

CRIMEWATCH: Brilliant knife-work suggested skill
in the wielding of lethal cutlery. Inexplicably,
supply of headless torsos suddenly dried up in
Cleveland in 1938. But six more turned up in
neighbouring Pennsylvania 1938-42. Prime
suspect, Frank Dolezal, a 52-year-old Bohemian
bricklayer. Hanged himself in jail in August
1939. Eliot Ness believed killer to be 'Gaylord
Sundheim' - pseudonym for young man of
influential family. The case remains wide open.

PRIME SOURCES:
Cleveland Murders. Edited by Oliver Weld Baver.
Duell, Sloan & Pearce, New York, 1947.
Butcher's Dozen. John B. Martin. Harper &
Brothers, New York, 1950.
Torso. Steven Nickel. John F. Blair, Winston-
Salem, North Carolina, 1989.
*In the Wake of the Butcher: Cleveland's Torso
Murders*. James Jesse Badal. Kent State
University Press, 2001.

Dr Carl Coppolino

The Deadly Doctor

MURDERER: Dr Carl A. Coppolino.

VICTIM: Dr Carmela Coppolino (32): wife.

LOCUS: 591 Bowsprit Lane, Longboat Key, Sarasota, Florida.

DATE: August 28th, 1965.

MEANS: Injection of succinylcholine chloride (a muscle relaxant used in anaesthesiology).

MOTIVE: The theory was that Coppolino wished to be free to remarry. There was also a life insurance of $65,000.

CRIMEWATCH: Coppolino (born May 13th, 1932) was twice tried for murder upon the information of a discarded, older mistress, Marjorie Farber. A jury in Freehold, New Jersey, in December, 1966, did not believe her evidence that Dr Coppolino had hypnotised her into a continuous waking trance, during which, on July 30th, 1963, he tried to influence her to inject her sleeping husband, Lieutenant-Colonel William E. Farber, with succinylcholine chloride. She further stated that Coppolino himself finished him off with a pillow. Dr Carmela Coppolino signed the death certificate, entering coronary thrombosis. For the State, Dr Milton Helpern said that he had found at autopsy no evidence of such thrombosis, and a normal heart for a man of fifty-two. However, he *did* find that the cricoid cartilage in the larynx was fractured. F. Lee Bailey, for the defence, argued that the injury occurred *post mortem*, during the process of late exhumation.

Freed, Dr Coppolino was again put up in Naples, Florida, in April, 1967. This time he was charged with murdering his wife, on August 28th, 1965, by use of the same drug. The death certificate specified coronary occlusion. Three weeks later, widowed Dr Coppolino married Mary Gibson, and the following day, Marjorie Farber went to the authorities. Carmela's body, too, was exhumed, and Dr Helpern found no evidence of any disease whatsoever. There was an apparent needle puncture in the left buttock. The toxicological evidence regarding succinylcholine chloride in the exhumed body was unsatisfactory, but the jury accepted it.

Coppolino was convicted of second-degree murder, and sentenced to life imprisonment. On October 16th, 1979, he was released on lifetime parole, for exemplary behaviour, and, in 1980, produced his own remarkable book about the events (and the atrocious prison conditions in Florida) in which he made worrying inroads into the medical evidence for the State.

PRIME SOURCES:
The Trials of Dr Coppolino. Paul Holmes. The New American Library, New York, 1968.
No Deadly Drug. John D. MacDonald. Doubleday, New York, 1968.
The Crime That Never Was. Carl A. Coppolino, M.D. Justice Press, Inc., Florida, 1980.

Dean Corll

The Lethal Candy Man

SERIAL KILLER

MURDERER: Dean Arnold Corll.

VICTIMS: At least 27 teenage boys.

LOCI: A succession of Houston addresses, according to Corll's two accomplices (see below). 3300 Yorktown. 6363 San Felipe. 3200 Mangum. 915 Columbia Street. 925 Schuler Street. 904 Westcott Towers. 1855 Wirt Road. And in Pasadena, at 2020 Lamar Drive.

DATES: 1970 - 73.

MEANS: Strangling and shooting.

MOTIVE: Sexual gratification, with torture and mutilation.

CRIMEWATCH: Corll, born in 1939, electrician and hander-out of candy, seduced two much younger accomplices, Elmer Wayne Henley and David Owen Brooks, and used them to procure boys from the Heights section of Houston. A pine 'torture-board' with handcuffs was the basis of Corll's equipment. The lost boys were buried under a boathouse, No. 11 Southwest Boat Storage, Silver Shell Road, Houston, at Lake Sam Rayburn, and at High Island Beach. In a final showdown on August 8th, 1973, Henley shot Corll dead, before Corll killed *him*. Henley (born 1956) and Brooks (born 1955) were convicted at San Antonio of six murders and were sentenced to life imprisonment.

PRIME SOURCES:
Mass Murder in Houston. John K. Gurwell. Cordovan Press, Houston, 1974.
The Man With the Candy. Jack Olsen. Simon & Schuster, New York, 1974.

Juan Corona

Madman with a Machete

SERIAL KILLER

MURDERER: Juan Vallejo Corona.

VICTIMS: 25 men of all ages.

LOCUS: On and around the Sullivan Ranch, near Yuba City, California.

DATES: Over about six weeks up to May, 1971.

MEANS: Stabbing, hacking the heads with a machete, and shooting.

MOTIVE: These were homosexual lust murders.

CRIMEWATCH: Fifteen years earlier, Corona had received in-patient treatment for full-blown schizophrenia, from which he had appeared to make a good recovery. Married, with children, he was a respected labour contractor, domiciled at 768 Richland Road, County of Sutter, hiring crews of men to harvest the ripe Californian crops. He put itinerant workers up in a bunkhouse at the Sullivan Ranch, and in shallow graves, dug, sometimes in advance, in the burgeoning orchards, he laid their desecrated bodies – vagrants, hobos, winos, not likely to be missed. But he scattered clues like fallen fruit, and even kept a ledger containing the names of the slain. He was sentenced, aged 38, to twenty-five terms of life imprisonment. In prison he was stabbed 32 times and blinded in one eye. On successful appeal – that he should have pleaded insanity, rather than denial which included alibi – he was moved to an institution for the criminally insane.

PRIME SOURCES:
Burden of Proof. Ed Cray. Macmillan, New York, 1973.
The Road to Yuba City. Tracy Kidder. Doubleday, New York, 1974.
Jury: The People vs. Juan Corona. Victor Villasenor. Little, Brown and Company, Boston, 1977.

Richard Cottingham

The New York Hotel Murders

MURDERER: Richard Francis Cottingham.

VICTIMS: Maryann Carr (26). Deedeh Goodarzi. Unidentified female. Valorie Ann Street (19). Jean Mary Ann Reyner (25).

LOCI: Locus of killing not known. Scream heard at victim's home – Apartment 112, Building 462, Ledgewood Terrace Apartments, Liberty Street, Little Ferry, New Jersey. Body found on parking lot of the Quality Inn, Hasbrouck Heights, New Jersey (Carr). Room 417, Travel Inn Motor Hotel, 515 West 42nd Street, Manhattan, New York (Goodarzi and Unidentified). Room 132, Quality Inn, Hasbrouck Heights, New Jersey (Street). Room 1139, Hotel Seville, East 29th Street, New York (Reyner).

DATES: December 15th, 1977 (Carr). December 2nd, 1979 (Goodarzi and Unidentified). May 4th, 1980 (Street). May 15th, 1980 (Reyner).

MEANS: Strangulation with a ligature. The lungs had collapsed: suffocated? Mouth was taped, and hands and legs handcuffed (Carr). Both bodies found badly burned, on twin beds, with their heads and hands missing. The severed parts were never discovered (Goodarzi and Unidentified). Strangled. Nude body stuffed under bed. Handcuffed, beaten, bitten and raped. Mouth sealed with adhesive tape (Street).Strangled and stabbed. Then breasts cut off and body set on fire (Reyner).

MOTIVE: The facts speak for themselves.

CRIMEWATCH: Cottingham, born November 25th, 1946, married, computer operator, was arrested in mid-flow at his favourite torture-ground, the Quality Inn, Hasbrouck Heights. There, on May 22nd, 1980, in Room 117, for three hours he had been enjoying himself with 18-year-old Leslie Ann O'Dell, until her screams were heard. He ran away, but was caught by a police officer. In his 'Trophy Room', at his home at 29 Vreeland Street, Lodi, New Jersey, clothing, jewellery, perfume, motel keys, and purses were found.

Maryann Carr was a nurse, but the rest of his murder victims were prostitutes. There were a number of other near-murders. Frightened girls testified that Cottingham had first drugged them with barbiturates. He was a savage biter, who went for the girls' breasts. Sentenced to life imprisonment after three separate trials.

PRIME SOURCE:
The Prostitute Murders. Rod Leith. Lyle Stuart, Secaucus, New Jersey, 1983.

Mary Ann Cotton

The West Auckland Bogey-Woman

MASS MURDERER

MURDERER: Mary Ann Cotton.

VICTIMS: Mass murderer – of her nearest and dearest.Some children might have died of natural causes, but 21 persons perished. William Mowbray: her first husband. Her 8 (or 9) children of that union. George Ward: her second husband.Margaret Stott: her own mother. John, James and Elizabeth Robinson: her stepchildren by her third husband, James Robinson. Mary Isabella Robinson: her first child by James Robinson. Frederick Cotton: her bigamous fourth husband. Margaret Cotton: Frederick Cotton's sister. Frederick Cotton and Charles Edward Cotton: Cotton's two sons. Robert Robson Cotton, her own child by Cotton. Joseph Nattras, a lover.

LOCUS: County Durham, England.

DATES: c. 1852 - 72.

MEANS: Arsenic.

MOTIVE: Financial gain from life insurance policies. Freedom to change marital partner.

CRIMEWATCH: Legendary Victorian bogey-woman. Administered arsenic brew in strong tea, having acquired the poison allegedly to anoint bed-legs against bedbugs. Ten-year-old Frederick Cotton, on his death-bed asked to be coffined in his black Glengarry cap. In Mary Cotton's defence, it was put that arsenic had been taken in from exudate of green wallpaper. Hanged – and it was botched – at Durham Prison on March 24th, 1873, aged 40. A rhyme that the local children used to chant runs:

> Mary Anne Cotton,
> She's dead and she's rotten,
> She lies in her bed,
> With her eyes wide oppen,
> Sing, sing, oh, what can I sing,
> Mary Ann Cotton is tied up with string,
> Where, where? Up in the air,
> Sellin' black puddens a penny a pair.

PRIME SOURCES:
When Justice Faltered. Richard Lambert. Methuen, London, 1935.
Mary Ann Cotton. Arthur Appleton. Michael Joseph, London, 1973.
Mary Ann Cotton: Dead but not Forgotten. Tony Whitehead. Privately published, 2000.

Dr Thomas Neill Cream

Pink Pills for Pale Prostitutes

Serial Killerr

Murderer: Dr Thomas Neill Cream.

Victims: Daniel Stott, (*c.* 61). Ellen Donworth (19). Matilda Clover (27). Alice Marsh (21). Emma Shrivell (18).

Loci: Grand Prairie, Boone County, Illinois (Stott). Waterloo Road, South-East London (Donworth). 27 Lambeth Road, South-East London (Clover). 118 Stamford Street, South-East London (Marsh and Shrivell).

Dates: June 14th, 1881 (Stott). October 13th, 1891 (Donworth). October 21st, 1891 (Clover). April 12th, 1892 (Marsh and Shrivell).

Means: Strychnine.

Motive: The sadistic pleasure of dosing unsuspecting prostitutes with a painful poison. Cream did not witness their sufferings, so the enjoyment must have come with the passing of the poison pills to the victim, and in the imagination thereafter.

Crimewatch: Donald Rumbelow, in *The Complete Jack the Ripper,* annihilates the old legend that Dr Cream was really Jack the Ripper, and confessed so to Mr. Hangman Billington. At the material time of the Whitechapel Killings, Cream was incarcerated in the Illinois State Penitentiary, at Joliet, for the murder by strychnine of Daniel Stott, husband of Cream's mistress. Although Cream's relatives may have thought him to be insane, and although he may have been in the habit of taking morphia, he was not McNaughton-mad. He knew the nature and quality of his acts, and he certainly fooled his fiancée, Miss Laura Sabbatini, of Chapel Street, Berkhamstead. On November 15th, 1892 (aged 42), Cream was hanged at Newgate.

Prime Sources:
Notable British Trial. Edited by W. Teignmouth Shore. William Hodge, Edinburgh, 1923.
A Prescription for Murder: The Victorian Serial Killings of Dr Thomas Neill Cream. Angus McLaren. University of Chicago Press, 1993.

Dr Hawley Harvey Crippen

The Horror at Hilldrop Crescent

MURDERER: Dr Hawley Harvey Crippen.

VICTIM: Cora Crippen *née* Kunigunde Mackamotzki, stage-name Belle Elmore (*c.*34): wife.

LOCUS: 39 Hilldrop Crescent, Camden, North London.

DATE: February 1st, 1910.

MEANS: Hyoscine.

MOTIVE: Elimination of a burdensome wife in favour of a new loved one: Ethel Clara le Neve.

CRIMEWATCH: The degree of premeditation is still arguable, the method of administration of hyoscine open to discussion. It is debated that the poison was given merely to quench Cora Crippen's unappreciated libido. Crippen buried the dismembered corpse in quick-lime under the cellar floor, imported Ethel into the household, arrayed her in his wife's finery, and inserted a notice of his wife's death in California in the *Era*. Suspicion forced an urgent passage to Quebec aboard the SS *Montrose*. The cellar was dug up. Hyoscine was found in the viscera, and an abdominal scar went towards identification. Le Neve, tried on her own, was acquitted. Crippen (born in 1862) was hanged at Pentonville Prison on November 23rd, 1910.

PRIME SOURCES:
Notable British Trial. Edited by Filson Young. William Hodge, Edinburgh, 1920.
Doctor Crippen. Max Constantine Quinn. Duckworth, London, 1935.
Dr Crippen. Michael Gilbert. Odhams Press, London, 1953.
Crippen: The Mild Murderer. Tom Cullen. The Bodley Head, London, 1977.
The Crippen File. Jonathan Goodman. Allison & Busby, London, 1985.
Walter Dew: The Man Who Caught Crippen. Nicholas Connell. Sutton Publishing, Stroud, Gloucestershire, 2005.

Jeffrey Dahmer

The Human Flesh-Eater of Milwaukee

SERIAL KILLER

MURDERER: Jeffrey Lionel Dahmer.

VICTIMS: Steven Mark Hicks (19). Steven W. Tuomi (25). James E. Doxtator (14). Richard Guerrero (22). Anthony Sears (24). Raymond Lamont Smith (31). Edward Smith (27). Ernest Miller (23). David Thomas (22). Curtis Straughter (18). Errol Lindsey (19). Anthony Hughes (31). Konerak Sinthasomphone (14). Matt Turner (20). Jeremiah Weinberger (23). Oliver Lacy (24). Joseph Bradehoft (25).

LOCI: Family home at West Bath Road, Bath Township, Ohio (Hicks). Ambassador Hotel, Milwaukee, Wisconsin (Tuomi). Dahmer's grandmother's home at 2357 South 57th Street, West Allis, Wisconsin (Doxtator, Guerrero, Sears). Apartment 213, Oxford Apartments, North 25th Street, Milwaukee, Wisconsin (all the other murders).

DATES: June 18th, 1978 (Hicks). September 15th, 1987 (Tuomi). January 16th, 1988 (Doxtator). March 19th, 1988 (Guerrero). March 25th, 1989 (Sears). May 29th, 1989 (Raymond Lamont Smith). June 14th, 1990 (Edward W. Smith). September 2nd, 1990 (Miller). September 24th, 1990 (Thomas). March 7th, 1991 (Straughter). April 7th, 1991 (Lindsey). May 24th, 1991 (Hughes).. May 26th, 1991 (Sinthasomphone). June 30th, 1991 (Turner). July 6th, 1991 (Weinberger). July 15th, 1991 (Lacy). July 19th, 1991 (Bradehoft).

MEANS: First the enticement to Dahmer's malodorous apartment – 50 dollars, perhaps, for a few photographs – then a chat, perhaps some consensual sexual activity if the young man were his type, followed by a drink heavily doctored with sleeping tablets provided for Dahmer by a kindly doctor. Finally, the murderous attack – strangling with a belt usually, then the longer period of pleasure *post mortem*, necrophilia, fiddling with the body, and dismemberment.

MOTIVE: In the continuing condition of being a serial killer, unstoppable by his own volition, the physical and mental need, compulsive, to select a victim, always male, usually black, to kill him and perform multiple atrocities on the corpse, taking photographs, before destruction, while preserving skulls and other parts as trophies to provide further reminiscent pleasure.

CRIMEWATCH: Dahmer was an exponent of indoor killing, unlikely to be caught in the act, with more time to enjoy the stages of the experience. The snag, especially when there was no garden, was storage and disposal. Dahmer was very good at all that, having had a lifetime's interest in bones and chemicals. His small, second-floor apartment was crammed with the by-products of his obsession.

Police found the head of Oliver Lacy in the refrigerator in the kitchen. There was a human heart in the freezer compartment, wrapped up like meat, with some flesh later identified as lungs, intestines, a liver, a kidney, and one bicep muscle. In a separate freezer chest, there were three more heads wrapped up and neatly sealed in plastic bags. The bed in the small bedroom was heavily stained with blood. A computer box was packed with two skulls and a photo album with images of Dahmer at work on dismembering the corpses.

Beside the bed, in a filing cabinet, he had stored away three skulls and a collection of bones. A gigantic kettle hidden in the bedroom cupboard held two cleaned skulls and a second kettle contained male genitalia and a pair of chopped off hands. There were three electric saws and containers of acid, chloroform, and formaldehyde.

Some of the skulls had been painted a greyish-blueish hue, like macabre artwork, so that at a pinch they could have been on open display. A massive, 57-gallon chemical drum, blue with a black lid, dominated the bedroom. Three headless torsos were sloshing about inside, slowly decomposing in acid, together with some skeletal remains. Some scummy pots and pans, still on the kitchen stove, had been used by Dahmer to boil flesh off bones. Was he a cannibal? By Dahmer's own account, he had been saving the heart to eat at his leisure, and he had already eaten a bicep, after seasoning it with salt, pepper and A-1 sauce. Eating his victims was not his main objective: he might have been showing off, or mulling over a defence of insanity. He confessed to 17 murders, and his trial at Milwaukee in 1992 was to test his plea of insanity.

Although he was clearly grossly abnormal and 'sick', Dahmer's case perfectly exemplifies our dilemma when we try to classify the behaviour of a serial killer. His activities, and the mind that compels him to re-enact them until he is caught, are offset by his reasoned cunning and premeditation. He *does* know that his murders are morally and legally wrong, and the insanity plea fails dismally. If he pities his victims he cannot continue, and so the compulsive urge overrides the humane spheres of his brain. How can we call him sane when he is reduced to a cold killing machine with unquenchable libido?

Dahmer's best chance of being judged schizophrenic lay in his desire to render the young men, while they still lived, into zombies by drilling holes in their heads and inserting acid or boiling water. If true (that he did so for that reason), here there might be a delusional content. Dahmer belongs to the 'killing for company' class of serial killers, admitting that if they wanted to leave him, his victims were lost. That was what happened when his very first murder came about, when he himself was only 18.

On that occasion, so the argument goes, he felt the primal loneliness of the serial killer because, as a result of a mistake by his warring parents, he had been abandoned, 'home alone'. He fits the pattern, too, in his boyhood hobby of picking over the bodies of dead animals, hopefully not killed by his own hands. He was horribly interested in their innards – a very bad precursor of the evil to come. His IQ was 117, above average but not brilliant. He was a drunkard from High School, and undoubtedly homosexual, although not happy in that skin. He often expressed racist sentiments.

Lionel Dahmer, his father, wrote a sad account of the family, in which he castigated himself and wondered if his scientific detachment had influenced the development of Jeffrey's personality. Little has been made of the mother's hypothyroidism which could explain much of her 'neurotic' symptomatology, which rendered her difficult to live with. A great deal was made in court of her ingestion of prescribed drugs for anxiety and depression while Jeffrey Dahmer was in the womb.

He was captured when Tracy Edwards, a clever young man who did not quaff down the prepared sedative because he was not a drinker, managed to escape and hail a patrol car. This incident, with hindsight, revived nightmare memories of 14-year-old Konerack Sinthasomphone, who also escaped, but was brought back to the apartment by the police.

Dahmer was not allowed the shield of insanity, and was sentenced to imprisonment for life. On Monday, November 28th, 1994, he was beaten to death in a prison lavatory by a fellow inmate, Christopher Scarver, who was sentenced to life imprisonment on May 16th 1995. Dahmer had always anticipated such a fate.

PRIME SOURCES:

Step into my Parlour: The Chilling Story of Serial Killer Jeffrey Dahmer. Ed Baumann. Bonus Books, Inc., Chicago, 1991.

Milwaukee Massacre: Jeffrey Dahmer and the Milwaukee Murders. Robert J. Dvorchak and Lisa Holewa, Robert Hale, London, 1991.

The Macabre Case of Jeffrey Dahmer: Massacre in Milwaukee. Richard W. Jaeger and M. William Balousek. Waubesa Press, Oregon, Wisconsin, 1991.

Jeffrey Dahmer. Dr Joel Norris. Constable, London 1992.

The Milwaukee Murders: Nightmare In Apartment 213: The True Story. Don Davis. True Crime, Virgin Publishing, London, 1992.

The Man Who Could Not Kill Enough: The Secret Murders of Jeffrey Dahmer. Anne E. Swartchz. Mondo, London, 1992.

The Shrine of Jeffrey Dahmer. Brian Masters. Hodder & Staughton, London, 1993.

A Father's Story: One Man's Anguish Confronting the Evil in his Son. Lionel Dahmer. Little Brown, London, 1994.

Albert DeSalvo

The Boston Strangler

SERIAL KILLER

MURDERER: Albert Henry DeSalvo.

VICTIMS: 13 women, aged 19-85. Anna Slesers, Mary Mullen, Nina Nichols, Helen Blake, Ida Irga, Jane Sullivan, Sophie Clark, Patricia Bissette, Mary Brown, Beverly Samans, Evelyn Corbin, Joann Graff, Mary Sullivan.

LOCI: Boston, Lynn, Salem, Cambridge, and Lawrence, USA.

DATES: June 1962 – January 1964.

MEANS: Strangulation with a ligature, typically stockings. Some variations: knifing, battering, manual strangulation.

MOTIVE: A continuum of sexual gratification, with rape usually before the murder, although there may have been some blurring of the sequence.

CRIMEWATCH: DeSalvo was never tried for the stranglings. He was protected by his status as an insane person, when he confessed in convincing detail to the Boston murders. At that time, he was an inmate of Bridgewater State Hospital, judged unfit to stand trial for a series of sexual assaults in his other personae, as 'The Measuring Man' and 'The Green Man', by reason of schizophrenia, of which there is precious little published evidence. Finally sentenced to life imprisonment on the lesser charges, aged 36, he was found, on November 26th, 1973, stabbed to death, the only occupant of the hospital block at Walpole State Prison, Massachusetts.

PRIME SOURCES:
The Boston Strangler. Gerold Frank. The New American Library, New York, 1966.
The Strangler: The Story of Terror in Boston. Harold K. Banks. Mayflower Paperbacks, London, 1967.
The Official Tape-Recorded Confessions of the Boston Strangler. Edited by George W. Rae. Tandem-Ortolan, London, 1967.
Boston Stranglers. Susan Kelly. Carol Publishing. New York, 1995.
A Rose for Mary. Casey Sherman. Northeastern University Press, Boston, 2003.

Baroness Susan de Stempel

Death Comes to Heath House

MURDERER: Baroness Susan de Stempel.

VICTIM: Thomas Simon Savage Dale (68): ex-husband.

LOCUS: Heath House, Hopton Heath, on the Shropshire-Herefordshire border.

DATE: *circa* September 11th, 1987.

MEANS: Bludgeoning.

MOTIVE: The prosection alleged frustration, hatred that had built up over the years, and the urgent need to get rid of her ex-husband.

CRIMEWATCH: The exotic marital title, the Baroness de Stempel, masks the natal identity of Susan Cecilia Mary Wilberforce. Born into the blue blood, on May 16th, 1934, a descendant of the slave trade abolitionist, William Wilberforce (1759-1833), she spent her childhood at Markington Hall, the family's stately home, near Ripon, in Yorkshire. At the age of five, she was sent to a Catholic boarding-school, St. Mary's Convent, Ascot. When she was twelve, Susan was expelled as a result of persistent self-willed and unco-operative behaviour. She was a rebel.

She went on to another Catholic boarding-school, Rye St. Anthony, at Oxford. Under the wing of Margaret, Lady Illingworth, her mother's sister-in-law, she 'came out' as a debutante, at the slighter later age than usual of nineteen, in 1953, and the Russian émigré aristocrat, Baron Michael Victor Jossif Walter de Stempel, was a guest at her coming-out ball.

In 1957, ignoring the shocked disapproval of the wealthy and snobbish Wilberforce clan, she married Simon Dale, an architect, 13 years her senior. He stood 6ft 3 in., was half-bald and half-blind, behind milk-bottle-bottom-thick glasses.

With money winkled out of a family trust, she bought, in 1959, for the absurdly modest sum of £2,000, a 30-room, dilapidated, seventeenth-century mansion, Heath House, at Hopton Heath, near Clungunford, and Leintwardine, on the Shropshire-Herefordshire border, to which she and Simon and their first child, Alexander, moved from their mansion flat in the Old Brompton Road, South Kensington.

At Heath House they raised a family of four sons – Alexander, Sebastian, Marcus, and Simon – and a daughter, Sophia. But the marriage did not prosper. Proverbially, as the wolf of poverty comes in at the door, love flies out of the window. So it was with the Dales.

Money was short, and they had encumbered themselves with the colossal, remorseless, cash-and-energy-consuming task of renovating a crumbling, rambling ruin. After 13 years, it all became too much for Susan Dale. She petitioned for divorce in 1972, on grounds of unreasonable behaviour.

She was later to state that her husband had been violent and abusive, hitting her repeatedly on the base of the spine. She also described his demands for sex as 'excessive' and 'unnatural', trying to insist on anal sex, which she had refused. She further claimed that he liked parading in women's clothes, wearing high heels and lipstick.

The decree nisi was granted in July, 1973. She stayed on at Heath House for a couple of months, then moved out. In the autumn of 1987, she leased Forresters Cottage, in the hamlet of Docklow, just outside Leominster, and about 30 miles from Heath House, and, true to type, immediately renamed what had been a simple farm worker's cottage, Forresters Hall!

On September 11th, 1984, at St. Helier, Jersey, Susan married Baron de Stempel. Their union was not a success. He refused to consummate

59

the marriage, and insisted on sleeping on his own in a tent in the garden of Forresters Hall. They divorced in December, 1986, but, characteristically, Susan hung on to the title.

Simon Dale, living an eremitic life in Heath House, still unsold, ten years on, and now near-blind, somehow coped on his own, occupying only three of the house's 30 rooms. He had a cleaning woman, Linda Williams, in for two hours once a week, and there were a number of friends who visited and kept an eye on him. Susan and her children would come regularly, assuredly not to see him, but to work on the restoration of the exterior of the house, hopefully preparing it for sale.

They had little or no truck with Simon, whose main interests had always been in historical matters, particularly anything to do with the legendary King Arthur, and archaeology. For some considerable time he had been engaged in writing a vast history of England, covering the period AD 300 - 600. Entrusted with the typing of his manuscript was Giselle Wall, a woman in her forties, who lived in nearby Kempton. She had promised to bring the typescript over as soon as it was ready.

It was now finished, and, on Sunday, September 13th, 1989, she arrived at Heath House with it at about 4.20 p.m. Upon her arrival, she rapidly realised that something was wrong. The sun was shining brightly, but there was a light on in the kitchen and the lobby, and the shutters were closed. As she neared it, she felt a terrible heat emanating from the kitchen, together with a dreadful smell. Pushing open the door, she saw Simon's body lying on the floor, in a ring of dark, congealed blood, and a red-hot ring glowing on the cooker; on top of it, a burnt-to-a-cinder supper of toad-in-the-hole.

Simon Dale had been murdered – his skull had been cracked by five blows from a straight-edged, heavy metal object, but the sixth and fatal blow had been to the throat, crushing the windpipe and smashing the larynx, causing him to inhale his own blood, and choke to death. That death had taken place, it was estimated, about two days before. Detectives found nothing in the house disturbed, no robbery. What, then, could have been the motive for so brutal an attack? Was it something personal?

On the preceding Friday (September 11th), Dale had entertained a party of friends. Interviewed, they recalled how, when they arrived at the house, a strange figure had come bearing down on them out of the gloom. It was Dale's former wife, and, thrusting her face close to the window of their car, she had snapped: ' I don't know why you're bothering to visit him, he'll be out in a month.'

When the police came to Forresters Hall to talk to the Baroness, they were very surprised by her and her children's total lack of reaction to the news of Simon Dale's violent death. She did not deny that there had been 14 years of wrangling over the sale of Heath House and her husband's refusal to get out of the place. Seeing her Peugot car parked outside, the detectives asked permission to look in it, and under the driver's seat they found a heavy brass poker, which was clean and shiny from recent polishing.

The Baroness said that she had cleaned it, and had been keeping it in the car for self-protection. She admitted taking it from Heath House on the day of the murder, and said she had hurried home that Sunday evening to watch Agatha Christie's 'Murder at the Vicarage' on television at 9 p.m.

Early in January, 1988, the decision was taken to charge Susan de Stempel, who had obviously had means, motive and opportunity, with the murder of her husband, and in the July she was put on trial at Worcester Crown Court. A witness, Ken Davison, a local farmer who had known the Dales for some years, told the Court that shortly before his death Dale had confided that he thought his wife was planning to kill him – 'I think I'm going to get knocked off. If I'm ever found dead, you'll know what's happened.'

Throughout the 14 days of her trial, the Baroness remained 'aloof, impassive, and imperious'. Haughty, detached, and cold, the press christened her 'The Ice Queen'. When prosecuting counsel, Mr. Anthony Palmer, Q.C., suggested that she had been driven to kill by her ex-husband's intransigent stance over the sale of Heath House, she looked at him very coldly and replied 'Bollocks.' And on August 1st, 1989, the jury delivered a verdict of Not Guilty.

But that was not quite the end of the story. The Baron and Baroness de Stempel, and Susan's children, Marcus and Sophia, were arraigned at Birmingham Crown Court on February 19th, 1990, to face trial for fraud. When the detectives had paid their visit to Forresters Hall in September, 1989, they had been astonished by the contrast between the very ordinary little house and its content of priceless antiques, superb pieces of furniture, silver and porcelain, jewellery, fine paintings, and Persian rugs. One officer observed: 'It was like a storeroom at the British Museum.'

A shrewd police eye had spotted a letter addressed to the Baroness' aunt, Lady Illingworth, who had died the previous year. One of the officers recognised the address on the envelope – Langford House – as that of a council-run local authority nursing home, not at all the sort of place in which you would expect a lady of her wealth and station to end her days.

Enquiries revealed that Lady Illingworth had developed Alzheimer's disease, and that was when, as if alerted by parasitic instinct, Susan suddenly descended, as out of a twenty-year purdah, back on the scene. She persuaded 'Aunt Puss' to leave her Kensington flat, and go to live at Forresters Hall with her. She arrived there, on February 29th, 1984, a rich woman, and left, on December 6th, 1984, denuded. She lasted for 23 months at Langford House. She was cremated at Hereford, the Baroness leaving the funeral bill unpaid.

The Baron, described by the judge, Mr. Justice Owen, as a con man, was jailed for four years. As he was being led from the dock, he turned towards the jury and said with a sneer, 'What can you expect from a working-class jury?' Sophia was sent to prison for two and a half years. Marcus was given 18 months. The last to be sentenced was the Baroness. She remained the tight-lipped and coldly aloof Ice Queen as Her Majesty's judge sent her to prison for seven years.

PRIME SOURCES:

The Trials of the Baroness. Terry Kirby. Mandarin, London, 1991.

Blood Money: The Story of the Baroness de Stempel Scandal. Kate Wharton. Ebury Press, London, 1991.

Who Killed Simon Dale? Kate Clarke. Logaston Press, Herefordshire, 1993.

Jeannie Donald

The Aberdeen Sack Murder

MURDERER: Jeannie Ewen or Donald.

VICTIM: Helen Wilson Robertson Priestly (8 years 6 months).

LOCUS: 61 Urquhart Road, Aberdeen.

DATE: April 20th, 1934.

MEANS: Asphyxia. Most likely due to inhalation of vomit. But possibly strangulation.

MOTIVE: Never discovered.

CRIMEWATCH: Helen, aged 8, was sent to buy a loaf. She never returned. At 5 a.m. next day her violated body was found in a sack at the foot of her tenement stair. Her injuries simulated rape. Special theory: The child used to taunt 38-year-old Mrs. Donald, calling her 'Coconut' and ringing her bell. Mrs. Donald caught her and gave her a good shaking. Helen, who had an enlarged thymus gland, passed into deep, deathlike unconsciousness. Thinking she had killed her, Mrs. Donald made it look like a male sexual attack. Sentenced to death, but respited to life, she was released in 1944.

PRIME SOURCE:
Notable British Trial, edited by John G. Wilson. William Hodge, Edinburgh, 1953.

Samuel Herbert Dougal

The Moat Farm Murder

MURDERER: Samuel Herbert Dougal.

VICTIM: Camille Cecille Holland (56).

LOCUS: Moat Farm, Clavering, Essex.

DATE: May 19th, 1899.

MEANS: Shooting in the head with a revolver.

MOTIVE: Financial gain: for four years, until the murder was discovered, 'Captain' Dougal, (born in 1846), adventurer and philanderer, forged Miss Holland's signature in order to milk her financial assets.

CRIMEWATCH: Lured to the lonely love-nest, Miss Holland survived only three weeks before Dougal struck. Her body lay hidden in a drainage ditch, covered and preserved by blackthorn bushes, until it was dug out on April 27th, 1903. And while Camille reclined amid the blackthorns, the gallant Captain amused himself by training nude girl bicyclists in the Moat Farm field. He was hanged on July 14th, 1903, at Chelmsford Prison.

PRIME SOURCE:
Notable British Trial. Edited by F. Tennyson Jesse. William Hodge, Edinburgh, 1928.

Diane Downs

Pistol Packin' Momma

MURDERER: Elizabeth Diane Frederickson Downs.

VICTIM: Cheryl Lynn Downs (7): daughter.

LOCUS: Old Mohawk Road, near Springfield, Oregon.

DATE: May 19th, 1983.

MEANS: Two .22 bullets in the back.

MOTIVE: Theoretical only: no confession. Could have been more psychologically complex, or more frankly disordered, than the State's construct that Diane Downs, who was divorced, tried to eliminate all three of her children because her married, and luke-warm, lover, Lewis Lewiston, 'never wanted kids – or to be a father'.

CRIMEWATCH: Diane Downs (27) blamed the ubiquitous Bushy-haired Stranger for the gun attack which killed her younger daughter Cheryl, and left her other children Christie (8) and Danny (3) permanently impaired. Assistant DA Fred Hugi later took the two survivors into his own home. Christie had recovered sufficiently to give evidence against her mother. The gun, a .22 semi-automatic Luger, numbered 14-57485, was not found. Immeasurably disturbed, Diane Downs gave a history of sexual abuse by her own father. Even so, she had given birth to a child under a surrogacy scheme. Sentenced to life imprisonment, she escaped from Oregon Women's Correctional Centre, and was transferred to Clinton, New Jersey, with no hope of parole until 2014.

PRIME SOURCE:
Small Sacrifices. Ann Rule. New American Library, 1987.
Best Kept Secrets. Diane Downs. Danmark Publishing, Springfield, Oregon, 1989.

John Duffy

The Railway Rape Murders

SERIAL KILLER

MURDERER: John Francis Duffy.

VICTIMS: Alison Day (19). Maartje Tamboezer (15). (Anne Lock (29). The judge ruled that there was insufficient evidence, and Duffy was acquitted at the trial).

LOCI: Beside a canal, near Hackney Wick Railway Station. Body found in canal. In woods near East Horsley Railway Station, Surrey. On a path near Brookmans Park Railway Station, Hertfordshire.

DATES: December 29th, 1985. April 17th, 1986. May 18th, 1986.

MEANS: Strangulation with a ligature – a strip torn from victim's shirt – by a technique known as a Spanish windlass, in which a stick is used to tighten the cloth. Strangulation by same method with her own scarf. Also beaten. Difficult to determine through deterioration of remains, although in all three cases the hands were tied behind the back.

MOTIVE: In the furtherance of rape, to prevent identification by the victim, or murder for its own sake.

CRIMEWATCH: The landscape of John Duffy's atrocities was the hinterland of Greater London's railway stations when they were at their loneliest. He knew the patterning of cinder-tracks, patches of scrubland, windswept car parks, lines of deserted garages. Not for him the risky sudden entry into the single compartments and empty carriages, which all women on their own try to avoid. He preferred to lie in wait in selected spots.

They called him 'The Railway Rapist' and later, 'The Railway Murderer'. Gingery Duffy was every woman's worst nightmare: zigzagging towards you along the deserted platform, grabbing you from behind as you unlock your bicycle, stretching a cable across a path to fell you as you come whizzing along on your bike, feeling safe and untouchable.

Once he had been an altar boy. The idea was that he hated women. All his victims, well, nearly all, spoke of his eyes piercing like lasers. He was supposed to be a loner, but he was perfectly clubbable, because he enthusiastically attended a martial arts club, and he had a close friend, David Mulcahy, not traced until implicated by Duffy years later, who went out with him and participated – an accomplice to rape and apparently murder as well. Mulcahy was taller and darker, and sometimes apologised to the rape victim afterwards. An artist's impression of Duffy was produced, but terror had so affected the photographic memory of the victims that it was not successful, more like the classic 'Bushy-haired Stranger'.

It transpired that Duffy had a special knowledge of the network of rail tracks and timetables because he had worked for British Rail as a carpenter, until they had sacked him for poor timekeeping. After his crime, he would sprint like a redshank to catch a train, and vanish. At other times, the two men travelled by car to likely stations where women were temporarily on their own. They called it 'hunting', and played a tape of Michael Jackson's 'Thriller'. Balaclavas and knives were their equipment. Home, from where Duffy ventured with increasing confidence, was in

Kilburn; exactly where Professor David Canter said it would be in his first and very successful application of American 'Psychological Profiling'. He was proved right in 13 out of 17 predictions.

Proactive Duffy showed unusual forensic awareness: he took with him a wad of paper tissues to wipe away any of his semen adhering to the victim's private parts and in one case set fire to tissues pushed into the girl. He used to comb through her pubic hair – using a small pocket comb – in order to remove any debris such as his own pubic hair. It would be a mistake to leap to the conclusion that this was a form of trophy collecting: his fancy was door keys, and he had a hoard of 33.

The police thought that he compounded the rapes by murder because he was afraid, as the inquiry progressed, that a survivor would identify him. There were at least 40 rapes. Previously, he had had no form, but he got himself on to the possibles list by virtue of an attack on his long-suffering wife, estranged Margaret, in 1985. 'The nice man I married,' she said, 'became a madman with scary, scary eyes.'

He had a number of hang-ups, which were thought to have inclined him towards violent crime: he was small, 5ft 4 in., troubled with adult acne and, worst of all in his mind, there were no children of the marriage. He blamed his wife, but it turned out that he had a low sperm count. There were fierce arguments, separations, and he took to tying her hands before sexual intercourse, just as he had tied his victims, although in their case the hands were behind the back. He collected hard-core pornography, and kept a lot of 'Kung Fu' weapons in his home.

It was after a separation in 1982, that Duffy first rode out by train with intent to rape. Always cunning and inventive, when he was questioned by the police, twice, and asked for a blood specimen, he persuaded a martial arts friend (who later confessed to his intervention) to rough him up, and then staggered into a police station and claimed amnesia. This bought him time: he was admitted to Friern Barnet Psychiatric Hospital as a voluntary patient. While there, he slipped out and raped a 14-year-old girl. He was tailed and arrested as he made for Copthall Park, the scene of a previous rape. He was now 29-years-old.

They searched his home, but the prize came from his mother's house, not far away, where a big ball of unusual twine, trade-named SOMYARN, was found under the stairs. This was what he used to tie the hands of his victims. John Duffy did not believe in confessing, and he was tried at the Old Bailey in 1987 on three counts of murder and five counts of rape. He was convicted of the first two murders and four rapes and sentenced to 30 years' imprisonment.

In prison in 1997, he admitted his crimes and implicated David Mulcahy in many of the rapes and, surprisingly perhaps, all the murders. Mulcahy was arrested, tried in 2000, and given three life sentences for the murders and seven rapes. In 2001, Duffy was sentenced to an extra 12 years for 17 further rapes.

PRIME SOURCES:
Criminal Shadows: Inside the Mind of the Serial Killer. David Canter. Harper Collins, 1994.
Mapping Murder: The Secrets of Geographical Profiling. David Canter. Virgin Books, 2003.
Contemporary Newspapers.

Theodore Durrant

The Girl in the Belfry Murder

MURDERER: William Henry Theodore Durrant.

VICTIMS: Blanche Lamont (21). Minnie Williams (20).

LOCUS: Emanuel Baptist Church, Bartlett Street, San Francisco.

DATES: April 3rd, 1895 (Lamont). April 12th, 1895 (Williams).

MEANS: Manual strangulation (Lamont). Suffocation, with pieces of victim's own dress, and stabbings (Williams).

MOTIVE: No certainty here. Sex enters. Frustration at rejection by Blanche Lamont is the most popular reconstruction. Frenzy is attached to the murder of Minnie Williams. Possibly she knew too much of the first murder.

CRIMEWATCH: Durrant (24) was a young man of good character, a medical student and an assistant superintendent of the Sunday School at the Emanuel Baptist Church. His sister was Maud Allan, the dancer. His mental disturbance unguessed at, he dragged Blanche's body up to the bell-less belfry, where she lay nude and white, indeed marmoreal, until discovery. Minnie was despatched gorily in the church library, her body stowed in a closet. Ridiculous rumours, such as the implication of the pastor, encrusted the case. Durrant was hanged at San Quentin on January 7th, 1898. 'Papa,' his mother is supposed to have said to Durrant's father as refreshment was fetched to the grieving parents, three feet from their son's cut-down corpse in its coffin, 'I'll take some more of that roast.'

PRIME SOURCES:
The Girl in the Belfry. Joseph Henry Jackson and Lenore Glen Offord. Gold Medal Books, Fawcett Publications, Greenwich, Connecticut, 1957.
Sympathy for the Devil. Virginia A. McConnell. Praeger, Westport, Connecticut, 2001.

Ruth Ellis

The Last British Woman To Hang

MURDERER: Ruth Ellis.

VICTIM: David Blakely (25).

LOCUS: Outside the Magdala public-house, at the foot of South Hill Park, Hampstead, London.

DATE: April 10th, 1955.

MEANS: Shooting with a .38 calibre, six-shot Smith & Wesson revolver.

MOTIVE: A crime of passion, of course. Ruth Ellis killed the thing she loved. There was sexual jealousy and rage at violent ill-treatment by her lover, a racing driver.

CRIMEWATCH: Ruth Ellis, born October 9th, 1926, was the last woman to be hanged in Britain – on July 13th, 1955, at Holloway Prison. Her case went towards the abolition of hanging. She had suffered a miscarriage very recently – on March 28th. It is thought that her distraught state of mind would have come under the Diminished Responsibility defence which reduces murder to manslaughter – but that was not enacted until the Homicide Act 1957. A defence of provocation had failed at the trial, because of the arguable degree of premeditation. Appeal failed. If a shot had not ricocheted and wounded the hand of an innocent bystander, Mrs. Gladys Yule, Ruth Ellis might have been spared.

PRIME SOURCES:
Ruth Ellis. Robert Hancock. Arthur Barker, London, 1963.
The Trial of Ruth Ellis. Jonathan Goodman and Patrick Pringle. Celebrated Trials Series, David & Charles, Newton Abbot, Devon, 1974.
Ruth Ellis: A Case of Diminished Responsibility? Laurence Marks and Tony Van den Bergh. Macdonald and Jane's, London, 1977.
Ruth Ellis, My Mother. Georgie Ellis. Smyth Gryphon, London, 1995.

Marie Marguerite Fahmy

The Savoy Hotel Murder

ACCUSED: Marie Marguerite Fahmy.

VICTIM: Prince Ali Kamel Fahmy Bey: husband (22). He was not, in fact, a prince, but a bey.

LOCUS: Suite No. 41, on the fourth floor of the Savoy Hotel, The Strand, London.

DATE: July 10th, 1923.

MEANS: Shooting with a .32 Browning semi-automatic pistol.

MOTIVE: Impulsive elimination of a threatening and oppressive figure.

CRIMEWATCH: Of humble origin, daughter of a Parisian cab driver and a charwoman, Marie Marguerite Alibert had advanced via prostitution and courtesanship to good position and considerable personal affluence. Motivated by avarice, she married spectacularly wealthy Prince Fahmy, aged 22 – ten years her junior. There was a six-month history of severe marital disharmony; threats and physical violence. Her husband's persistent demands for "unnatural intercourse" – he insisted on anal sex, and was not interested in ordinary vaginal penetration – had caused her to suffer from severely painful haemarrhoids. Marguerite Fahmy shot the Prince in hot blood during a violent thunderstorm. Defence by Marshall Hall, unashamedly racial, presented Madame Fahmy as the alleged victim of oriental cruelty and the unnatural sexual practices of a vengeful bisexual husband. A sympathetic occidental jury acquitted her.

PRIME SOURCE:
Scandal at the Savoy. Andrew Rose. Bloomsbury, London, 1991.

Albert Howard Fish

The Child-Eater of Wisteria Cottage

SERIAL KILLER

MURDERER: Albert Howard Fish.

VICTIMS: Murdered at least 15 children.

LOCI: Grace Budd, aged 12, was murdered at Wisteria Cottage, Irvington, Westchester County, New York, and other unidentified children all over America.

DATES: June 3rd, 1928 (Grace Budd). Others over a period of years up to his arrest in 1934.

MEANS: Strangulation, knifing, and other horrors unguessed at.

MOTIVE: Sexual satisfaction in a grossly deviant personality. Cannibalism was the dominant drive, with antecedent sado-masochistic acts. There was a strong family history of mental illness.

CRIMEWATCH: At sixty-six, decidedly elderly for a serial killer, stooped, seamed house-painter Albert Fish (born May 19th, 1870), was captured six years after he had slain, and eaten, what he fancied of Grace Budd, in isolated Wisteria Cottage. Good detective work traced him to 200 East 52nd Street, New York City, through his use of a printed envelope to enclose a taunting descriptive letter to Grace Budd's mother. A product of an orphanage, where he had become coprophagous, he had been married, with six children, but for years had been mastered by his sado-masochistic urges. At least a hundred serious sadistic acts on children, not amounting to actual murder, are attributed to Fish. He would pounce upon his victims in the nude. Sometimes his painter's overall would carry ambiguous red splashes. In his own words, 'I learned to like the taste of human flesh many years ago during a famine in China. It is something like veal. Little girls have more flavour than little boys.' A routine X-ray disclosed 29 separate needles which Fish had inserted into the skin around his testicles. He looked forward to his electrocution at Sing Sing on January 16th, 1936, as the ultimate thrill. He helped the executioner to attach the electrodes to his leg. The first charge of electricity failed, perhaps short-circuited by his cache of needles.

PRIME SOURCES:

Trail of Blood. Michael Angelella. Bobbs--Merrill, Indianapolis/New York, 1979.

Deranged. Harold Schechter. Pocket Books, New York, 1990.

The Cannibal: The Case of Albert Fish. Meil Heimer. Lyle Stuart, Inc., New York, 1971.

Billy Flynn

A Murder for the Teacher

MURDERER: Billy Flynn.

VICTIM: Greg Smart (24).

LOCUS: Apartment 4E of the condominium on Misty Morning Drive, Derry, New Hampshire.

DATE: May 1st, 1990.

MEANS: Shooting.

MOTIVE: The elimination of the husband of his lover, Pamela Smart.

CRIMEWATCH: The police of the small New Hampshire town of Derry were puzzled. The crime scene to which they had been called, at Apartment 4E of the two-storey, up-market condominium complex on Misty Morning Drive, on the night of May 1st, 1990, bore all the classic signs of a burglary that had gone wrong.

The young man stretched face down on the floor, a bullet hole in his head, had obviously walked in, surprised burglars in his home, and been killed by them. And yet . . . why had the intruders decided to break into an apartment complex in the evening instead of during the day, when there would have been fewer people around?

And, as they continued to investigate, even bigger question-marks raised even uneasier doubts. Why had the burglars not taken the credit cards from the dead man's wallet? Why leave his diamond ring lying under his body? It just didn't make criminal sense.

The young couple who lived in 4E, Greg and Pamela Smart, were still six days shy of their first wedding anniversary. Greg, aged 24, was a strongly upwardly mobile insurance salesman with the Metropolitan Life Insurance. Pam (22), who had nursed a fierce ambition to succeed as a TV anchorwoman, had sacrificed it for marital bliss, and taken a job as media centre director at School Administrative Unit 21, in nearby Hampton.

The marriage was, in fact, in trouble. Pam had found out that, in December, 1990, Greg, while away on a business trip, had had a one-night stand. She had never forgiven him for this lapse, and, in February, 1991, started an affair herself – with a 15-year-old schoolboy, Billy Flynn, a pupil at Winacunnet High, which was just across the car park from the School Authority Unit building.

Pam had got to know Billy when she was taking time off from her public relations job to lead an alcohol and drugs awareness course at Winacunnet, and subsequently helping some of the students to make a video about orange juice, in connection with a competition they were entering. Before they became lovers, Pam gave Billy a stack of photographs of herself, wearing a bikini and striking provocative poses.

They had sex for the first time that February. They spent the night at her place. Greg was off on a course in Rhode Island. It was the morning after that she first issued the fatal ultimatum, telling Billy that if he wanted to keep on seeing her, he was going to have to get rid of her husband.

To begin with, Billy thought that she was joking, but as the weeks slipped by and she kept on about it, he was not so sure. By now, they were very heavily sexually committed. They were copulating every chance they got – in Billy's room, in her room, in the back of her car, al fresco on the beach – up to seven times a day.

By April, things had reached a crescendo. Pam was in love with Billy, and determined to get Greg out of her life. The trouble was that if she divorced him he would, she believed, get everything; and that would include her dearly loved little Shih-Tzu dog, Halen. And so she sat down and hatched a plot to rid herself of Greg – permanently.

Her plan moved into action at 9 p.m. on the night of May 1st, 1990. Greg Smart parked his Toyota pick-up, strode across the condominium parking lot to his home, turned the key in the front-door, and stepped into the darkened hall. As he did so, he was seized by the coat. Another pair of hands grabbed him by the hair, and threw him full force against the wall. He was gruffly ordered to get down on his knees. He did so. He saw that his assailants were two teenagers. One of them had a carving-knife which he had taken from the Smarts' kitchen in his hand. He had intended to cut Greg's throat, but his nerve failed him. The other was grasping a Charter Arms .38 revolver. He clapped it to the kneeling Greg's head, pulled the trigger, and in cold blood shot him dead.

Then Billy Flynn, for it was he who was the gunman, and his schoolfellow, Pete Randall, fled through the back door, and, holding tight to the bag of jewellery that they had stolen from upstairs, pelted across some waste ground to where their friends, Vance Lattime (17) and Raymond Fowler (18), were waiting in an old Chevrolet Impala to whisk them off top speed to their home ground, the southern area of the coastal town of Seabrook.

The clock hands stood at precisely 10.10 p.m. when, according to careful plan, Pamela, who had been attending a school meeting that evening, drove her silver 1987 Honda CRX into the parking lot beside her husband's Toyota, and headed up the path towards the front-door. She well knew what to expect, but at the sight of Greg's prone corpse fetched forth a most wonderful cacophony of variegated screams, which brought the hair-raised neighbours running.

They came. They saw. They called the police. Initially, the officers of the law toyed with theories. Greg had liked a gamble. Had he got in too far; left debts unpaid? Was it a Mafia hit made to look like a burglary? They found a marijuana joint in the Toyota. Was it a drugs-related rub-out? Only gradually did the grieving

widow come into the frame. She did shed the odd mandatory tear, but appeared more worried about her dog – safely shut away in the cellar by the considerate burglars – and as to how she was going to rescue her contact lens' solution from the now forensically-sealed house.

Greg's parents also found their daughter-in-law's behaviour peculiar. She struck them as being more concerned about the mess the fingerprint men had made of her beautiful white sofa than with her husband's death. And they were upset when, two days later, she delivered all of Greg's belongings to them in plastic bin bags. Her conduct at the pre-funeral wake was weird, too. She absolutely refused to look at Greg's body. Then, when the coffin had been finally closed, she spent fifteen minutes weeping by it, and screaming, over and over again, 'Why?'

It was Raymond Fowler's teenage cousin, Fred Welch, who lived with the Lattime family, who eventually let the cat out of the bag. He had overheard Vance Lattime and Pete Randall talking about what had happened. Welch told Mr. and Mrs. Lattime, and they told the police. Billy Flynn, Pete Randall, and Vance Lattime were arrested. Raymond Fowler later turned himself in.

Billy, Pete, and Vance struck a deal. They all agreed to testify against Pam, in return for the charges against them being reduced to second degree murder. They all duly received reduced sentences. Even so, they will be middle-aged men before they are released.

At her trial, Pamela Smart lived up to her name, being impressively smartly dressed in different stylish clothes each day. She also comported herself with a dignity and reserve that earned her the title of 'The Ice Princess' from an admiring press. And so she remained to the bitter end, unmelting, withdrawn and distant, accepting her sentence of life imprisonment without possibility of parole, without a flicker of emotion.

PRIME SOURCES:
Teach Me to Kill. Stephen Sawicki. Avon Books, New York, 1991.
Contemporary newspapers.

Sidney Fox

The Margate Matricide

MURDERER: Sidney Harry Fox.

VICTIM: Rosaline Fox (63): Mother.

LOCUS: Room 66, Hotel Metropole, Paradise Street, Margate, Kent.

DATE: October 23rd, 1929.

MEANS: Strangulation.

MOTIVE: Financial gain from life insurance policies.

CRIMEWATCH: Convicted con man and forger, Sidney Fox, (born January, 1899), aping his betters, lived by the skin of his teeth, bilking hoteliers. His silver-haired mother tottered along with him, a part of his stock-in-trade. Their only luggage was a brown paper parcel. Even Mother was expendable. To cash in, Fox had to show that she had died by accident before the midnight of October 23rd. After he had despatched her on the bed, he lit a fire under a chair, and when the smoke was dense, he called the alarm at 11.40 p.m. Sir Bernard Spilsbury alone discerned a small bruise on the larynx indicative of strangulation. The hyoid bone, unusually but not uniquely, was intact. Sidney Fox was hanged at Maidstone Gaol, on April 8th, 1930.

PRIME SOURCE:
Notable British Trial. Edited by F. Tennyson Jesse. William Hodge, Edinburgh, 1934.

Augusta Fullam & Henry Clark

The Agra Double Murder

MURDERERS: Augusta Fairfield Fullam and Henry Lovell William Clark.

VICTIMS: Edward McKean Fullam (44): husband. Louisa Amelia Clark (*c*. 55): wife.

LOCI: 9 Metcalfe Road, Agra, India (Mr. Fullam). 135 Cantonments, Agra, India (Mrs. Clark).

DATES: October 10th, 1911 (Fullam). November 17th, 1912 (Clark).

MEANS: Poisoning by arsenic, finally, probably by gelsemine and cocaine (Fullam). Procured slaying by assassins with sword-slashes to the head (Clark).

MOTIVE: Freedom from matrimony so that the surviving partners could marry each other.

CRIMEWATCH: Augusta, daughter of a Bengal river pilot, minor memsahib of the British Raj, a tubby temptress with claws of steel, shockingly fell in love with half-Indian Dr Clark (born August 15th, 1868). Before they met, he had already tried to poison his wife, Louisa, and it was he who instigated the double murder plan, which Augusta enthusiastically embraced. Unwisely, she kept in a trunk her own incriminating letters to Clark, in which she discussed the slow poisoning of her husband by packets of arsenic masked as 'tonic powders', sent by post to her by Clark. Louisa was tougher, more poison-proof than Eddie Fullam, and the murderous pair had recourse to the bazaars of Agra for the recruitment of a band of 'badmashes', who killed Louisa in her bed while Clark was absent setting up a false alibi. Upon interrogation, he fluffed and fumbled the details of that alibi. The trunk of letters was found. Augusta and Clark were tried jointly at Allahabad High Court in 1913. Both were found guilty and sentenced to death. Clark was hanged on March 26th, 1913, but Augusta's sentence was commuted to penal servitude for life, because she was pregnant by Clark. A son was born in prison. He survived and lived a good life, but Augusta died of heatstroke in Naini Prison, aged 38, on May 28th, 1914. The assassins were tried separately: three were hanged, one got off on alibi.

PRIME SOURCES:
The Agra Double Murder. Sir Cecil Walsh. Ernest Benn, London, 1929.
Khaki Mischief. Molly Whittington-Egan. Souvenir Press, London, 1990.

John Wayne Gacy

The Killer Clown

SERIAL KILLER

MURDERER: John Wayne Gacy.

VICTIMS: 33 boys and young men.

LOCUS: 8213 Summerdale Avenue, Norwood Park Township, Chicago.

DATES: 1972-78

MEANS: Strangulation.

MOTIVE: Sexual gratification. Sadistic sodomitic rape, with beating and whipping.

CRIMEWATCH: Gacy, born March 17th, 1942, who had a long history of sexual perversion, loved to attend children's parties dressed as a clown. He stowed victims' bodies in the crawl space under his house and in the garden, and dumped extra ones in rivers. At his emotional trial, the Prosecution placed photographs of 22 identified victims on a ten-foot-high wooden board facing the jury. Paramedics stood by to attend weeping relatives. Sentenced on March 13th, 1980, to the electric chair, Gacy survived on Death Row, Stateville Correctional Centre, through the process of appeals. On April 8th, 1991, a judge scheduled a hearing on a writ of Federal habeas corpus which argued constitutional errors in the trial. But he was executed by lethal injection at Stateville Prison, Illinois, on May 10th, 1994.

PRIME SOURCES:
The Man Who Killed Boys. Clifford L. Linedecker. St. Martin's Press, New York, 1980.
Killer Clown. Terry Sullivan with Peter T. Maiken. Grosset & Dunlap, New York, 1983.
Buried Dreams. Tim Cahill. Bantam Books, New York, 1986.

Gerald Gallego alias Feil
The Sex Slave Murders

SERIAL KILLER

MURDERER: Gerald Armand Gallego.

VICTIMS: Rhonda Scheffler (17). Kippi Vaught (14). Brenda Judd (15). Sandra Kaye Calley (14). Stacy Ann Redican (17). Karen Chipman-Twiggs (17). Linda Teresa Aguilar (21). Virginia Mochel (34). Craig Raymond Miller (22). Mary Beth Sowers (21).

LOCI: Near Baxter, 15 miles east of Sacramento, California (Scheffler and Vaught). Somewhere in the vicinity of Reno, Nevada, but bodies never found (Judd and Colley). Near Lovelock, Nevada (Redican and Chipman-Twiggs). Some nine miles south of Gold Beach, Oregon (Aguilar). Skeletal remains near Sacramento, California (Mochel). Remote spot near Bass Lake Road, Eldorado County, California (Miller). Cow pasture somewhere between Rocklin and Loomis, north-east of Sacramento, California (Sowers).

DATES: September 11th, 1978 (Scheffler and Vaught). June 24th, 1979 (Judd and Colley). April 24th, 1980 (Redican and Chipman-Twiggs). June 16th, 1980 (Aguilar). July 17th, 1980 (Mochel). November 1st-2nd, 1980 (Miller and Sowers).

MEANS: Shooting, bludgeoning to death. Aguilar, after being beaten severely about the head with a hammer, was buried alive.

MOTIVE: All sexually motivated killings, except in the case of Miller, who had to be killed because he happened to be in the company of the victim.

CRIMEWATCH: Born in 1947, son of a three-times killer who had been despatched in the Mississippi gas chamber at the age of 28. Seven times married, twice to the same woman, Gallego, a Sacramento, California, nightclub bartender, had been sodomising and sexually abusing his own daughter since she was six. Pursuing a compulsive fantasy, he sought the perfect lover and sex-slave. In fact, he had found her in his wife, Charlene, who, acting as pander, lured young girls picked up in such places as the Sacramento shopping mall, into his van with promises of marijuana. She would sit complacently in the front, while on a crude bed in the back of the van her satyriasic husband ravaged and savaged and killed his victims. She then helped to bury them. The Gallegos were caught after a friend of their last victim's managed to jot down the number of the kidnap car. In a plea-bargaining deal which gave her a 16-year prison sentence plus immunity from any further prosecution, Charlene finally agreed to testify against her husband. Twice tried – in California and Nevada, respectively – twice condemned to die, Gallego was still awaiting execution, when, on July 18th, 2002, in prison in Nevada, he died of rectal cancer.

PRIME SOURCES:
All His Father's Sins. Lt. Ray Biondi and Walt Hecox. Prima Publishing, Rocklin, California, 1988.
The Sex Slave Murders. R. Barri Flowers. St. Martin's Press, New York, 1996.
A Venom in the Blood. Eric van Hoffman. Donald I. Fine, 1990.

William Gardiner

The Peasenhall Murder

ACCUSED: William George Last Gardiner.

VICTIM: Rose Harsent (23).

LOCUS: Providence House, Rendham Hill, Peasenhall, Saxmundham, Suffolk.

DATE: May 31st–June 1st, 1902.

MEANS: Throat cut.

MOTIVE: Eliminatian of inconveniently pregnant girl.

CRIMEWATCH: Bucolic crime in turn-of-the-century primitive village community. Sex and incest behind the innocent hedgerows. Gardiner, Methodist Elder, Sunday School Superintendent, 36-year-old father of six, accused of sexual dalliance with 23-year-old Rose, servant at Providence House, was charged with her murder. After two juries disagreed, the Crown lodged a *nolle prosequi*. Gardiner, who moved to Southall, Middlesex, and took over a grocer's shop, has traditionally been held to have been fortunate, but latest research, based on the comparison of Gardiner's handwriting with that of an unsigned assignation note sent to Rose on the day of the murder, is held by some to go towards Gardiner's innocence. However, that innocence seems very highly unlikely.

PRIME SOURCES:

Notable British Trial. Edited by William Henderson. William Hodge, Edinburgh, 1934.
The Peasenhall Mystery. John Rowland. John Long, London, 1962.
The Peasenhall Murder. Edwin Packer. Yoxford Publications, Saxmundham, Suffolk, 1980.
The Peasenhall Murder. Martin Fido and Keith Skinner. Alan Sutton, Stroud, Gloucestershire, 1990.

Edward Gein

The Original of Hitchcock's *Psycho*

PROBABLE SERIAL KILLER

MURDERER: Edward Theodore Gein.

VICTIMS: Mary Hogan (51). Bernice Worden (58). Quite probably others.

LOCUS: Gein farm, near Plainfield, Waushara, Wisconsin.

DATES: December 8th, 1954 (Hogan). November 16th, 1957 (Worden).

MEANS: Shooting with a Mauser pistol (Hogan) and a rifle (Worden).

MOTIVE: Sexual and emotional gratification, with disordered thinking.

CRIMEWATCH: It was Mother who screwed up young Eddie. Augusta Gein (pronounced 'Geen') reared him to have nothing to do with women. But he was very, very interested in them. And when Augusta died, and he was 39, he nailed up her room and went out to the graveyards to dig himself up some women to play with. About nine of them. He did not like their smell, and the murders were a natural extension of his activities.

The decapitated body of Mrs. Worden, his last victim, was found hanging by the heels from a crossbar hoisted by a block and tackle in a shed at the neglected Gein farm. The body was gutted and dressed out like a deer from the local woods. Dark rooms held more secrets: skulls on the bedposts, a belt of nipples, bowls made from skull-caps, a wastepaper basket, lampshades, and chair-seats made out of human skin, a knife-handle of human bone, a shade-pull with a pair of woman's lips attached, skin puttees, nine vulvas in a shoe-box (one trimmed with red ribbon), four noses, Mary Hogan's mask of skin and hair, nine more masks, Mrs. Worden's head, with bent nails ready as hooks in the ears, and her heart in a saucepan on the stove.

There was the skin of a woman's torso, with breasts, stiff and tanned like leather. Gein admitted that he used to tie it on and, with a real-face mask and with a vulva or two tied on to his genitalia, dance in the yard in the moonlight. He kept the skin nicely oiled.

Three graves were opened to check Gein's confession. They were, indeed, empty or violated. He was incarcerated as insane through schizophrenia (although he instructed Counsel remarkably well), died at Mendota Institute, aged 78, and was interred beside Mother.

He took with him a ghastly mystery: two of his collection of vulvas were judged to have come from girls of about fifteen, but the records of local cemeteries showed that no girls aged 12 to 18 had been buried there during Gein's time. So there must have been two more live victims.

PRIME SOURCES:
Edward Gein: America's Most Bizarre Murderer. Judge Robert H. Gollmar. Chas. Hallberg, Delavan, Wisconsin, 1982.
Deviant. Harold Schechter. Pocket Books, New York, 1989.

Andrew George
The Case of the Murdered Rose-Grower

MURDERER: Andrew Harold George.

VICTIM: Miss Hilda Murrell (79).

LOCUS: 'The Moat' (a copse) Hunkington Lane, Hunkington, Nr Shrewsbury.

DATE: March 21st, 1984.

MEANS: She was left to die in the open with penetrating knife wounds which, in themselves, were not sufficient to cause death, and hypothermia was the decisive factor. She had been knocked about and the collarbone was broken.

MOTIVE: Burglary that went wrong.

CRIMEWATCH: *Hilda Murrell* is the conspiracy that never was. It was a very important case, with questions asked in the House of Commons, but the police never wavered from their belief that the murder arose from a burglary, and they have been proved right, with the conviction of, Andrew Harold George, now aged 37, but only 16 at the time of the crime.

Miss Murrell lived alone in her large Victorian house, Ravenscroft, 52 Sutton Road, Shrewsbury, with neighbours nearby. With many friends and contacts, she was still regarded as mildly eccentric, but that may be an unfairness. There was an individuality about her, a passion for issues which marked her apart perhaps from most women of her age.

She was a graduate of Newnham College, Cambridge, and probably the first such to be murdered. Once, she had grown beautiful roses, become an expert, but now she lay without aid on a lonely knoll, cold, cold, her life sliding away. If ever there was a burglary that went wrong, this was it.

She had returned to her home from a shopping trip before going out to lunch with a friend, to find the burglary in progress. Nearly £50 in cash was taken and the telephone wires were tampered with. There was a struggle, youth against age, and a banister rail was broken. The boy, in a panic, knocked her about

and broke her collarbone. There was a sexual assault not amounting to rape.

George was not the first burglar to become sexually excited by having a helpless woman, however old, in his power. She became shocked, and may have been drifting in and out of consciousness. He considered – if you could call it that – his options, and, armed with a knife, possibly her kitchen knife, bundled her into her own Renault 5 car, and abducted her, with what intent? It was an unusual decision. To delay investigation and identification, to kill her elsewhere, just to abandon her, or what?

He was not a good driver, and he was agitated. Many people saw his fast, erratic flight, as if with no goal in mind, while, slumped beside him in the passenger seat was the figure of Miss Hilda Murrell, still, bizarrely, wearing her brown, broad-brimmed hat, not yet dead

It was a dreadful last journey. Six miles away, in deep countryside, the car was driven into a ditch. They got out, there could have been another struggle, and somehow he goaded or dragged her 500 yards further up to a spinney. There were severe abrasions on her knees. There was no blood in the car and, either in the meadow or at the top, George inflicted painful knife wounds. There were defence cuts on her hands.

Then he left her to die in the cold, a process which would have taken five to ten hours. A kitchen knife, Miss Murrell's hat, and her spectacles were found by a hedge, with her moccasin shoes further up, 200 yards from the place of her death. She may have crawled about for a while, even cried for help. If someone had discovered her sooner, she might have lived, but her body lay from the Wednesday, March 21st, to Saturday, March 24th.

The memories of what he had done stayed with George for two decades. He had already been in trouble with the police at the time, and was living at a children's home in Shrewsbury. More offences, particularly burglary, some of violence, were to follow, but certainly not murder. He was one of the 1,860 people loosely classified as suspects in 1984, because he was a known burglar and had been missing from his school or college at the relevant time. He said that he had spent all day in Woolworths playing 'atomic games'.

The investigation relied on card indexing, and DNA technology was not available then. In 2003, scientists perfected the DNA Low Copy Number, which yields DNA profiles from very few cells. Miss Murrell's petticoat, stained with semen, had been carefully preserved over the years, and a match to George's DNA was obtained. The police said that he was on the DNA database because he was a career criminal.

The trial of Andrew George began at Stafford Crown Court on April 8th, 2005. It emerged that his fingerprints were on a button tin of beer, and a lavatory seat at Miss Murrell's home. George, who did admit burglary at Ravenscroft, accused his own, older brother, Steven George, 17 at the time, of having committed the violence and abduction, and he was brought to the witness-box by the Prosecution, but the jury did not believe the accusation. No forensic evidence was cited to link Steven to the crimes. Interestingly, Mr Justice Wakerley told the jury that they could consider manslaughter as an alternative to murder, but they convicted George of kidnap and murder. He was sentenced to life imprisonment, to serve a minimum of 13 years and 30 days before being considered for parole.

While summing up, the judge had instructed the jury to ignore as 'absolute rubbish' the conspiracy theories which the case had spawned. Miss Murrell was a committed conservationist and well-informed anti-nuclear campaigner, and was preparing a paper to present at the Sizewell Enquiry. The theory was that security forces, men in dark suits, had seen to it that she was found dead in the woods, in order to silence her special knowledge. Alternatively, it was suggested that Miss Murrell's nephew, Commander Robert Green, who held a key position in Naval Intelligence during the Falklands War and the sinking of the *Belgrano*, had deposited vital secret documents with Miss Murrell, and a search of her home by the Intelligence Services had gone wrong, and been covered up.

It is very curious that she had telephoned friends, Gerard and Fern Morgan-Grenville, on February 25th, 1984, to say that, 'If they don't get me first, I want the world to know that one old woman has seen through their lies.' No one qualified or competent to discern a late paranoid illness developing has come forward to say so. Dr PR Acland, who carried out the first post-mortem examination on Miss Murrell and gave evidence at the inquest, finding himself caught in the toils of the conspiracy speculations, wrote to *The Times* on January 1st, 1985, to defend his position, and contributed the prophetic comment that 'I don't know who killed Miss Murrell, but I have a strong suspicion that some two-penny-halfpenny thief is gloating over a pint of beer in a pub not many miles from Shrewsbury about all this media interest'.

PRIME SOURCES:
Who Killed Hilda Murrell? Judith Cook. New English Library, 1985.
Death of a Rose-Grower: Who Killed Hilda Murrell? Graham Smith. Cecil Woolf, 1985.
Enemies of the State. Gary Murray. Simon and Schuster, 1993.
Unlawful Killing: The Murder of Hilda Murrell. Judith Cook. Bloomsbury, 1994.
Shropshire Star, May 7th, 2005.

Barry George

The Jill Dando Murder

MURDERER: Barry George aka Barry Bulsara.

VICTIM: Jill Dando (36).

LOCUS: 29 Gowan Avenue, Fulham, London, SW6.

DATE: April 26, 1999.

MEANS: Shooting.

MOTIVE: Impossible logically to determine.

Left: Barry George (convicted)
Right: Jill Dando (victim)

CRIMEWATCH: At 11.32 a.m. on Monday, April 26th, 1999, Jill Dando died on the doorstep of her London home from a single bullet wound to the head. The nation was horrified. One of television's most popular presenters, she was 36 years old, born November 9th, 1962, at Weston-super-Mare, and was to have married her fiancé, Alan Farthing, a successful London gynaecologist, in the September. For some time she had indeed been living with him at his home in Chiswick, and her house – No.29 Gowan Avenue – in Fulham was in process of being sold. She would visit it from time to time, specifically to collect faxes, which, for one reason or another, she did not want arriving at Chiswick.

That morning, she had left Chiswick just after 10 a.m., driving her blue convertible BMW, and before turning into Gowan Avenue, popped into Rymans to buy some stationery, into the King's Mall, Hammersmith, branch of Dixon's to buy an ink cartridge for her fax machine, and into Cope's fish shop on Fulham Road, where she bought two fillets of Dover sole. Then she drove to Gowan Avenue, was lucky to find a parking space right by her house, clicked open the front garden gate, walked up the tiled pathway to the front-door, and was about to insert the key in the lock when she was suddenly gripped from behind by the arm – so violently that the pathologist, Dr Iain West, would later note a bruise on her right forearm.

She was forced to the ground, and while, with his right arm he held her there, with his left hand the killer fired a single shot into her left temple, holding the gun pressed so hard against her skull that the imprint of the muzzle could be seen on her scalp afterwards. The bullet entered her head just above and behind the left ear, parallel with the ground, killing her instantly. It came out of the right side of her head and lodged in the door, leaving a mark 22 cm. above the doorstep.

So clean, clinical, and confident was the killing, that it was at first thought to be the defiantly impudent craftsmanship of a professional hit man. But who would be likely to put out a contract on Jill Dando? One of her former lovers? A resentful ex-girlfriend of one of her lovers? An obsessed fan of the Beatle-killing variety? A disgruntled criminal brought to book through the 'Crimewatch' programme which she had fronted? A vengeful Serbian terrorist?

Three days before the Dando shooting, Nato had bombed the Serbian television headquarters in Belgrade, killing ten journalists. And, on April 3rd, Dando had presented an appeal for Kosovar refugees, and subsequently received a hostile letter of criticism from a Serb.

The witnesses to her untimely demise began to come forward. Just after 10 a.m., a postman had seen a suspicious-looking man, wearing a dark jacket and 'of Mediterranean appearance', standing outside Dando's house, and, at approximately the same time, a woman traffic warden had noticed a man sitting in an illegally parked blue Range Rover nearby. Four more witnesses claimed that, between 10.40 a.m. and 11.30 a.m., they had seen a man standing in Gowan Avenue. He was either talking on a mobile phone, or just looking agitated.

Their descriptions of him varied. One of them said that he was wearing black-framed glasses, which were too big for his nose. The police made an unsuccessful attempt to pinpoint a mobile phone call made from outside Dando's house about half an hour before the murder. A number of sightings spoke of a man in a dark suit. He was often seen running in and around Fulham Palace Road, which is a couple of minutes away from Gowan Avenue.

One witness, whose description of the man provided the police with the details for their officially issued E-fit picture, vividly recalled the presence of a profusely sweating man, with a mark on the bridge of his nose, like that left by spectacles, waiting at the bus stop outside No.389 Fulham Palace Road. It was believed that he boarded a No.74 bus to Putney Bridge tube station, where he was lost sight of. There was a witness who saw a young man in a wax jacket talking on a mobile phone in nearby Bishop's Park.

Dando's visits to her Gowan Avenue house were both sporadic and absolutely random. How could the killer have known that she would be there that particular morning? Had someone just been watching at the house for days, perhaps weeks, on end, on the off-chance? There were no reports to support this idea. Was she followed there from Chiswick? If so, the killer knew that she was living with Farthing, and had located and staked out his house. Did someone close to Dando inadvertently tip off her killer? Or was it someone close to Dando who was her killer? Her murder seemed to bear all the hall-marks of a ruthless, well-thought-out killing. The advantages of the close-up, single-shot method were speed of execution, probable freedom from blood and flesh spattering on the trigger man, and the benison of silence; for, whereas the gases escaping when a gun is discharged normally cause a loud external report, the explosion in this case would have taken place within the victim's head, so that there would have been little or no noise of a shot to hear.

At the end of thirteen abortive months, the detectives suddenly produced the man who they said was the killer. His name was Barry George, but being a fantasist and a fanatical devotee of the late Freddie Mercury, of Queen, who, he claimed, was his cousin, and whose real name was Bulsara. George had changed his surname to that of his idol, the dead singer. Barry George was forty years old, educationally subnormal, and had an IQ of 76. Hardly, you might think, qualifications for the elaborate planning and skilful execution necessarily involved in such an operation as the Dando murder.

Described as an unemployed musician, he had not had a job for twenty years, and was, frankly, unemployable. He lived, conveniently, within 800 yards of the spot where Jill Dando died. His flat, at 2B Crookham Road, Fulham, was what is colloquially termed 'a tip'. Cluttered and uncleaned, it was crammed with piles of old newspapers, 736 of them, on the floor, posters of Queen, and some 2,597 rolls of undeveloped film of some 400 women, whom he had followed and covertly photographed on the streets.

He was well known in the area as an oddball, who had a habit of trailing and talking to women. And he had a history of psychological problems. He had been jailed for attempted rape – according to his wife, he was guilty of frequent marital rape – and had convictions for indecent assaults, and for impersonating a police officer. The likelihood of his guilt of the murder of Jill Dando does not seem overwhelming.

The killer had used a semi-automatic 9mm 'short' – as opposed to the longer standard 9mm – gun. Examination of the bullet and cartridge case yielded two unusual clues. There were no obvious rifling marks on the bullet. There were, close to the rim, six tiny indentations or crimping marks: as the cartridge case was tightened around the bullet, they were slightly irregular. That suggests that they were handmade.

Barry had neither the expertise in weaponry nor the resources to modify them. He had no money. He had no car. In spite of a raking search of the premises, no forensic evidence against him was found in his flat. Only two witnesses, Richard Hughes, who lived next door to Dando, and Geoffrey Uphill-Brown, who lived opposite her, had actually seen the gunman. Both failed to pick out Barry George in an identity parade. In fact, there was not one piece of direct, or even persuasive, evidence to link him to the crime. No guns or ammunition were traced to his possession. The solitary so-called evidence, was a sub-visible speck of explosives' residue found on the lining of one of his coats. It could have come from fireworks. It was said to be a 'close match' to particles found in Dando's hair. George's coat had been sealed in an evidence bag, taken from his flat to be photographed in a police studio, where it was placed on a dummy with an officer's shirt underneath, photographed, and put back in the bag, all *before* it underwent forensic scrutiny. It could easily have been contaminated at any one of several stages of this sloppy procedure. In July, 2001, Barry George was convicted of the murder of Jill Dando by a majority jury verdict of ten to one. That conviction sits uneasily on many people's minds.

PRIME SOURCES:
Jill Dando: Her Life and Death. Brian Cathcart. Penguin Books, London, 2001.
Dead on Time. John McVicar. Blake, London, 2002.
All About Jill: The Life and Death of Jill Dando. David James Smith. Time Warner Books, London, 2002.

Harvey Glatman

The Deathly Photographer

SERIAL KILLER

MURDERER: Harvey Murray Glatman.

VICTIMS: Judy Ann Van Horn Dull (19).
Shirley Ann Loy Bridgeford (24). Ruth Rita Mercado (24).

LOCI: Beside the highway, in the desert, near India, California (Dull). Beside Butterfield Stage Road, Anza Borrego, Desert State Park, California (Bridgeford and Mercado).

DATES: August 1st, 1957 - around midnight (Dull). March 9th, 1958 (Bridgeford). July 24th, 1958 (Mercado).

MEANS: Strangulation from behind. Victim so trussed and bent backwards that the cord securing the ankles and legs also acted as a garrotte.

MOTIVE: Rape – followed by disposal to avoid identification.

CRIMEWATCH: Jug-eared Glatman (born 1928), unattractive to the opposite sex, had given up normal methods of approach. For robbing women, in which connection he was known as 'The Phantom Bandit', he had already been sentenced to five years in Sing Sing. He did not like prison. Posing as a professional photographer, while really a television repair man, brought him closer to the good-lookers who would otherwise have scorned him. In the desert, he tied them up (he had a thing about ropes) and raped and photographed them, right up to the end. That was the extent of his perversions. Dull and Mercado were models, but he got hold of Bridgeford through a dating agency. Dangerous. If his next potential victim, model Lorraine Vigil (27), had not fought back and grabbed his gun, a Belgian Browning, he might have continued his course for years. A Highway patrolman came to her rescue when he saw the couple wrestling in the sand. Photographs of the three dead girls – and a collection of ropes – were found in Glatman's sordid Los Angeles bungalow, at 1011 South Norton Avenue. He confessed, pleaded guilty, and was despatched in the San Quentin gas chamber on September 18th, 1959. No doubt there are some photographs, somewhere.

PRIME SOURCES:
Rope. Michael Newton. Pocket Books, New York, 1998
Contemporary newspapers.

John Glover

The Granny Killer

SERIAL KILLER

MURDERER: John Walter Glover aka John Wayne Glover.

VICTIMS: Gwendoline Mitchelhill (82). Lady Winfreda Isabelle Ashton (84). Margaret Frances Pahud (85). Olive Cleveland (81). Muriel Falconer (93). Joan Violet Sinclair (61).

LOCI: Camellia Gardens Apartment Block, Military Road, Mosman. Raglan Street Apartment Block, Mosman. Passageway near the Ridgeway Apartment Block, in Austin Street, Lane Cove. Wesley Gardens Retirement Village, in Belrose, on the northern beach peninsula. No.3 Muston Street, Mosman. Pindari, 14 Pindari Avenue, Beauty Point.

DATES: March 1st, 1989. May 9th, 1989. November 2nd, 1989. November 3rd, 1989. November 24th, 1989. March 19th, 1990.

MEANS: Bludgeoning with a hammer. Strangulation.

MOTIVE: Extremely complex. A rage against life. He had been dominated by women since his childhood. He hated his mother, Freda. She had had four husbands, and numerous other men, and Glover believed her to have abandoned him at the age of nine, to move in with her second husband, leaving him to live with his father. He hated his mother-in-law, Essie Rolls. The feeling was mutual. She had never liked him, saw him as a fortune-hunter, and went out of her way to make it clear that he was only a tolerated guest in the Rolls' house in Wyong Road; it did not belong to him. All this erupted into a periodic psychological frenzy, a red mist which only cleared after a vicious and brutal killing.

CRIMEWATCH The notorious Australian 'Granny Killer' was a Four X , no, a Six X (he killed six elderly ladies), British export. John Walter Glover was born on November 26th, 1932, in the Victoria Hospital, at Lichfield (the name appropriately means 'Field of corpses') in Staffordshire, and spent his first twenty-three years living in and around Wolverhampton.

In 1956, he left his home, at 28 Lower Villiers Street, Wolverhampton, and sailed aboard the P&O liner *Strathnaver* on Christmas Day. At the beginning of February 1957, 24-year-old Glover stepped ashore at Prince's Pier, Melbourne. He was one of the 'Ten Pound Poms' – young, assisted-passage immigrants, hopeful of chiselling out a good new life for themselves in the Antipodes. He started off as a tram conductor, and was arrested for peeping and prying and assaulting two women. Over the

years he had known a lot of women; loved them, bedded them, and left them. Then, in Melbourne, he met a girl.

Her name was Jacqueline Gail Rolls – 'Gay', for short. She was both personally ambitious and ambitious for him. She made him go to night-classes, better himself, saw him ending up as a sales representative, a member of the 'suit and tie brigade'. For his part in the upwardly mobile stakes, he set his sights on her parents' very pleasant house, nestling in the harbour-side hills of the affluent North Sydney suburb of Mosman.

There was, he saw, a dividend in marrying her. Only child; parents getting on; she would end up inheriting their luxurious Wyong Road house. They married on June 1st, 1968. After a spell in East St.Kilda, they settled in with Gay's parents, John and Essie Rolls, in Sydney, where their first daughter, Kellie, was born in 1971. A second daughter, Marney, arrived in 1976.

There is no doubt that there was a powerful streak of criminality in Glover's make-up. He had left behind him in England a record of larceny and various other petty offences. The Australian police believed him to have been guilty of a murderous attack on 72-year-old Mrs. Myrtle Ince, in Sydney, in September, 1962, and of the August, 1984, killing, in her Ettalong home, of Mrs. Josie McDonald, aged 73. During the week following this murder, six other elderly women reported that they had been beaten, raped, and sexually attacked.

At the time, Glover, a travelling meat pie salesman, was doing the rounds in that Central Coast district. On November 21st, 1986, Wanda Amudsen (83) was found dead in her cottage, only eight blocks away from where Josie McDonald died. She, too, had been attacked with murderous ferocity. And between 4.30 p.m. and 5 o'clock on January 11th, 1989, Mrs. Margaret Todhunter (84), walking along Hale Road, Mosman, on her way to her sister-in-law's house in Macpherson Street, saw a grey-haired man walking towards her. They had just passed each other, when she felt a brush on her left shoulder, followed by a dull thump on the top of her head. As she fell to the pavement, the man snatched her white vinyl handbag from her grasp, and pelted off. The bag contained 200 dollars. It took 14 stitches to close the profusely bleeding wound in her scalp.

For these attacks and deaths, Glover may, or may not, have been responsible. There is no proof either way. It is a different matter though as regards his killing spree on the north shore, which created a real reign of terror. It could, in psychological terms, have been a sort of celebration, a liberation, for, in January, 1989, Essie Rolls had died, and, early in 1989, his mother, Freda, had died of breast cancer.

The first killing of the series took place on March 1st, 1989. The victim was an 82-year-old widow, Gwendoline Mitchelhill. It was 3.50 p.m. when Glover spotted her. She was walking home along Military Road, Mosman, to her flat in the Camellia Gardens apartment block. He took a claw hammer from his Ford station wagon, stuck it under his shirt, walked rapidly after her, and, as she rounded a corner where she was hidden from view, punched her with all his might. She fell, six ribs shattered, to the ground. Still conscious, she stared up in horror as he crashed the hammer down on her head. Discovered still alive, she was taken to the Royal North Shore Hospital, where she died at 8.45 p.m. The fact that her purse had been stolen made it look like a robbery that had gone wrong.

Killing No.2. May 9th, 1989. At half-past two that Tuesday afternoon, Lady Winfreda Ashton, widow of 84, left the Mosman Returned Servicemen's Club to return to her apartment block, in Raglan Street, Mosman. Glover, the predator, hovering, saw the old lady in the bright red raincoat walking slowly with a stick. He followed her to her block, where, instead of going up to her flat, she went into the ground-floor bin room to dispose of some rubbish. Glover was at her heels. He entered the bin room behind her, and dragged her backwards to the concrete floor. He pulled her head up, and bashed it again and again on the concrete. Then he removed her nylon tights, wrapped them round her neck, and strangled her. He pocketed her gold wristwatch, wallet, and two purses, and walked calmly back to his car. Again, it looked like a robbery with violence.

On October 18th, 1989, Doris Cox (86) was set upon at the Garrison Retirement Village, in Spit Road, Mosman. Her head was repeatedly bashed into a wall, and her purse stolen. That she survived, may have been because she was suffering from Alzheimer's Disease, and this stopped her from going into shock. Although it was never brought home to him, the crime bore all the authentic Gloverian hall-marks.

But it was definitely Glover who, on November 2nd, 1989, struck for the third time. He was on a pie-selling visit to Lane Cove, another suburb on Sydney's north side. He saw an old woman dressed in a two-piece black summer suit walking down Longueville Road. She was Margaret Pahud, 85 years of age. Coming from the shops she was carrying two bags of groceries. It was just after 3 p.m. when she turned into a narrow private passage, her usual short cut to her home in the Ridgeway apartment block, in Austin Street. Glover descended on her like a tornado, delivering a lightning trio of skull-shattering blows with his Stanley Hercules hammer. The private passageway was uncomfortably public from his point of view. It was overlooked by a retirement village on one side, and a house on the other. Cars were flashing by at the end of the lane, and there was the possibility of a stray pedestrian approaching at any second. So . . . Glover, eschewing his normal ritual strangulation, seized her handbag, with its content of 400 dollars, and, as the parlance has it in such circles, 'legged it' – but fast!

The very next day – November 3rd, 1989 – Glover was at it again. Mid-afternoon he drove into the Wesley Gardens Retirement Village, on Forest Way, Belrose, on the northern beach peninsula. There, he chanced upon an old woman sitting peaceably on a garden seat outside the home. She was Olive Cleveland (81). Glover walked over to her and tried to start up a conversation, but she was not inclined to talk. She got up and began to walk back to the front-door of the building. With pantherine speed, Glover bounded after her and pounced. He manipulated her past the doorway and down a sloping pathway to the right. He hurled her to the ground, caught her head in his hands, and kept pounding it on the bitumen until she lost consciousness. He pulled up her skirt, removed her thick stockings, tied them round her neck, and strangled her. Finally, he took 60 dollars from her.

It was now that the frightening realisation came: a ruthless killer was at work in the community. Three weeks all but a day passed. Thursday, November 23rd, 1989. The killing fever in his blood broke out again. Glover selected his next intended. She was Mrs. Muriel Falconer, 93 years old, practically blind, and very deaf. She was a brave soul and would trundle off regularly from her Bungalow, No.3 Muston Street, Mosman, to Clancy's Supermarket, where she was a well-known shopper. She was last seen at half-past four, making her way homewards along Military Road, laden with her grey-striped shopping bag. Glover, having 'tooled' himself up with hammer and gloves from his car, was just in time to see Mrs. Falconer rounding the corner into Muston Street, and he followed her through the gate in her hedge, and up the garden path to her front-door. It is likely that, being sensorially impaired, she never knew anything until, as he pushed her in through the door which she had just opened, a split-second later the hammer came down on the back of her head and she crumpled on the beige hall carpet. He left her semi-naked, her dress up over her head, her buttocks exposed. He helped himself to 300 dollars, which he found in a drawer, and left.

Glover's Hercules hammer rose and fell for the last lethal time on March 19th, 1990, and the skull that it bit into was that of a 61-year-old grandmother and divorcée, his friend and former dalliance partner, Joan Sinclair. He telephoned her that Monday morning and arranged to call round to see her at her bungalow, No.14 Pindari Avenue, in the suburb of Beauty Point, high above the waters of Quakers Hat Bay, with a tennis court and swimming pool behind it. It was around half-past ten that Glover arrived, carrying a black leather attaché-case with his trusty claw hammer nestling in it beside a bottle of whisky, purchased en route from Liquorland bottle shop, in Spit Junction.

They were together in the living-room when Mrs. Sinclair turned her back on him. There was a sickening crunch as the hammer homed on its unprotected cranial target. Mrs Sinclair slumped to the floor. Glover rained hammer blows on her. He pulled up her dress, pulled off her knickers and tights, looped the tights around her neck and strangled her. Her genitals were damaged. He left the body face-down, her legs apart, pushing her buttocks up obscenely. This is significant, for the posture replicated that of a pornographic photograph of his mother which he had come upon with shock many years before.

He then undressed, ran a hot bath, rummaged through the bathroom cabinet for pills, swallowed Tryptanol, Panadol, Panamax, and whatever else he could find, by the handful, and, flushing them down with swigs of whisky, lowered himself into the steaming bath. His suicide attempt failed. The police found him, and he was rushed to the Royal

North Shore Hospital, where he was revived.

The irony is that at the time of the Sinclair murder the police had Glover under surveillance. He had been identified as the sex offender who had interfered with 82-year-old Daisy Roberts at the Greenwich Hospital, not far from Lane Cove, on January 1st, 1990. He had thereafter made a suicide attempt, leaving a note saying 'No more grannies', which should have told them everything. On the morning of March 19th, 1990, a surveillance team had been shadowing Glover. They knew that he had telephoned his boss, Morris Grant, at Four 'N Twenty Pies, telling him that he would not be at work that day because he had to see a solicitor, and they thought that he was visiting the solicitor at the house in Pindari Avenue. However, after nearly eight hours had elapsed, realising that no one could possibly afford the fee for spending so long a time consulting a lawyer, the watching police concluded that Glover must be conducting a liaison with a lady friend in there, and, with praiseworthy delicacy, hesitated to intrude. In the end, though, the decision had to be taken, and they forced their way in. The trial took place at Darlinghurst Supreme Court, Sydney, in November 1991. Originally, 59-year-old Glover pleaded not guilty by reason of insanity, but later changed his plea to guilty. The jury agreed. The man who had once announced 'If I got my hands on the Granny Killer, I'd cut his balls off', was sentenced on November 29th, 1991, to spend the rest of his natural life in jail.

PRIME SOURCES:
Granny Killer: The Story of John Glover. Les Kennedy and Mark Whittaker. Angus & Robertson, Australia, 1992.
Garden of Evil. Larry Writer with Steve Barrett and Simon Bouda. Ironbark Press, New South Wales, 1992.
Australian Crime. Edited by Malcolm Brown. Lansdowne, Australia,1993.
The Killer Next Door. Lindsay Simpson and Sandra Harvey. Random House, Australia, 1994.

John George Haigh

The Acid Bath Murderer

Mass Murderer

Murderer: John George Haigh.

Victims: William Donald McSwan (34). Donald McSwan (70) and his wife, Amy McSwan (65). Dr Archibald Henderson (52) and his wife, Rosalie Henderson (41). Mrs. Olive Henrietta Helen Olivia Roberts Durand-Deacan (69). Haigh confessed to nine murders in all. Three remain unknown and were probably apocryphal.

Loci: The McSwans in the basement of 79 Gloucester Road, Kensington, London, S.W.7. The Hendersons and Mrs. Durand-Deacon in a storehouse belonging to Hurstlea Products, Ltd., in Giles Yard, Leopold Road, on the outskirts of Crawley, Sussex.

Dates: William Donald McSwan. September 9th, 1944. Donald and Amy McSwan. *c.* July 2nd, 1945. Dr Archibald and Rosalie Henderson *c.* February 13th, 1948. Mrs. Durand-Deacon, February 18th, 1949.

Means: Shooting in the cases of the Hendersons and Mrs. Durand-Deacon. The McSwans were most probably killed by blows to the head.

Motive: The purest of all motives – money.

Crimewatch: Pretending interest in commercial idea of Mrs. Durand-Deacon, fellow guest at the Onslow Court Hotel, Queen's Gate, South Kensington, of manufacturing plastic finger-nails, Haigh drove her to Crawley, shot her and, pausing briefly to eat an egg on toast at Ye Anciente Priory Restaurant, dissolved her body in a drum of sulphuric acid, before going off to dine at the George Hotel. Bone fragments, gallstones, and an undissolved acrylic plastic denture in the resultant sludge led to his arrest. Hazarding an insanity defence, he claimed to have drunk his victims' blood. Vampiric plea rejected, he was hanged, aged 40, at Wandsworth Prison on August 10th, 1949.

Prime Sources:
Notable British Trial. Edited by Lord Dunboyne. William Hodge, Edinburgh, 1953.
Haigh: The Mind of a Murderer. Arthur La Bern. W. H. Allen, London, 1973.
The Acid Bath Murders. David Briffett. Field Place Press, Broadbridge Heath, West Sussex, 1988.

Archibald Hall alias Roy Fontaine

The Monster Butler

MASS MURDERER

MURDERER: Archibald Thomson Hall aka Roy Fontaine.

VICTIMS: David Wright (30): blackmailer of the butler. Dorothy Alice Scott-Elliot (60): wife of employer. Walter Travers Scott-Elliot (82): employer. Mary Coggle (51): accomplice to murder of the Scott-Elliots. Donald Hall (36): brother of the butler.

LOCI: Woodland by Kirtleton Hall, near Waterbeck, Dumfriesshire (Wright). 22 Richmond Court, Sloane Street, Chelsea, London (Dorothy Scott-Elliot). Glen Affric, Inverness-shire (Walter Scott-Elliot). Middle Farm Cottage, Newton Arlosh, Cumbria (Coggle and Hall).

DATES: August/September, 1977 (Wright). December 8th, 1977 (Dorothy Scott-Elliot). December 14th, 1977 (Walter Scott-Elliot). December 17th, 1977 (Coggle). January 1st, 1978 (Hall).

MEANS: Shooting with a .22 rifle (Wright). Suffocation with a pillow (Dorothy Scott-Elliot). Strangling and hitting with a spade (Walter Scott-Elliot). Battering with a poker (Coggle). Chloroform (Hall).

MOTIVE: Broadly, financial gain, and the concealment thereof. Finally, the concealment of those murders themselves.

CRIMEWATCH: The monster butler was a con man and a jewel thief. He was good at his job. First, he shot Wright, blackmailer from prison days, who threatened to expose him. Next, the butler killed Scott-Elliot, ex-MP, and his wife, in pursuit of their antiques and assets. By now, he had two accomplices, Michael Kitto (39) and Mary Coggle. The butler got rid of Coggle because she refused to relinquish Mrs. Scott-Elliot's incriminating mink coat. Finally, so deep in blood that he could not draw back, the butler silenced his own brother, another weak link and a liability. After hearings at the Edinburgh High Court and the Old Bailey, both Hall (born July 17th, 1924) and Kitto were sentenced to life imprisonment. Hall died in prison in October 2002, aged 78.

PRIME SOURCES:
The Monster Butler. Norman Lucas and Philip Davies. Arthur Barker, London, 1979.
The Butler. James Copeland. Panther Books, 1981, London.

James Hanratty

The A6 Killer

MURDERER: James Hanratty.

VICTIM: Michael Gregsten (*c.* 36). Married lover of Valerie Storie. (23).

LOCUS: A lay-by off the A6, at the top of Deadman's Hill, near Ampthill, Bedfordshire.

DATE: August 23rd, 1961.

MEANS: Two shots from a .38 Enfield revolver.

MOTIVE: Probably a panic reaction.

CRIMEWATCH: Man approached Gregsten and Storie, love-making, *circa* 9 p.m., in car parked in remote cornfield, at Dorney Reach, near Maidenhead, Berkshire. He forced Gregsten at gunpoint to drive to Bedfordshire, shot him dead, raped Miss Storie, then shot and paralysed her. Hanratty was arrested. Claimed conflicting Liverpool and Rhyl alibis. Peter Louis Alphon confessed to the killing, triggering a controversy still raging long after 25-year-old Hanratty's hanging at Bedford on April 4th, 1962. Issue complicated by the weird circumstance that both Hanratty and Alphon had stayed in the seedy Vienna Hotel, Maida Vale, London, where two cartridges from the A6 murder gun were found.

Around 4 a.m on Thursday, March 22nd, 2001, the body of James Hanratty was exhumed from his grave in Carpenders Park Cemetery, Oxhey Lane, Watford, in order to obtain from it specimens for DNA testing. It was widely reported that DNA evidence had been found to link Hanratty to the crime. The Hanratty appeal was heard by the Court of Appeal in April-May, 2002, and was rejected on the basis that the DNA evidence, in the words of Lord Woolf, the Lord Chief Justice, established 'beyond doubt that James Hanratty was the murderer'. Predictably, family and long-campaigning friends of Hanratty challenged the forensic scientists' findings, contending that material found on the pair of Valerie Storie's knickers which she was wearing when she was raped, and on a handkerchief that had been wrapped around the murder weapon, could have been contaminated with DNA from Hanratty's clothing.

The full story of how and why the killer came to be in the cornfield is still to be told.

PRIME SOURCES:
The A6 Murder. Louis Blom-Cooper. Penguin Books, London, 1963.
Murder vs. Murder. Jean Justice. Olympia Press, Paris, 1964.
Deadman's Hill: Was Hanratty Guilty? Lord Russell. Secker & Warburg, London, 1965.
Who Killed Hanratty? Paul Foot. Jonathan Cape, London, 1971.
The Case of James Hanratty. Report of Mr C. Lewis Hawser, Q.C., HMSO, April 1975, Cmnd. 6021.
Hanratty: The Final Verdict. Bob Woffinden. Macmillan, London, 1997.

Neville Heath

The Sadist of Notting Hill

MURDERER: Neville George Clevely Heath alias Group Captain Rupert Brooke.

VICTIMS: Margery Aimee Brownell Gardner (32). Doreen Marshall (21).

LOCI: Room 4, Pembridge Court Hotel, 34 Pembridge Gardens, London, W.2. (Gardner). Branksome Dene Chine, Bournemouth (Marshall).

DATES: June 21st, 1946 (Gardner). July 4th, 1946 (Marshall) .

MEANS: Suffocation, with beating with a riding whip and sexual mutilations inflicted *ante mortem* (Gardner). The throat was cut, with sexual mutilations inflicted *post mortem*. (Marshall).

MOTIVE: Sexual gratification.

CRIMEWATCH: A sado-masochistic encounter in Room 4, with bondage and flagellation, went wrong: apparently there had been previous such transactions. In the alternative, Heath (29) had intended the worst. When he saw what he had done, he thirsted for more. Doreen Marshall, not a masochist, was enticeable, and he did as he pleased with her in the bushes of the gladsome resort. His defence of insanity was doomed to failure, and it was an incorrigible psychopath that they hanged at Pentonville on October 26th, 1946.

PRIME SOURCES:
Notable British Trial. Edited by Macdonald Critchley. William Hodge, Edinburgh, 1951.
Borstal Boy: The Uncensored Story of Neville Heath. Gerald Byrne. John Hill Productions, London.
Portrait of a Sadist. Paul Hill. Neville Spearman, London, 1960.
Rotten to the Core? Francis Selwyn. Routledge, London, 1988.

Gary Heidnik

The Sex Slave Cellar of Horror

SET ON COURSE FOR A SERIAL KILLER

MURDERER: Gary Heidnik.

VICTIMS: The dead: Sandra Lindsay (25). Deborah Johnson Dudley (23). Prisoners: Josefina Rivera (26). Lisa Thomas (19). Jacquelyn Askins (18). Agnes Adams (24).

LOCUS: 3520 North Marshall Street, Philadelphia.

DATES: November 26th, 1986: Josefina Rivera picked up. November 29th, 1986: Sandra Lindsay captured. December 22nd, 1986: Lisa Thomas imprisoned. January 1st, 1987: Deborah Johnson Dudley captured. January 18th, 1987: Jacquelyn Askins kidnapped. March 23rd, 1987: Agnes Adams captured.

MEANS: Sandra Lindsay, after dangling by one wrist from an overhead beam for a week, choked to death on a lump of bread forced down her throat. Deborah Dudley was electrocuted – by a live wire lowered into the water-filled pit in the cellar into which Heidnik had put her.

MOTIVE: Who knows? To punish insubordination on the part of sex slaves? *Pour encourager les autres?* We are in muddied psychiatric waters here.

CRIMEWATCH: Legally, Heidnik was not insane. By no stretch of the imagination, however, could he be proposed as a personification of normalcy. His I.Q. was high - 130-148 on various testings - yet he deliberately elected intimacy with severely mentally retarded black women. He had considerable flair for investment, and by its shrewd deployment was possessed of more than half a million dollars – yet chose to live meagrely and filthily in a black slum. He indulged strangely conflicting fancies. He founded the United Church of the Ministers of God – and it was not wholly a scam. The stock market apart, his main interests – hobbies, really – were pornography, black prostitutes, and top-class cars. He had a plan to start his own baby farm in the basement, and went out hunting black girls to bear his children. He kept them chained and shackled prisoners. He killed two. He fed the survivors on dog meat mixed with the minced flesh of his victim (Lindsay), put them in a black pit, and drove screwdrivers down their ears. He was captured after Josefina Rivera managed to slip out of his clutches, and led incredulous police to his church-cum-torture-house. Convicted of two first-degree murders, he was executed by lethal injection on July 6th, 1999.

PRIME SOURCE:
Cellar of Horror. Ken Englade. Angus & Robertson, London, 1989.

Elbert Homan

The Avenger

MURDERER: Elbert Ervin Homan.

VICTIM: William List (57).

LOCUS: Todville Road, Seabrook, Texas.

DATE: October 17th, 1984.

MEANS: Shotgun.

MOTIVE: Scrawled on the wall above wreckage wrought to List's luxury home – chandeliers smashed, furniture broken and scattered, along with food on the floor, acid poured into the Jacuzzi, a 50,000-dollar crystal water fountain reduced to smithereens – 'No more pain. Bill List is a sick man. No more fist for List. Have a nice day'.

CRIMEWATCH: Homan, born December 23rd, 1965, started off in life with big ambitions. He dreamt of becoming a lawyer or a policeman. The son of divorced parents, his unstable background undoubtedly contributed to his status as a troublemaker at school. He graduated to street-wise life via the Covenant House, Houston, Texas, home for runaways and street kids. Life became an up and down affair of drug-induced highs and desperate shifts-for-a-living lows. The pseudo-glamour of Westheimer Boulevard hooked him. October 13th, 1984, standing outside a Westheimer grocery store, Homan was picked up by homosexual oil rig trailer maker, multimillionaire, William List. He took the teenager to his 30-room mansion and invited him to live there with him and three other youngsters. Here was undreamt of luxury, and Bill was generous with drugs. But, as always in life, there was a price to be paid. No such thing as a free lunch! Bill's 'guests' were forced to strip nude and submit to torture. They were required also to minister to List's highly weird anal erotic needs. Enough for him was more than enough for his house guests. Homan freed them all from List's tacky embraces – by sacrificing his own freedom for 45 years.

PRIME SOURCE:
Contemporary newspapers.

Donald Hume

Body Parts from the Sky

Murderer: Brian Donald Hume aka Donald Brown, John Stephen Bird.

Victims: Stanley Setty aka Sulman Seti (46). Arthur Maag (50).

Loci: 620 Finchley Road, Golders Green, London (Setty). Zurich (Maag).

Dates: October 4th, 1949 (Setty). January 30th, 1959 (Maag) .

Means: Stabbing with German S.S. dagger (Setty). Shooting with Manhurin 7.65 mm pistol (Maag).

Motive: Spur of the moment quarrel – with incidental financial gain (Setty). Attempting to evade capture (Maag).

Crimewatch: Clever, calculating, cold, psychopath. Tried for the murder of his spivvish criminal partner, Setty, whose corpse, after dismemberment, he dropped piecemeal from an aircraft which, accompanied by his Alsatian dog, Tony, he himself piloted, into the English Channel. One of the parcels containing Setty's headless torso was washed up on the Essex mud flats at Tillingham, where it was found by a farm labourer. The jury disagreed. Hume pleaded guilty to second indictment as accessory after the fact. Sentenced to 12 years. While he was in prison, the crime reporter, Duncan Webb, made off with Hume's wife Cynthia. Released in February, 1958. Sold confession of guilt to *Sunday Pictorial*. Returned to a life of escalating crime and violence. In January, 1959, Hume killed again, while robbing the Gewerbe Bank, Ramistrasse, Zurich. Sentenced by Swiss court to life imprisonment. His victim was Arthur Maag, a taxi driver, who unwisely 'had a go'. Brought back to England and Broadmoor in 1976. Transferred in 1988, aged 69, to St. Bernard's Psychiatric Hospital, Southall, Middlesex. Died 1998.

Prime Sources:
Hume: Portrait of a Double Killer. John Williams. Heinemann, London, 1960.
Trials of Brian Donald Hume. Ivan Butler. David & Charles, Newton Abbot, Devon, 1976.

Ian Huntley

The Killing Caretaker

MURDERER: Ian Kevin Huntley aka Ian Nixon.

VICTIMS: Holly Marie Wells (10), Jessica Aimee Chapman (10).

LOCUS: 5 College Close, Soham, Cambridgeshire.

DATE: August 4th, 2002.

MEANS: Unestablished. Possibly strangulation. Possibly smothering.

MOTIVE: Sexual.

CRIMEWATCH: The truth as to what exactly befell the two ten-year-olds, Holly Wells and Jessica Chapman, lies locked away in the mind of 28-year-old Ian Huntley. The empirical facts are few, simple, and straightforward.

On the afternoon of Sunday, August 4th, 2002, Holly's parents, Kevin and Nicola Wells, had invited their friends, Rob and Trudy Wright, round to a barbecue in the garden of their home in Red House Lane, in the village of Soham. Holly's friend, Jessica, also arrived, bearing a present she had bought for her on her fortnight's holiday in Minorca, from which she had just returned the previous day.

The two girls spent most of the afternoon upstairs in Holly's bedroom. Around five o'clock, they popped down to see how things were going with the grown-ups. The two were wearing matching outfits – bright-red, David Beckham number-seven Manchester United shirts, and black Adidas shorts, with a couple of white stripes down each side, and Holly's mother, Nicola Wells, took a snapshot of them, standing smiling next to each other. The hands of a clock on the wall behind them pointed to four minutes past five. Within two hours they would be dead. Murdered.

After being photographed, the girls went back to Holly's room and played on her computer until, some minutes before 5.30 p.m., they decided they were bored, and went out for a walk. No one had heard them leave the house, and when, some time later, Holly's parents went to look for them, there was no sign of either of the girls. As the tally of minutes

mounted into hours, the worry became acute.

At 10 p.m. Jessica's mother, Sharon Chapman, telephoned the police. Twelve days of appalling anxiety were to drag by. Then, on the thirteenth day, the dwindling flame of hope was doused. On August 17th, two naked, decomposing, little bodies were found in a remote, nettle-filled ditch in woodland near the American air base at Lakenheath, in Suffolk.

And, earlier that morning, the scorched and burnt remnants of the girls' red T-shirts, along with their trainers and other clothes, had been found hidden in a bin in a locked school building known as the hangar. All last lingering fragments of hopeful doubt regarding the children's fate were now mercilessly erased.

Suspicion had for some time been forming in the minds of the detectives that Ian Huntley, the local school caretaker, and Maxine Carr, his live-in mistress, knew a lot more than they were disclosing.

Ian Kevin Huntley was born in Grimsby Maternity Hospital on January 31st, 1974. Poverty, instability, and uncertainty were his cradle companions. Bullied and unhappy at school, he grew into a resentment-filled loner. Sexually precocious, he was early an exploiter of the vulnerable, choosing the weakest and youngest girls for his victims; defenceless schoolgirls were to be his most particular targets.

Having been bullied himself, he became a bully – a control freak. He loved to dominate and abuse women. He indulged in endless paedophiliac affairs with under-age girls, revelling in violent sex with children, and enjoying it best when they were frightened. He kept a 16-year-old girl locked up without food or water for two weeks when she resisted his sexual demands.

In 1995, he married 18-year-old Claire Evans. He began battering her almost as soon as they set up home together, and would, for no reason, give her terrible daily doses of domestic violence. None of this could, of course, be revealed to the Court at the time of his trial, for fear of prejudicing the jury. There was a streak of savage cruelty in him.

As a teenager it was his hobby to roam the streets looking for stray cats and dogs. He would pour paraffin over the dogs and set them on fire. To both cats and dogs he would strap bangers, and blow them up. From the age of 16 to 27, he worked his way through a series of menial, dead-end jobs. His great opportunity came in December 2001, when, under the name of Ian Nixon – actually his mother's maiden name – he applied for, and landed, the position of Residential Senior Site Officer (newspeak for caretaker) at Soham Village School. With it went a house, a salary of £16,000 a year, and a staff of four working under him.

The mandatory police checks as to the characters of all persons applying to work with children showed no record of any sexual offences under the name of Nixon, and, as a result of mistake or negligence, the record held under the name of Huntley seems never to have been brought to light. A tragic circumstance that was to lead to circumstances even more tragic. Huntley brought with him to the new job at Soham his partner, 25-year-old Maxine Carr.

Born Maxine Ann Capp, on February 16th, 1977, at that same Grimsby Maternity Hospital as Huntley, she, too, had endured a somewhat emotionally disturbed childhood. She had harboured so great an anger against her absentee father that she had changed her name from his name, Capp, first to Benson, and then, by deed poll, to Carr. Her school days in the Lincolnshire village of Keelby had, however, been happy, and it became her ambition to qualify as a teacher.

It had been in the course of one of their customary Grimsby binge evenings of pub and club crawling, that, one summer night in 1998, Huntley and Carr's slightly weaving paths crossed, and they discovered instant mutual attraction. Within days they were lovers. In no time at all, she had moved in with him. The fact that he was a sexual rough rider counted for plus rather than minus points in Carr's carnal ordinal, for Maxine was a masochist, receiving pleasure from the pain it was Huntley's pleasure to inflict.

Moving with him to Soham, she gratefully took on the minor rôle of temporary teaching assistant at St. Andrew's Primary School, which occupied the same site as the College, hopeful that it would eventually lead to that of a permanent primary school teacher. All did, indeed, seem set fair for them both. But, true to flawed type, Huntley had to spoil it.

The police belief is that the murders were not planned, but opportunistic: he yielded to suddenly presented temptation. He was in his front garden, washing his Alsatian, Sadie, when Holly and Jessica, both of whom were, like quite a few of the girls, said to have had a bit of a crush on the passing handsome young caretaker, were going past on their walk. They went across to pat Sadie and have a chat with Huntley. The police felt sure that he enticed them into the house, saying that Carr, who was their teacher, and of whom they were exceptionally fond, was upstairs, and would come down to see them. He waited with them in the dining-room.

It is likely that he gave them alcohol, or perhaps glasses of squash laced with the date-rape drug, Rohypnol. At some point, probably after flirtatious talk, he must have made a grab for one of the girls. Her reaction, and that of her friend, threw him into one of his ungovernable rages, and in an explosion of anger he killed them both.

There may have been some blood-spilling in the room. If so, the fantastically thorough cleaning to which it, and the entire house, was subjected, removed every last trace of it. The likelihood, however, is that he strangled Holly first, and then smothered Jessica, by holding her down and covering her nose and mouth with his palm. After the girls were dead, he carried them upstairs and laid them on his bed. What his purpose was is not known, but can well be guessed. The cock and bull story which Huntley himself told was that Holly drowned in the bath while trying to stem a nosebleed, and that he accidentally killed Jessica while endeavouring to stifle her screaming. To compare Huntley and Carr with Brady and Hindley is quite wrong. Carr was away visiting her parents in Grimsby that Sunday. She had no hand in the murders. Her intelligence was not of the highest order, and it is likely that she would believe any tale that the infinitely cunning Huntley chose to spin. What story it was that he pitched to her she has never revealed. That he invented some legitimate-seeming reason for her helping him to wipe the house clean is plain, but that she shared his guilty secret is far from being anything like a foregone conclusion. When she did at last realise the truth about him, her classic words in court were: 'I am not going to be blamed for what that thing in that box has done to me or those children.' Both were tried before Mr. Justice Moses at the Old Bailey in December 2003. Maxine Carr attracted a sentence of three and a half years for perverting the course of justice by providing Huntley with a false alibi. She was released on May 10th, 2004. The trial judge told Huntley: 'You are the one person who knows how you murdered them. You are the one person who knows why. You destroyed the evidence. But you showed no mercy and you show no regret. It is plain that once you killed one you had to kill the other in your attempt to avoid detection.' Ian Huntley was sentenced to two terms of life imprisonment.

On September 29th, 2005, under a new procedure whereby the trial judge sets the tariff, Mr. Justice Moses ordered that Huntley should serve at least 40 years imprisonment before being considered for parole. He had taken into account the fact that there had been no proof of abduction, and that there was no evidence of sexual activity. Under these circumstances the law did not permit a life means life sentence.

PRIME SOURCES:

Beyond Evil. Nathan Yates. John Blake, London, 2004.

Soham: A Story of Our Times. Nicci Gerrard. Short Books, London, 2004.

Colin Ireland

The Self-Made Serial Killer

SERIAL KILLER

MURDERER: Colin John Ireland.

VICTIMS: Peter Walker (45). Christopher Dunn (37). Perry Bradley (35). Andrew Collier (33). Emmanuel Spiteri (43).

LOCI: Wealdstone, North of Harrow, Middlesex. Brechin Place, South Kensington, London, S.W.7. Dalston Lane, Stoke Newington, London, E.6. Hither Green Lane, London, S.E.

DATES: March - June, 1993.

MEANS: Suffocation and strangulation.

MOTIVE: To achieve the status of a serial killer.

CRIMEWATCH: To Colin Ireland, Hannibal Lecter, the human-liver-eating, serial killer psychiatrist in Thomas Harris' *The Silence of the Lambs*, was a new hero to be added to two old favourites, the Yorkshire Ripper and Dennis Nilsen, to make a heroic trio. The 39 years of his own life had, he felt, been a uniform failure. He wanted to be famous, written about, remembered. And that was when he decided that he, too, would become a serial killer.

He made it his New Year's resolution for 1993. The New Year and his resolve were barely nine weeks old when, on March 8th, 1993, he took the first step towards the realisation of his strange ambition. That Monday, he caught a train from Southend, in Essex, to London. He took with him his murder bag. It contained a pair of gloves and a length of nylon sailing cord – his murder kit. The bag would also be useful to carry away anything he had touched without gloves, and anything he might want to steal.

He had already made up his mind that he would target homosexuals, not only because he hated them, but also because he thought that their deaths would arouse less public sympathy. Prostitutes and promiscuous cruising homosexuals are the most vulnerable victims, and, since their killers have no known or demonstrable connection with them, their murders are the most difficult to solve.

Accordingly, he made his way to the Coleherne, a public-house at the Earl's Court end of Old Brompton Road, then a well known haunt of cruising homosexuals. He positioned himself near the door of the men's lavatory. Peter Walker, a 35-year-old theatre director, made the approach, deliberately brushing against him and spilling a splash of drink on his coat. They went together by taxi to Walker's flat in Vicarage Crescent, Battersea.

Indicating his desire to play the passive part in a sado-masochistic ritual, Walker, spread-eagled naked on his four-poster bed, allowed Ireland to tie him by the wrists and ankles to each of the four bedposts. Walker quickly realised that this was to be no erotic game. 'I am going to die,' he said. 'Yes,' said Ireland, 'you are.' And he put a plastic bag over his head and suffocated him. Later, he singed the dead man's pubic hair – 'Just to see what it smelt like.'

Next day, Ireland telephoned the *Sun* newspaper. 'I did it,' he announced. 'It was my New Year's resolution to murder a human being.' He went on to describe the killing. 'Is that of interest to you?' He was visualising the headlines. He telephoned the Samaritans, too. He gave them the address in Vicarage Crescent, telling them that Walker's Labrador, Bess, and Alsatian, Sam, needed to be fed and exercised. What he did not know was that Walker's body had already been found.

When he had failed to turn up at the Prince of Wales theatre for rehearsal of the new West End musical, *City of Angels*, his colleagues had alerted the police. At first, the detectives thought that what they were looking at was just another case of autoerotic asphyxia gone wrong. That is to say, self-induced strangulation or suffocation during masturbation, which reputedly enhances orgasm, but carries the serious risk of incidental accidental death. The practice is frequently associated with bondage and transvestism. The subsequent discovery that £200 had been removed from Walker's bank account with his cash card, suggested that his had not been a solitary sex session. Ireland had read in Robert Ressler's *Crime Classification Manual*, that in order to qualify as a *bona fide* serial killer you had to have killed more than four people. He was, consequently, planning further excursions into homicide. His second such was the killing of Christopher Dunn (37), a librarian. Changing from his sober daytime wear into his night-time gear of black leather jacket and trousers and a studded black leather collar around his throat, on Friday, May 28th, 1993, the flamboyantly attired cruiser set course for the Coleherne. And who should be waiting there for him, but Colin Ireland. Back they went to Dunn's flat in Wealdstone. There it was the mixture as before, except that when Chris refused to tell him the PIN number of his bank card, Colin burned his testicles with his` cigarette lighter. Ireland was later the richer by another £200. He struck again on June 4th. His happy hunting ground was once more the Coleherne. His elected one, Perry Bradley, from Sulphur Springs, Texas. His flat was in Brechin Place, South Kensington. The American was soon trussed up. This time Ireland did not resort to a plastic bag tied tightly round the head as in his previous two murders. He varied his *modus*, strangling him instead. Ireland's fourth victim, Andrew Collier (33) , also encountered at the Coleherne drinking pool, was accompanied home to Dalston Lane, Stoke Newington, and duly despatched in the same ritualistic manner as his predecessors. Riffling through the dead man's papers, he discovered that he had been HIV positive. 'He had not told me he was an AIDS carrier. I was the killer, but he could have killed me.' Ireland felt blind fury. 'He loved his cat. That was his life.' Venting his

rage, Ireland seized the pet cat, tied a sailing rope noose round its neck, tossed the poor terrified creature over a door, and hanged it. He then took its still twitching body and dropped it on to its dead master's corpse. He arranged the end of its tail in Collier's mouth, and the cat's mouth around Collier's penis, both tail and penis sheathed in a condom. It was a Maltese chef, Emmanuel Spiteri (43), his fifth mortal statistic, who enabled Ireland to achieve his longed-for, hard-earned status of Ressler recognised, full-blown serial killer. Spiteri was spotted outside the Coleherne, and seen again, by pure malignant chance, at Earl's Court underground station. They made eye contact, got into conversation, and travelled together to Catford, changing from underground to overground train at Charing Cross. At Spiteri's home in Hither Green Lane, the killing followed the usual pattern, terminating with the strangling of the naked man lying bound hand and foot on the bed. A new element introduced, was Spiteri's killer's unsuccessful attempt to burn the place down, to get rid of any evidence. Colin Ireland was now a serial killer, but he was also a marked man. He had been caught on a video surveillance camera at Charing Cross railway station with Spiteri. And he had left a single fingerprint on the concealed face of a window grille. There had been some sort of disturbance in the street outside as the two men sat having a pre-sex session drink. They went over to the window to see what was going on, and Ireland had accidentally left his fingerprint on the grille. He was arrested on July 23rd, 1993. Detectives were surprised to find that the six-foot, 15 stone, crop-haired Ireland was not himself a homosexual. He had two failed marriages behind him. He also had a lengthy police record, starting with persistent petty thefts, which led to Borstal, and graduating to blackmail and robbery, and several terms of imprisonment. Born in Dartford, Kent, in 1954, he was the illegitimate son of a newsagent's assistant. He enjoyed a secure childhood, living with his mother and grandparents in a council house in Myrtle Road, Dartford. When he was twelve, the family moved to the Isle of Sheppey, and his mother married. It seems that it was after this that he became 'difficult'. He was taken away and put in a special school for maladjusted children. During a two-year spell in the army he had undergone survival training, and he liked to spend periods living rough on the Thames Estuary marshes, eating rabbits and birds and snake meat. He had also tried to join the Foreign Legion. He was brought to trial at the Old Bailey in December, charged with five counts of murder. He pleaded guilty to them all, and on December 20th, 1993, received five life sentences. The judge, Mr. Justice Sachs, told him: 'You expressed your desire to be regarded as a serial killer, that must be matched by your detention for life.'

PRIME SOURCES:
The 1995 Murder Yearbook. Brian Lane. Headline, London, 1994.
Landmarks in 20th Century Murder. Robin Odell. Headline, London, 1995.
Contemporary newspapers.

Identity Unknown

Jack the Ripper

SERIAL KILLER

MURDERER: Jack the Ripper. Unidentified.

VICTIMS: Mary Ann Nichols (42-45). Annie Chapman (47). Elizabeth
Stride (44-45). Catherine Eddowes (43). Mary Jane Kelly (25).

Elisabeth Stride (victim)

LOCI: Buck's Row, Whitechapel (Nichols). Backyard of 29 Hanbury Street, Spitalfields (Chapman).
Dutfield's Yard, Berner Street, Whitechapel (Stride). Mitre Square, City of London (Eddowes). 13
Miller's Court, Dorset Street, Spitalfields (Kelly).

DATES: August 31st, 1888 (Nichols). September 8th, 1888 (Chapman). September 30th, 1888 (Stride and
Eddowes). November 9th, 1888 (Kelly).

MEANS: Cutting of the throat, followed by *post mortem* selective mutilation, with uterine bias, and
evisceration.

MOTIVE: Sexual gratification achieved by mutilation.

CRIMEWATCH: Peripatetic sexual psychopath. Has
been suggested that he first pointed his toe to
England from Russia or Poland. Certainly
beyond the Pale behaviour. Definitely no
connection with the British royal family. Most
unlikely to be any of the well-known
personages bruited as the innominate one. Nor
a cricketing barrister. Victims all prostitutes.
Abdomens routinely ripped open. Surgical
skill, highly questionable. Dubiously alleged to
have written taunting notes to the police.
Vanished after fifth and final – indoor orgy –
murder. Despite all and many subsequent
rumours, no real clue to the Ripper's true
identity has ever been discovered.
Contemporary top brass at the Yard, all in
denial and conflict.

PRIME SOURCES:
The Mystery of Jack the Ripper. Leonard Matters,
Hutchinson. London, 1928.
Jack the Ripper in Fact and Fiction. Robin Odell.
Harrap, London, 1965.
Autumn of Terror. Tom A. Cullen. Bodley Head,
London, 1965.

The Complete Jack the Ripper. Donald Rumbelow.
W. H. Allen, London, 1987.
Jack the Ripper: The Bloody Truth. Melvin Harris.
Columbus Books, London, 1987.
The Jack the Ripper A to Z. Paul Begg, Martin Fido
and Keith Skinner. Headline, London, 1991.
The True Face of Jack the Ripper. Melvin Harris.
Michael O'Mara Books, London, 1994.
The Complete History of Jack the Ripper. Philip
Sugden. Robinson, London, 1994.
The Lodger: The Arrest and Escape of Jack the Ripper.
Stewart P. Evans and Paul Gainey. Century,
London, 1995.
The Ultimate Jack the Ripper Sourcebook. Stewart P.
Evans and Keith Skinner. Robinson, London,
2000.
Jack the Ripper: Letters from Hell. Stewart P. Evans
and Keith Skinner. Sutton Publishing, Stroud,
Gloucestershire, 2001.
Jack the Ripper: The Facts. Paul Begg. Robson
Books, London, 2004.
The Quest for Jack the Ripper. Richard
Whittington-Egan. Patterson Smith, New
Jersey, 2005

Identity Unknown
Jack the Stripper
The Hammersmith Nudes Murders

SERIAL KILLER

Irene Lockwood (victim)

MURDERER: Jack the Stripper. Unidentified.

VICTIMS: Hannah Tailford (30). Irene Lockwood (26). Helen Catherine Barthelemy (22). Mary Fleming (30). Margaret McGowan (21). Bridget (Bridie) Esther O'Hara (28). Possibly – Gwynneth Rees (22).

LOCI: In the river Thames – bumping up against the pontoon pier beside the London Corinthian Sailing Club, Hammersmith Reach, West London (Tailford). Floating among weeds and a tangle of bankside branches in the Thames at Duke's Meadow, a large area of riverside grassland at Chiswick, West London (Lockwood). In an alleyway ten yards off Swyncombe Avenue, Brentford, West London (Barthelemy). On the parking space in front of the garage of a house in Berrymede Road, Chiswick (Fleming). Under a pile of rubble in a car park in Hornton Street, 100 yards from Kensington High Street (McGowan). Sprawled on a bed of bracken behind a store-shed off Westfield Road, Acton, West London (O'Hara). In an ash-tip near Chiswick Bridge (Rees).

DATES: Bodies discovered: February 2nd, 1964 (Tailford). April 8th, 1964 (Lockwood). April 24th, 1964 (Barthelemy). July 14th, 1964 (Fleming). November 25th, 1964 (McGowan). February 16th, 1965 (O'Hara). November 8th, 1963 (Rees).

MEANS: Exact cause of death of Tailford unestablished, but head injuries indicate possible knocking about. Exact cause of Lockwood's death not known, but marks on back of head. Strangulation (Barthelemy, McGowan, O'Hara). Cause of death of Rees unascertainable.

MOTIVE: Sexual alleviation. Ex-Detective Assistant Commissioner John du Rose, in charge of the investigation, believed the killer to be a man in his forties, who originally formed no intent to kill, but was subject to orgasmic frenzy, in which the women died. A curious feature was the extraction of teeth *post mortem*. Three of Barthelemy's front teeth were missing and one of McGowan's.

CRIMEWATCH: All the victims were prostitutes working the North Kensington, Bayswater and Soho areas. All were small in size, between 4ft. and 5ft. 3in., three at least bore tattoos, all were found naked. Whether Rees was his seventh victim is questionable. The other six were picked up, driven by car or van to the killing spot and attacked from behind. After death the body was stripped, stored somewhere where sprayed paint microscopically contaminated it, and, later, wrapped in a tarpaulin and dumped. Vital clues: tiny multicoloured specks of paints, found on Barthelemy, Fleming and McGowan, and the fact that O'Hara's corpse was partly mummified, which indicated storage near a heat-source. Samples of paint flakes found beneath a covered transformer (heat source) behind a building on the Heron Estate, Acton, facing a paint-spray shop. That victims vanished between 11 p.m. and 1 a.m. and were dumped between 5 a.m. and 6 a.m., suggested a nightworker. Nightwatchman? Policeman? Security guard? It has been said – but with absolutely nothing revealed to substantiate it – that a man who committed suicide in South London in March, 1965, was Jack the Stripper.

PRIME SOURCES:
Murder Was My Business. John du Rose, W. H. Allen, London, 1971.
Found Naked and Dead. Brian McConnell. New English Library, London, 1974.

Dr Mario Jascalevich

Fatal Doses of Curare

ACCUSED: Dr Mario Enrique Jascalevich.

VICTIMS: Carl Rohrbeck (73). Nancy Savino (4).
Margaret Henderson (26). Frank Biggs (59). Emma Arzt (70).

LOCUS: Riverdell Hospital, Bergenfield, New Jersey.

DATES: December 13th, 1965 (Rohrbeck). March 20th, 1966 (Savino). April 23rd, 1966 (Henderson).
August 28th, 1966 (Biggs). September 23rd, 1966 (Arzt).

MEANS: It was alleged that Jascalevich administered a lethal dose of curare by route of intravenous drip.

MOTIVE: 'He wanted to have the power of life and death in this hospital as chief of surgery. He wanted to play God.' - words of State attorney, Sybil Moses. Professional jealousy.

CRIMEWATCH: The defence was that Dr Jascalevich was the victim of a conspiracy. The accusation against chief surgeon Jascalevich was alleged to have been motivated by feuds and jealousies of hospital politics. The story of the series of sudden and unexplained deaths that plagued the suburban New Jersey Hospital in 1966, was broken in 1976 by journalist Myron Farber, who was nominated for a Pulitzer Prize for his 'Dr X' articles in the *New York Times*. These articles led to the trial of Jascalevich. The doctor had been seen near the victims of unexpected death, but 'There is no proof that this man ever put anything into anybody.' Eighteen vials of curare were found in his locker, but he claimed that he used it for vivisection on dogs. Although there was suspicion and enquiry in 1966, Jascalevich was not tried until 1978, when, aged 51, he was acquitted on all charges. The scientific proof of curare found in exhumed bodies ten years interred had been hotly debated. Jascalevich is said to have removed to Argentina.

PRIME SOURCES:
Final Treatment: The File on Dr X. Matthew L. Lifllander. W. W. Norton, New York, 1979.
Somebody is Lying: The Story of Dr X. Myron Farber. Doubleday, New York, 1982.

Arthur Albert Jones

The Strangling of Little Brenda Nash

MURDERER: Arthur Albert Jones.

VICTIM: Brenda Nash (12).

LOCUS: Yateley Common, Yateley, Hampshire.

DATE: October 28th, 1960.

MEANS: Manual strangulation.

MOTIVE: Sexual gratification. And to escape detection.

CRIMEWATCH: The awful tragedy of Brenda Nash began with the lesser tragedy of a little girl whose identity was protected under the name of 'Barbara'. Barbara was eleven years old and she was a Girl Guide. On the evening of Friday, September 9th, 1960, she had gone to a Guides' meeting in a church hall at Twickenham, Middlesex. It was at about 9.15 p.m., as she was cycling the three miles home along the Staines Road, that she saw a man standing beside a black car parked at the roadside. The man stepped out, holding up his hand. She stopped.

He told her that he was a police officer, and showed her a wallet with a badge on it. He said that he was investigating bicycle thefts, and hers looked like one of the stolen ones. He instructed her to leave it leaning against a tree and to get into his car. He would, he said, take her home, and then to the police station.

As they drove off, he gave her a peppermint. The sweets were in a pocket next to the front seat. She ate it, putting the wrapper in her blazer pocket. Then he showed her a revolver, telling her it was loaded and that 'All policemen have one.'

He drove some 20 miles to a deserted lane in the Sunningdale area of Berkshire, where he stopped, looked at his watch, drove on a little further, and came to a full stop. He ordered her to remove some of her clothing. She refused. He punched her in the face, forced her into the back of the car, and raped her, telling her, 'Don't scream. Don't be silly. All girls do this.' He put his hands round her throat and squeezed tightly. 'I did that to frighten you,' he told her

matter-of-factly. Then he dragged her out of the car, spread a blanket from the boot on the ground, and raped her again.

He bundled her back into the car, and drove her to within half a mile of her home. Before letting her go, he asked: 'Do you think you'd recognise me again?' Her reply probably saved her life. 'No,' she said. 'I've only seen you a little while.' He drove off.

She had undergone nearly three hours of abuse. It was 1.20 a.m. when she staggered into her home and the arms of her distraught parents. She was a sorry sight. Her face was bruised, her lips badly swollen and covered with blood. But she was able to supply a splendid description of her assailant.

He was forty-ish, thickset, about 5 ft 8in. tall, dark hair going grey at the sides, a reddish face, slanting eyes, and with a starfish-shaped scar on his right cheek. The car was a Vauxhall Wyvern. Arthur Albert Jones, who fitted her description in every detail, was a 44-year-old, £18-a-week fitter-welder. Married for 23 years to Grace Amelia, he lived in a council house in Ely Road, Hounslow, had a 22-year-old married daughter, a 16-year-old son, Martyn Robert, and a 1952 black Vauxhall Wyvern

He also had an alibi: on September 9th, accompanied by his wife and son, he had been staying with his wife's sister, Mrs. Ivy Eldridge, at Beckenham. When this was exposed as bogus, he offered another fake alibi involving a visit to a London prostitute. He was tried at the Old Bailey, and sentenced on March 7th, 1961, to fourteen years.

Meanwhile, back on Sunday, December 11th, 1960, three boys – brothers Alistair (12), Keith (9), and Ian Muir (5) – playing on Yateley Common, near the Hampshire village of Yately, had come upon a grim sight. Lying in a slight hollow, hidden by the long grass, was the body of a young girl. She was wearing the blue uniform of a Girl Guide. Clearly marked on the shoulder tabs was the legend, 5th Heston Company Girl Guides. Brenda Nash had been found.

It had been on the night of Friday, October 28th, 1960, that the 12-year-old girl had left her council estate home at 9 Bleriot Road, Heston, Middlesex, as she did every Friday night, to go to the Heston Girl Guides' meeting. That evening there had been a special Girl Guide Divisional First Aid Contest for a silver cup, held at Heston Junior School. It was all over by 9.20 p.m., and Brenda, with her two friends, Pamela Dwyer and Glynis Blight, left on foot. They went to a fish-and-chip shop and bought a bag of chips. At 10.05 p.m., they parted company at the junction of Armytage Road and Cranford Lane, a quarter of a mile from Brenda's home. She was never seen again.

Following Jones' sentencing for the rape of Barbara, his photograph was plastered all over the newspapers, and he was promptly recognised and officially identified by two men, Frederick Holloway and Cuthbert Wakefield, who had seen him hanging around Heston in his black Vauxhall Wyvern on the night that Brenda vanished. Professor Keith Simpson had conducted a post-mortem, which had established the cause of death as asphyxia resultant upon strangulation, and also showed that, although she had been sexually interfered with, she had not been raped.

Jones, of course, denied everything, even produced an almost identical prostitute alibi for the night of the 28th, but no one, least of all the Old Bailey jury, believed him. On June 19th, 1961, he was found guilty of the murder of Brenda Nash and given life, the sentence to run consecutively to the 14 years which he was already serving.

One psychiatric view is that Jones was motivated by an enormous incestuous stimulation when his own daughter reached, or nearly reached, the age of puberty. She was a Girl Guide, and, for some perverse reason, the image of a young girl in Guides' uniform became an ongoing source of irresistible sexual excitement and desire. The need to murder Brenda Nash was not sexual, but in the hope that it would enable him to escape detection. In May, 1963, his wife was granted a divorce.

PRIME SOURCES:
Famous Criminal Cases – 7. Rupert Furneaux. Odhams, London, 1962.
My Own Case. Ex-Detective Chief Superintendent Walter Jones. Angley Books, Maidstone, Kent, 1966.
Occupied With Crime. Sir Richard Jackson. Harrap, London, 1967.
The Child Killers. Norman Lucas. Arthur Barker, London, 1970.
Forty Years of Murder. Keith Simpson. Harrap, London, 1978.
Public Prosecutor. Sir Norman Skelhorn. Harrap, London, 1981.

Patrick Kearney

The Trash Bag Murders

SERIAL KILLER

MURDERER: Patrick Wayne Kearney.

VICTIMS: Probable total of 32 male homosexual victims.
Indicted for the killing of Albert Riviera (21). Arturo Marquez(24).
John Le May (17).

LOCI: Dumped along the highway, right from south Los Angeles, following the California coastline, to Newport Beach, down towards the Mexico border. Dismembered portions discovered in ditches by the roadside and on freeway shoulders, obviously thrown from a car. A plastic-wrapped head turned up on the conveyor belt at a recycling plant. A left leg was found on a junk heap outside a Sunset Beach saloon.

DATES: 1972 – 77. The first of the bodies was discovered on Christmas Day, 1972.

MEANS: Shooting in the head with small-calibre gun. All the victims were nude. Several were dismembered after being shot.

MOTIVE: Almost all the victims were young male drifters haunting the homosexual cruising areas and hangouts around Hollywood and LA. Kearney specifically refused to articulate any motive for his gay slaughtering spree.

CRIMEWATCH: Bearded, bespectacled, 38-year-old (born 1940), avowed homosexual, Kearney had worked as an electronics engineer for the LA aerospace firm, Hughes Aircraft Co. For 15 years he had been room-mates with David D. Hill (34), his best friend. Latterly, they lived at Redondo Beach. In their home there, investigators turned up a hacksaw stained with what proved to be Le May's blood. They found, too, hair and carpet fibres which matched those adhering to tape on victims' bodies. Kearney and Hill, who had fled to Mexico, walked in on the authorities on July 1st, 1977, pointed to a wanted poster with their pictures on it, and announced, 'We're them.' They had listened to the advice of relatives to turn themselves in. On July 13th, 1977, Kearney was indicted on three counts of murder. Charges against Hill were not pressed for lack of evidence. After pleading guilty to 21 killings in exchange for the promise that he would not receive the death penalty, Kearney proceeded to provide details of a further 11 homosexual murders. In 1978, he was sentenced to life.

PRIME SOURCE:
Contemporary newspapers.

Edmund Kemper
The Co-ed Killer

SERIAL KILLER

MURDERER: Edmund Emil Kemper.

VICTIMS: (At age of 15). His grandparents, Maude and Edmund Kemper. (At age of 23). Six hitch-hiking girl students: Mary Ann Pesce (18). Anita Luchessa (18). Aiko Koo (15). Cindy Schall (18). Rosalind Thorpe (23). Alice Lui (21). His own mother, remarried and now Clarnell Strandberg, and her friend, Mrs. Sara (Sally) Taylor Hallett.

LOCI: The Kemper farm at North Fork, near Tollhouse, Madera County, California (Grandparents). Side roads in Central California (Hitch-hikers). A duplex numbered 609A Ord Drive, Aptos, Santa Cruz, California (Mother and friend).

DATES: 1963 – 73.

MEANS: Shooting, strangling, butchering. For mother – a blow with a claw hammer.

MOTIVE: A mixed psychopathology. Resentment of mother-figures. Sexual gratification (rape, necrophilia, cannibalism).

CRIMEWATCH: Giant Kemper, 6ft 9in tall, 20 stone, with a high IQ of 136, was a child cat-killer and rejected by his parents. Mother used to lock him in the basement under a trap-door. Grandparents on a remote farm had a go at rearing him, but he repaid their strict kindness with a bullet in the head, and Grandma, a children's writer, was slashed to pieces with a knife. For this, they sent him to Atascadero State Hospital, where he learnt all about rape. Released after five years, now aged 20 (born December 18th, 1948), rejected by the police as too tall, he found work as a flagman for the California Division of the Highways. Cruising the freeways, he practised his technique in picking up student hitch-hikers. After rape, his paramount pleasure was the dissection and decapitation of their bodies. He used a Polaroid as he was at his work. With a body in the boot of his car, he felt, he said, like a fisherman with a prize catch. He cooked and ate some bits. He decapitated his mother and her friend, too. Then he gave himself up, pleaded insanity; but, on November 8th, 1973, was found guilty on all eight counts of first-degree murder and sentenced to life imprisonment.

PRIME SOURCE:
The Co-ed Killer. Margaret Cheney. Walker & Company, New York, 1976.

Constance Kent

The Road Hill House Murderess

MURDERER: Constance Emily Kent.

VICTIMS: Francis Saville (Savile, Savill), Kent
(3 years 10 months): half-brother.

LOCUS: Road Hill House, near Trowbridge, Wiltshire.

DATE: June 29th, 1860.

MEANS: Throat cut with razor. Head practically severed from body. Stab wound in left side. Has been said that there was evidence of preliminary stifling.

MOTIVE: To pay out stepmother (whose child he was) for taking the place of, and making disparaging remarks about Constance's real mother and the children of the first marriage.

CRIMEWATCH: Sixteen-year-old Constance was arrested for the murder, but released by the Trowbridge magistrates. The child's nurse, Elizabeth Gough (22), was then accused. She, too, was discharged at the police court. The mystery seemed impenetrable until, five years later, Constance, who, under the benign influence of the Reverend Arthur Wagner, devout Puseyite, in whose Conventual Home of St. Mary, in Brighton, she had, in search of solitude and retreat, become a paying guest, and most passionately embraced religion, came cathartically forward to confess her guilt. She who had sought revenge, now sought redemption. Tried and found guilty at Salisbury Crown Court, spared death, her ordained purgatory was to spend the succeeding twenty years in prison. Released at the age of 41, calling herself now Ruth Emilie Kaye, she went to Australia. There she trained as a nurse, and tended lepers and the tuberculous. Later, she was appointed matron of an institution for problem girls, and finally became proprietress of a nurses' home in Maitland. Constance Kent died, aged 100, on April 10th, 1944, at Strathfield, New South Wales.

PRIME SOURCES:

The Great Crime of 1860. J. W. Stapleton. E. Marlborough & Co., London, 1861.

The Road Murder: Being A Complete Report and Analysis, by A Barrister-At-Law. London, n.d.

The Case of Constance Kent. John Rhode. Geoffrey Bles, London, 1928.

Saint – With Red Hands? Yseult Bridges. Jarrolds, London, 1954.

Cruelly Murdered. Bernard Taylor. Souvenir Press, London, 1979.

Ronald and Reginald Kray

The East End Icon Gangsters

MURDERERS: Ronnie Kray and Reggie Kray.

VICTIMS: George Cornell (38). Frank Mitchell (38). Jack McVitie (38).

LOCI: The Blind Beggar Public-House, Mile End Road, Whitechapel (Cornell). Barking Road, East Ham (Mitchell). 65 Evering Road, Stoke Newington (McVitie).

DATES: March 9th, 1966. December 24th, 1966. October 28th, 1967.

MEANS: Shooting. Stabbing.

MOTIVE: To prove their toughness and sustain their reign by fear.

CRIMEWATCH: The whole thing is ambered in time, with the cut of the '50s and '60s. Ronnie and Reggie, Mrs. Kray's twins, born on October 24th, 1933, had fought their way upward through the same East End streets haunted by Jack the Ripper fifty years before.

By the 1950s and swinging sixties, after much sweat and bloodshed, they had grown wealthy from the huge rake-off of their fear-enforced protection and extortion rackets. They had become, with their elegant Savile Row suits, shiny Jaguars, the clubs they owned, and their shoulder-rubbing with sporting and show business celebrities, East End icons. But woe betide any who decided to face up and decline to pay up. They would, at the mildest, have their buttocks slashed with a razor – 'So every time the bastards sit down they remember me,' explained Ronnie. And he wasn't smiling.

There was a scarifying additional menu of disasters, both personal and to the business premises, if the shell-out reluctance persisted. But it was when the violence escalated to murder at a personal level, that the writing appeared on the wall. The scene of the first of the twins' hands-on murders was the saloon bar of the Blind Beggar public-house, almost opposite the Royal London Hospital, in the Mile End Road. The victim was George Cornell, a mouthy hard man, torturer in chief to the Richardson Brothers' outfit, a rival south

London gang to the Kray twins' Firm. He had made the fatal, as it proved, mistake of bad mouthing Ronnie to his face, calling him a 'fat poof', and telling him to 'bugger off.'

At half-past eight on the evening of March 9th, 1966, Ronnie Kray evened up the score with a 9 mm Mauser automatic. Cornell was sitting on a high stool, sipping whisky. 'Well, look who's here,' he said mockingly. They were the last words he ever spoke. Ronald Kray clapped the revolver to the side of his head and pulled the trigger. As Cornell slumped, dying, to the floor, Kray turned on his heel and marched smartly out.

Within ten minutes the police arrived – and, surprise, surprise, no one had seen anything! The Krays were questioned for 36 hours. They supplied no meaningful answers. But the incident had set up a sort of mental barrier between the twins. Ronald had killed a man, ruthlessly, in cold blood. 'I have done my one,' he told Reggie. 'Now you do yours.'

Their chosen victim was Jack 'The Hat' McVitie, so nicknamed because, acutely sensitive to his premature balding, he wore a perpetual natty trilby. It was on October 28th, 1967, that they lured him, with promises of a rip-roarer of a Saturday night party, to 'Blonde Carole' Skinner's basement flat, in Evering Road, Stoke Newington. No sooner was he through the door, than Reggie put a gun to his head and pulled the trigger. Nothing happened. It had misfired. McVitie thought he was the butt of a cruel practical joke. But when, twice more, Reggie pulled the trigger, and twice more nothing happened, McVitie suddenly realised that this was in deadly earnest.

Struggling for his life, he tried to jump out of the window. 'Come on, Jack, stand up and die like a man,' Ronnie taunted him as he dragged him back and seized him in a bear hug. In a split second, Reggie was on him with a carving-knife, stabbing him in the face, just below the eye, and then, repeatedly, in the stomach. He fell to the ground. Reggie stood over him and plunged the knife into his neck. They wrapped him in a candlewick bedspread and spirited his corpse away.

The third murder had not been a hands-on job. It had taken place back in December, 1966. For some reason best known to themselves, the twins had taken it into their heads to 'spring' Frank 'Mad Axeman' Mitchell from Dartmoor, where he was serving a life sentence. On December 12th, Mitchell, out on a work party, asked permission to walk across the moor to feed some wild ponies. After a very rough start at the prison, Mitchell had eventually calmed down and turned into a model prisoner, so the guard did not have second thoughts about granting his request. But Mitchell never came back.

Picked up by a nearby waiting car, he had been whisked off to a specially prepared flat in Barking Road, East Ham. An immense man, 6 ft 4in. tall, weighing in at 17 stone, big and fit as an ox, Mitchell's brain power did not match up with his physique. He was said to have the mind of a 10-year-old boy, and was easily bored. Cooped up in the not over large Barking Road flat, he soon became restless and alarmingly fractious. So the Krays sent a blonde nightclub hostess, Lisa, to occupy and console him. He fell in love with her.

He wanted to marry her, and started writing letters to the newspapers asking the Home Secretary for a release date. Sensing danger for themselves, the Kray brothers decided to eliminate a liability. On Christmas Eve, telling him that he was going to be moved to the country, and that Lisa would be following him there, they sent a van round for him. He hugged and kissed Lisa goodbye, and allowed himself to be escorted out by a couple of heavies to the waiting van. Almost immediately after he had left the flat, there was the sound of three shots. 'They've shot him. Oh, God, they've shot him,' screamed Lisa.

They had. Ronnie and Reggie were never found guilty of that killing which they had ordered, but they were tried for the murders of Cornell and McVitie at the Old Bailey, and sentenced to life by Mr. Justice Melford Stevenson on March 5th, 1969. They never came out. Ronald died in Broadmoor on March 9th, 1995, aged 61, having been behind bars for 26 years. Reggie, released from prison on compassionate grounds in August, 2000, died in his sleep in the honeymoon suite of the Town House Hotel, at Thorpe St. Andrew, near Norwich. His second wife, Roberta (41), was at his bedside. He died of inoperable bladder cancer on October 1st, 2000. He was within three weeks of his 66th birthday, and had served 30 years. Reggie was the last of the Kray clan. The twins' elder brother, Charles, had died of cancer in 1999, while serving a 12-year sentence for drugs offences. They will be missed – not greatly, but gratefully.

PRIME SOURCES:
Me and My Brothers. Charles Kray with Jonathan Sykes. Everest Books, London, 1976.
The Profession of Violence. John Pearson. Granada, London, 1984.
Our Story. Reg and Ron Kray with Fred Dinenage. Sidgwick & Jackson, London, 1988.
My Story. Ron Kray with Fred Dinenage. Sidgwick & Jacson, London, 1993.
A Way of Life. Reg Kray. Sidgwick & Jackson, London, 2000.
The Krays: Unfinished Business. Martin Fido. Carlton, London, 2000.
The Kray Brothers: The Image Shattered. Craig Cabell. Robson Books, London, 2002.

Peter Kürten

The Düsseldorf Monster

SERIAL KILLER

MURDERER: Peter Kürten.

VICTIMS: The full tally of his victims is unknown. He was charged with nine murders. Those of Christine Klein (10); Rosa Ohliger (8); Rudolf Scheer (45); Maria Hahn; Gertrud Hamacher (5); Luise Lenzen (14); Ida Reuter; Elisabeth Dörrier; Gertrud Albermann (5). He was also charged with seven attempted murders: Frau Kühn; Anna Goldhausen; Frau Mantel; Gustav Kornblum; Gertrud Schulte; Frau Meurer; Frau Wanders.

LOCI: An inn on the Wolfsstrasse, Köln-Mülheim (Klein). Building site, Kettwiger-Strasse, in the Flingern district of western Düsseldorf (Ohliger). In the Hellweg, in the Flingern district of Düsseldorf (Scheer). A meadow close to the Morp-Papendell highway (Hahn). At Flehe, on the market garden allotments (Hamacher and Lenzen). Meadows beside the Rhine, near Düsseldorf (Reuter). On the banks of the Düssel near Grafenberg (Dörrier). The vicinity of the Haniel house, near the Lenaustrasse, Düsseldorf (Albermann).

DATES: Summer, 1913 (Klein). February 8th, 1929 (Ohliger). February 12th, 1929 (Scheer). August 11th, 1929 (Hahn). August 24th, 1929 (Hamacher and Lenzen). September 29th, 1929 (Reuter). October 11th, 1929 (Dörrier). November 27th, 1929 (Albermann).

MEANS: Strangling, stabbing, throat-cutting, and bludgeoning.

MOTIVE: Sadistic sexual gratification – especially satisfied by the sight of spurting blood.

CRIMEWATCH: Born in Cologne-Mülheim, third of thirteen children of a brutal, alcoholic, incestuous father, Kürten was unquestionably the victim of a vicious background – bad home and poor heredity. Seduced, around age nine, to cruelty by a sadistic dog-catcher, he grew powerfully bonded to a sexuality fused with blood and suffering. He killed men, women, children, animals – anything he found – was an arsonist, and a petty thief, and served many prison sentences. When he did work, it was as a sand moulder in a factory, where he was a very active trade unionist. Arrested in May, 1930, he was tried in April, 1931. During that waiting year his psychopathology was studied in great detail by psychiatrist Professor Karl Berg. Guillotined, aged 48, at Klingelputz prison, on July 2nd, 1932, after a hearty meal of Wiener-Schnitzel and white wine (second helpings), he went to his death proclaiming that the pleasure to end all pleasures would be to hear the sound of his own blood gushing from the stump of his neck.

PRIME SOURCES:
The Monster of Düsseldorf. Margaret Seaton Wagner. Faber and Faber, London, 1932.
Peter Kürten. George Godwin. The Acorn Press, London, 1938.
The Sadist. Karl Berg. William Heinemann, London, 1945.

Leonard Lake & Charles Ng

The California Torture Duo

SERIAL KILLERS

MURDERERS: Leonard Lake aka Charles Gunnar. Charles Chi tag Ng (pronounced Ing).

VICTIMS: Made away with an estimated 25 men, women and children. Many of the decomposed remains still unidentified. Various friends, neighbours, and chance acquaintances were murdered. Some victims had responded to advertisements offering video equipment for sale. Others, like Paul Cosner, came to sell a car to Lake. Known named victims include Kathy Allen, Brenda O'Connor, her friend, Scott Stapley, and her 2-year- old son, Lonnie Bond, Jr., (scattered baby teeth found), and, very probably, Lake's disagreeable younger brother, Donald, Lake's best friend from his Vietnam years, Charles Gunnar, and Ng's prison friend, Michael Carrol, whose girlfriend was Kathy Allen.

LOCI: A survivalist compound at the Mother Lode, Humboldt County, California (Gunnar, Donald Lake). Two-room cabin off Blue Mountain Road, Wisleyville, Calaveras County, California. (Allen, O'Connor, Bond and many others).

DATES: *c.* 1981 – 85.

MEANS: Not known (save in the cases of 'snuff' video victims), but assuredly following prolonged torture.

MOTIVE: Complicated. Basically sexual, of course, but linked with a belief – perhaps genuine, perhaps adapted and adopted - that an inevitable nuclear holocaust impended.

CRIMEWATCH: Lake – born July 20th, 1946, in San Francisco – balding, black-bearded, powerful-looking, former Marine and Vietnam veteran, was into war-games. Through this mutual interest met, in 1981, Ng (24), ex-Marine, ex-convict, fugitive. Lake had developed, too, an interest in survivalism. The stockpiling of food supplies, weapons and women sex slaves, through whom he would repopulate the post-holocaust world, went well with his obsessional personality, expressed in hypergraphia, compulsively minute genetic experimentation with rats and mice in his boyhood, the indulgence in continual hand-washing rituals, and the absolute insistence that his victims should take a shower before the torture session began. On June 2nd, 1985, Ng was seen shoplifting at a San Francisco hardware store. He ran off, but Lake, arrested, committed suicide, swallowing a cyanide capsule. Police sent to search his house for other stolen goods found mutilated bodies, skeletal remains, torture implements, and home-made 'snuff' videos, combining violent sex scenes with actual murders committed on camera. Ng, captured at Calgary, Alberta, Canada, in July, 1985, after another shoplifting incident, served a prison sentence there. Extradited, he is currently on death row at San Quentin.

PRIME SOURCES:
Eye of Evil. Joseph Harrington and Robert Burger. St. Martin's Press, New York, 1993.
Die for Me. Don Lasseter Pinnacle Books. New York, 2000.
No Kill No Thrill. Darcy Henton and Greg Owens. Red Deer Press, Calgary, Canada, 2001.
Contemporary newspapers.

David Lashley

The Killing of Janie Shepherd

MURDERER: David Lashley.

VICTIM: Janie Shepherd (24).

LOCUS: Ladbroke Grove, West London.

DATE: February 4th, 1977.

MEANS: Strangulation by throat crushing.

MOTIVE: Sexual – admixed with an element of revenge.

CRIMEWATCH: Janie Shepherd, step-daughter of John Darling, chairman of British Petroleum, Australia, left the family home in Sydney in 1971 to go to London, where she went to live with her cousin, Camilla, and her husband, Alistair Sampson, in their Clifton Hill luxury apartment, in the St. John's Wood area of north-west London. Provided with a generous allowance, she had no need to work, but she chose to, and found a job at an art gallery, the Caelt Gallery, in Westbourne Grove, Bayswater.

She also found a boyfriend, Roddy Kinkead-Weekes, old Etonian, in merchant banking, Middlesex county cricketer. On Friday, February 4th, 1977, planning to spend the weekend with him at his flat in Lennox Gardens, Chelsea, Janie set forth in her blue Mini Clubman from Clifton Hill at about 8.30p.m. En route, she popped into the Europa Supermarket, in Queensway. Roddy had asked her to pick up something for their supper. She bought a couple of trout, tomatoes, chicory, cheese, and yoghurt.

When, by 9.30.p.m., Janie had failed to arrive, Roddy was not unduly worried. London traffic on a Friday night could be pretty awful. Even so, he rang through a check call to cousin Camilla. Yes, she had definitely left at half past eight. It was a three-mile drive. It should have taken her about twenty minutes. By 10p.m., when there was still no sign of Janie, Roddy really began to worry. Thereafter, he rang

Camilla at regular intervals up to midnight. After that, they all rang round hospitals, and later, alarmed now, reported Janie missing to the police.

Four days passed. A police patrol car spotted Janie's Mini. It was parked on a yellow line in Elgin Crescent, Notting Hill. An examination of the car revealed cause for worry. There were signs of a fierce struggle. There were two deep slashes in the soft, vinyl sun-roof. Janie's boots were in the car. So was her red shoulder bag. As far as money was concerned, her purse, in which there had been £40-odd, was empty, but the tell-tale receipts, from the Europa for food purchases, and for petrol bought at a self-service petrol station in Bayswater, which centred the search around Queensway, were discovered there. Janie had topped up her seven-gallon fuel tank with three gallons of four star petrol. Calculating from the amount remaining, the car was estimated to have covered a round trip of 75-80 miles.

On Easter Monday, April 18th, 1977, two school friends, Neil Gardner (10) and Dean James (11), out cycling at Devil's Dyke, a part of the common known as Nomansland, near Wheathampstead, in Hertfordshire, saw, in a hollow barely fifty yards off the B651 Wheathampstead to St. Albans road, what they thought was a bundle of rags. In fact, it was the badly decomposed body of Janie Shepherd.

She was fully clothed. A ligature on her left

ankle, together with other marks, showed that her arms and legs had been bound. The congestive condition of her heart and lungs indicated that she had died of asphyxia, following compression of the neck. She was identified by her teeth and the jewellery found with her. Such was her state of decay that, although it was strongly suspected, it was impossible to say for sure whether she had been sexually assaulted.

A trawl through police records of sex offenders with links to West London revealed that, in July, 1971, a woman sitting at midnight in a parked car outside her flat in Chesterton Road, Notting Hill, less than half a mile from where Janie's Mini was found, had been raped at knife point.

Her assailant had come up to the car window and asked her the time. As she glanced down at her watch, he had wrenched open the door, threatened to kill her if she screamed, and forced her over into the front passenger seat. He then drove the car to an isolated spot, raped her twice, tried to strangle her, and, before jumping out of the car, slashed one of her wrists with a knife. She was lucky. She survived to give a description of a black man with a scar on his face.

The man the police thought to be the most likely culprit was David Lashley, a van driver who had been convicted in 1970 of committing five rapes on young women in cars, and sentenced to 12 years. He had recently been released on parole. But there was no mention on his record of his having a scar on his face. So he was not in the frame.

However, on February 17th, 1977, Lashley was taken by detectives from his Southall, north London, home, put on an identity parade, and picked out by the Chesterton Road rape victim. In December, 1977, he was sentenced to 15 years. In the end, it was a fellow rapist who brought Lashley to book.

Daniel Reece (that is not his real name) was white. He and the black man had palled up at Frankland Maximum Security Prison, in County Durham. They shared a passion for weight-lifting, as well as for buggery and rape, for which Reece was serving a long sentence. They spent a lot of time together in the prison gym. It was there that Lashley confided how he had grabbed a 'nice-looking blonde', and raped and murdered her in a secluded part of Ladbroke Grove.

After hearing from the 50-year-old father of two how, since his brutalised wife left him in the 1960s, David Lashley had developed a murderous hatred of all blonde white women, Reece, in a rare moment of civic conscience, had conveyed this intelligence to the authorities, confessedly fearful of what might ensue if Lashley was ever to be permitted the freedom of the streets again.

So it came about that, on March 19th, 1990, thirteen years to the month since Janie Shepherd's death, her killer stood in the dock at St. Albans Crown Court, to hear himself being jailed for life, with Mr. Justice Alliott expressing the view that he was such an appallingly dangerous man that 'the real issue is whether you can ever be allowed your liberty again in your natural lifetime.'

PRIME SOURCE:
Contemporary newspapers.

John Watson Laurie

The Arran Murder

Murderer: John Watson Laurie.

Victim: Edwin Robert Rose (32).

Locus: Goatfell, Isle of Arran, Scotland.

Date: July 15th, 1889.

Means: Probably battering with a stone.

Motive: Robbery. Premeditated? Insane sudden impulse? Quarrel? Homosexual undertones?

CRIMEWATCH: Two men went to climb, went to climb a mountain. One came down. The other stayed up, hidden in a tomb of stones. Holiday acquaintances, Laurie (26), a skilled artisan, and Rose, a dandiacal clerk from Upper Tooting, were lodging together on the island. On July 15th, they began the ascent of Goatfell. Three hours later, a shepherd saw Laurie coming down alone. He left the island. Rose was missed on July 18th. On August 4th, a search party of 200 tackled the misty mountain. A fisherman found Rose's robbed body hidden under stones plugged with heather. The face, left side of head, and left shoulder-blade were frightfully smashed. Run to earth in a wood near Glasgow, Laurie said, 'I robbed the man, but I did not murder him.' At the trial in Edinburgh, on November 8th, 1889, the defence was that Rose had fallen to his death. Laurie was convicted by a majority of one, seven voting for Not Proven, but the death sentence was commuted to life after a petition claiming insanity. He died in Perth Criminal Asylum on October 4th, 1930.

PRIME SOURCE:
Notable British Trial. Edited by William Roughead. William Hodge, Edinburgh, 1932.

Jean Lee

Australia's Last Woman To Hang

Murderer: Jean Lee (born Marjorie Jean Maude Wright).

Victim: William ('Pop') Kent (73).

Locus: Mallow House, 50 Dorrit Street, Carlton, Melbourne, Australia.

Date: November 7th, 1949.

Means: The actual cause of death was strangulation by the thumb and fingers of a right hand, but there were precedent blows and cuts to the face and body. Lee's part in the attack was almost certainly confined to the lesser wounds and bruises.

Motive: This was a joint enterprise with two male accomplices, all habitually under the influence of alcohol, and in the pursuit of robbery. The murder was probably not premeditated, but executed by one person in a panic, to keep the victim quiet and prevent identification. There was, however, an undoubted element of sadism.

Crimewatch: Jean Lee was the last woman to be hanged in Australia. She looked quite like a film star in the Joan Crawford mode, except for her brilliant red Rita Hayworth hair. Perhaps she could have gone along that route, but she took a lower road to prostitution. There is nothing in her early history to explain her descent into vice and crime, although those who had known her would point to the bad influence of certain men. She was a victim, always getting knocked about.

Born on December 10th, 1919, in Dubbo, NSW, she came from a good, but not affluent, home. Her father was a railway ganger, and she was the youngest of five siblings. Although bright at school, where she asked too many awkward questions, she never settled, and took menial jobs. One daughter, Jill, was born, but Jean's mother had to bring her up.

And so Jean drank far too much, and drifted from town to town with various men, some of them pimps. She worked in brothels, and eventually she deteriorated to the 'badger trick'. Her last lover, and pimp, Robert David Clayton, three years older than Jean, was a confirmed criminal, but she loved him to the end. He suffered, officially, from 'anxiety neurosis', after the Second World War, and was violent to her.

The dubious pair were flashy dressers, keeping up appearances, and they frequented low-grade hotels and race-tracks, fuelled by alcohol throughout every waking moment and living on their wits. Their only income was what they could obtain on the day. It was felt in Australia at that time that she was a disgrace to womanhood. Her crime was unusual, and stood out from domestic murders, where there were mitigating circumstances.

On the day in question, Jean Lee and Clayton were hanging around with Norman Andrews, another hardened criminal, all three attracted to the racing fixtures in Melbourne. They booked into the Great Southern Hotel, and went out to drink at the inappropriately named University Hotel. In the Ladies Bar, Jean was weighing up a likely looking target, who was obviously very interested in her. She pretended to be an exotic dancer.

William Kent, known to everyone as 'Pop', was 73, but he still liked female company and was not averse to taking a woman to his home across the street. He made a bit of an income as a bookmaker, and also rented out rooms in his once-elegant house, a 19th-century building of Italianate brick, with a green plaster façade, three arches spanning a veranda with a wrought-iron balustrade. Carlton had become a poor neighbourhood.

Now, they were all drinking hard, and Kent, drawn by the glamour of the red-haired dancer, made the mistake of inviting the three friends, all fuelled-up, to join him at home for more drink and cigarettes. They crowded into his one shabby little room, with its old iron bed, chamberpot and faded carpet. The fireplace was filled with ashes and stuffed with newspapers. Glasses chinked and the cigarette smoke choked the stale air.

Jean Lee sat on Pop's lap and there was some fumbling, and possibly more. What she was really doing was trying to get into his top pocket to extricate the wad of money, which he foolishly allowed the strangers to see, but he was too fat, and she grew impatient. He twigged what was going on, and the atmosphere changed.

They robbed him and tortured him to make him divulge where the rest of his bookmaker's stash was hidden, but, like them, he lived from hand to mouth, and there was nothing more. Two penknives were used as extempore weapons. In a statement, which she later repudiated, Jean said that she hit him with a piece of wood and a bottle, which broke, cutting her finger. There was a lot of noise, and a couple of interruptions: Mallow House was not a private place.

The three murderers had been seen entering with Pop Kent at 6.15 pm. They were all tipsy and giggling, and 'joking up a treat.' The three were seen leaving without old Pop at 9 pm. Inside, the room was in chaos where it had been ransacked, and a harmless old man with an eye for the ladies, lay dead on the floor, nearly invisible under the rubble.

The autopsy findings were that the nose had been flattened, and both nasal bones fractured. An incised wound ran into the nasal cavity. Both lips were swollen and bruised. A half-inch wound through the upper lip communicated with a large tear in the under surface. A tooth had been loosened. There were large bruises: one like a tennis ball on the right cheek, and another the size of a dinner plate on the left thigh. The wrists had been tied together, and were bruised accordingly, and the thumbs were tied with a bootlace. The police had previously noted cigarette burns.

Dark fluid blood in the heart was consistent with asphyxia, and the presence of blood in both main bronchi, and haemorrhages on the surface of the lungs, indicated strangulation. Appropriate scratches on both sides of the neck were present. The larynx was bruised and broken on each side and dislocated. It would have taken considerable manual force to fracture the larynx, and one to two minutes of such force would have had to be applied to produce the death by asphyxiation.

The police did a good job of tracking down the trio to their hotel, where they had been trying to clean bloodstained clothing, and had booked a flight to Adelaide. During their interrogation, the police made a number of procedural errors, such as failure to caution, which were of importance at the trial, which took place in the Supreme Court at Melbourne on March 20th, 1950.

There had at first been an element of blaming the others, but by now things had been patched up, and the three defendants, tried together, each with their separate counsel, behaved oddly, giggling and conspiratorial, even though they had been dry for months. Apparently, the distaste for what they had done was almost palpable in the courtroom. All three were convicted and sentenced to death.

It is rather disturbing that Jean Lee never, however much it was explained to her, understood the legal concept of a joint enterprise, where all are liable for the murder, even if, as here, only one administered the *coup de grâce*. No doubt it was Jean's own beloved Robert Clayton who throttled the life out of poor old Pop. There was an appeal to the Privy Council in London, but it failed.

Execution day at Pentridge Prison, Coburg, was February 19th, 1951. Jean's mental state had deteriorated alarmingly. She had been officially written-up for a sedative the night before, but there must have been a further, powerful dosage or two because she was carried to the scaffold, totally unconscious. There, she was placed on a chair, and the chair, on a rope, went down with her.

There had been a rumour that she had died

of fright the night before, and had to be propped on the chair because *rigor mortis* had set in, but in fact the autopsy report stated in terms that *rigor* was not present. The neck had been broken cleanly. The hanging beam, made of oak, had been shipped out from England in the 1850s, when executions ceased at Newgate, where it had been in continuous use for at least two centuries. Then it was Clayton's turn, and Andrews', side by side in their hoods. They wished each other goodbye. Andrews was lucky, but you could say that Clayton was hanged by the old-fashioned, Calcraftian method – slowly strangled to death. By a curious ceremony of Common Law, the hangman and his assistant were formally charged with three homicides at a closed hearing at a Coroner's Court held at the prison, and then discharged on the finding of judicial executions. The grotesque spectacle of Jean Lee, descending on her chair in front of an audience of journalists, sickened the nation, and there was no repetition.

PRIME SOURCE:
Jean Lee: The Last Woman Hanged in Australia.
Paul Wilson, Don Treble & Robyn Lincoln.
Random House, Australia, 1997.

Ronald Light

The Green Bicycle Case

ACCUSED: Ronald Vivian Light.

VICTIM: Annie Bella Wright (21).

LOCUS: Gartree Road, also known as Via Devana, near Little Stretton, Leicestershire.

DATE: July 5th, 1919.

MEANS: Shooting in head.

MOTIVE: Unknown.

CRIMEWATCH: Ronald Light, born in October, 1885, was recovering from shell-shock. When arrested, he was a master at a school at Cheltenham. Giving evidence on his own behalf, he admitted bicycling with Bella Wright, whom he had not known previously. He said that they had parted at a junction near the spot where her dead body was found, a spent bullet beside it. He admitted throwing his green bicycle into a canal, because he was frightened. The jury believed him. A dead rook or crow was found nearby, and some there were who thought that the shooting was an accident, perhaps a ricochet.

PRIME SOURCES:
The Green Bicycle Case. H. R. Wakefield. Philip Allan, London, 1930.
The Green Bicycle Mystery. A. W. P. Mackintosh. Published in aid of the Bella Wright Memorial Fund, n.d.

Bobby Joe Long

The Sex Maniac Murders

SERIAL KILLER

MURDERER: Robert Joe Long.

VICTIMS: The identities of all his 8 victims are not known. Generally accepted as his first victim was Ngeon Thi Long (19), a go-go dancer in the strip bars along North Nebraska Avenue, Tampa, Florida. Other named victims were Michelle Denise Simms (22), Virginia Johnson (18), and Kim Swann. Long was also the 'Classified Ad Rapist', operating in Fort Lauderdale and Ocala, Florida, raping and robbing housewives who innocently placed 'for sale' advertisements in the local newspapers. At that time, he displayed no homicidal violence, but is reputed to have committed more than 50 rapes in Florida between 1980 and 1983.

LOCI: A field outside Tampa (Ngeon Thi Long). Other bodies left along the side of the road in rural areas around Tampa.

DATES: May 1983 - November 1983. Body discovered May 13th, 1983 (Ngeon Thi Long). Body discovered May 27th, 1983 (Simms).

MEANS: Bound, strangled, sometimes stabbed to death.

MOTIVE: To satisfy raging hypersexuality. During the latter part of his marriage was requiring intercourse two or three times a day, in addition to masturbation at least five or more times per day. Also, an element of revenge against womankind, as typified by his forceful mother and dictatorial ex-wife.

CRIMEWATCH: Born in Kenova, West Virginia, October 14th, 1953. Presents a curious psychiatric history. At age 11, developed female breasts – a familial, congenital, endocrinal dysfunction consequence – and became fearful of being transformed into a women. Surgically corrected, but continued to experience lunar premenstrual cycle. In 1973, married Cindy Jean Guthrie, whom he had been dating since he was 13. Two children. Divorced 1978. In 1973, Long, then serving in the army, where he hoped to become a qualified electrician, sustained massive head injuries in a motorcycle accident. Said to have undergone personality change to hypersexuality and hair-trigger violence. Arrested November 16th 1984, after allowing a 17-year-old girl, whom he had kidnapped and raped, to go free to identify him, Long said that he was tired of killing and wanted to be caught. At his trial, he pleaded guilty to seven murders and received six life sentences. For the murder of Virginia Johnson, he was sentenced to death. When it was learned that Long had been interrogated by the police after he had requested a lawyer, the Florida Supreme Court ordered a new trial. At his second trial – in 1989 – the jury recommended the death penalty. He is currently on Death Row at Starke, Florida.

PRIME SOURCES:
Bound to Die. Anna Flowers. Pinnacle Books, New York, 1995.
Bobby Joe: In the Mind of a Monster. Bernie Ward. Cool Hand Communications, Boca Raton, Florida, 1995.
Contemporary newspapers..

Lord Lucan

Murder Most Aristocratic

MURDERER: Richard John Bingham, Seventh Earl of Lucan.

VICTIM: Sandra Rivett (29).

LOCUS: 6 Lower Belgrave Street, London S.W.1.

DATE: November 7th, 1974.

MEANS: Bludgeoning with lead piping.

MOTIVE: To get rid of his wife and so settle personal and financial problems.

CRIMEWATCH: The scene of the crime was Lord Lucan's £250,000 house in the heart of London's Belgravia. The time, shortly before 9p.m. The basement was in darkness. His lordship had deliberately removed the single electric light bulb. A woman's slight figure came gingerly down the stairs. Fast as a panther, Lucan sprang out from where he was crouching behind the banisters, and delivered a rain of savage blows with the length of lead piping in his hand on to her head and shoulders. In a spray of blood, she fell to the floor. He picked up the limp body, bent it in half, and crammed it into the mailbag he had waiting for it. Then, he heard movement above. Someone came to the top of the stairs. A woman's voice called 'Sandra! Sandra!'

In that instant, the earl suddenly realised that he had made his first terrible mistake. Sandra Rivett, the children's nanny, was not supposed to be there. Thursday was her night off. How could he possibly have known that this week she had changed it to another night? He had killed the wrong woman.

He crept up the stairs to the hall and set about his true target, Veronica, with the length of lethal lead piping. Then, in a careless, unguarded moment, he made his second mistake. He let his battered wife make her escape. As, at 9.45 p.m. on Thursday night, November 7th, 1974, the door of the Plumbers' Arms public-house in Lower Belgrave Street

burst open, the drinkers were transfixed by the spectacle of a petite woman, clad only in a nightdress, smothered in blood, crying for help. She was taken swiftly off by ambulance to St. George's Hospital, at Hyde Park Corner, where it was ascertained that she was the Countess of Lucan.

It was in November 1963, that Richard John Bingham had married Veronica Mary Duncan. The daughter of an army major, she was regarded by the Lucan clan and their friends as socially inferior. Two months after their marriage, Lucan's father died, leaving him £250,000, and vast estates in England and Ireland. After Eton, Lucan had taken a commission in the Coldstream Guards. Back in civvy street in 1955, he had joined William Brandts, the City merchant bankers. The first thing he did after coming into his inheritance was to quit his job, and, encouraged by a lucky win of £20,000 at *chemin de fer*, which, incidentally, had brought him the nickname 'Lucky', launch himself as a professional gambler.

Sadly, he did not live up to his name. Lady Luck rapidly deserted Lucky Lucan. Night after long night at the tables of his friend John Aspinall's Clermont Club, in Berkeley Square, brought him only the gradual, but steady, loss of his fortune, until he was finally reduced to having to sell the family silver. To make matters worse, his marriage had turned sour.

In January, 1973, the couple separated. Veronica was given the custody of their three children, and she kept the Belgravia house. Lucan moved into a flat in Elizabeth Street, Chelsea. Losing at the tables, losing his children and his home, Lucky began to brood grimly. And he reached a dreadful conclusion. He must kill Veronica. Then he would get his children and his home back, and he could sell it and pay off all his debts with the proceeds. He planned to drive Veronica's corpse to the Sussex coast in the boot of a friend's borrowed car, take the body out to sea in a speedboat, and drop it, weighted, into one of the deeps of the English Channel. But everything went wrong.

At 1.15 a.m. on November 8th, 1974, Lucan, driving a Ford Corsair borrowed from his friend, Michael Stoop, turned up unexpectedly at the Uckfield, Sussex, house of his friends, Ian and Susan Maxwell-Scott. After writing two letters and refusing the offer of a bed for the night, Lucan drove off. And that is the last that anyone has ever seen of him. The Ford Corsair was later found abandoned at Newhaven. Is Lucky Lucan dead or alive? Theories abound.

Ex-Detective Chief Superintendent Roy Ranson, the officer who led the original hunt for Lord Lucan, feels certain that he is dead, his body lost in the English Channel. On the other hand, Chief Inspector David Gerring, another veteran of the case, remains convinced that Lucky is alive, his escape engineered by powerful friends. The simple truth is that no one knows. Or if they do, they are keeping shtoom.

PRIME SOURCES:
The Lucan Mystery. Norman Lucas. W.H. Allen, London, 1975.
Trail of Havoc: In the Steps of Lord Lucan. Patrick Marnham. Viking, London, 1987.
Lucan Not Guilty. Sally Moore. Sidgwick & Jackson, London, 1987.
Looking for Lucan: The Final Verdict. Ex-Detective Chief Superintendent Roy Ranson. Smith Gryphon, London, 1994.
Lord Lucan: What Really Happened. James Ruddick. Headline, London, 1994.
Lucan Lives. Chief Inspector David Gerring. Robert Hale, London, 1995.
Dead Lucky: Lord Lucan The Final Truth. Duncan Maclaughlin. John Blake, London, 2003.

Henry Lee Lucas
The Texas Multicide

SERIAL KILLER

MURDERER: Henry Lee Lucas.

VICTIMS: Has claimed between 360 and 600 killings. Subsequently retracted, saying that he had told tall tales because he enjoyed the notoriety and wanted to embarrass the police. Stated that he had committed only one murder - that of his mother. But convicted of three murders in Texas.

LOCI: Based on original claims, wide-splaying blood trail striking across Arkansas, California, Florida, Georgia, Indiana, Illinois, Louisiana, Michigan, New Mexico, Ohio, Texas, Virginia, Washington, and Wisconsin. Also a brief foray into Canada.

DATES: Mainly between 1975 and 1983.

MEANS: Stabbing, strangling, stomping, suffocating, hanging, bludgeoning, and shooting. Liked to mutilate and dismember victims alive, and to fillet them like fish, after old American Indian torture fashion.

MOTIVE: Chiefly sexual gratification and spree-killing blood-lust, but with an infrastructure of pure hatred (especially in the case of his mother).

CRIMEWATCH: Born August 23rd, 1936, in Virginia hill country. Son of unnamed client of his half-American Indian, half-Irish prostitute mother. Classic deprived childhood. Privation, severe physical and sexual abuse by mother and brutal live-in boyfriend. Dressed as a girl up to age 5. In and out of prison for theft from age 14. Sentenced to 40 years in 1960 for murdering his mother. Paroled in 1970, he warned 'If you release me now, I will kill again.' They did. And he did. Again. . . and again. . . and again. . . .In Jacksonville Prison for attempted abduction, 1970-1975. Released and teamed up with homosexual, cannibalistic Ottis Elwood Toole (28). While living in a trailer on the camp ground of Pentecostal preacher Stanley Shane's community, House of Prayer For All People, at Stoneburg, Texas, Lucas stabbed to death Becky Powell, his 15-year-old common law wife, with whom he had been living since she was nine, and knifed Katherine Rich (80). He was arrested on June 11 th, 1983. Most unusually for a serial killer, Lucas purports to have undergone a death-cell religious conversion. A committed Christian, he was awaiting events on Death Row, Huntsville, Texas, when his death sentence was commuted by George W. Bush He died of a heart attack on March 12th, 2001.

PRIME SOURCES:
Hand of Death. Max Call. Prescott Press, Lafayette, Louisiana, 1985.
The Confession of Henry Lee Lucas. Mike Cox. Pocket Star Books, New York, 1991.

Michael Lupo

The Strangler Wore Silk

SERIAL KILLER

MURDERER: Michele De Marco Lupo.

VICTIMS: James Burns (36). Damien McClusky. Unknown Man. Anthony Connolly (26).

LOCI: Warwick Road, Earl's Court, London (Burns). Cromwell Road, Kensington, London (McClusky). Charing Cross Railway Bridge, London (Unknown man). Hut beside main railway line, Brixton (Connolly).

DATES: March – April, 1986.

MEANS: Strangulation.

MOTIVE: Sexual gratification, enjoyment of killing, and revenge.

CRIMEWATCH: On March 16th, 1986, the savaged corpse of 36-year-old James Burns, who worked as a guard with British Rail, was carried out from the dusty basement of a once-elegant five-storey house in a Victorian terrace on Warwick Road, Earl's Court. He had been strangled, and his neck showed livid bruising where a ligature had been pulled so tightly that its material had bitten deeply into the flesh. Most of his clothing had been torn off, but from its style it was plain to see that he had been a homosexual. His body was covered with bite-marks. His tongue had been practically bitten through.

Subsequent enquiries elicited that he had been a 'leather' man, and a frequenter of gay pubs. On the night he died he had been in one, the Coleherne, in Brompton Road. Some three weeks later, on April 5th, 1986, the body of Anthony Connolly, an unemployed man of 26, was discovered in a dirty, rubbish-filled plate-layer's hut alongside the main railway line, near his Brixton home. He had been strangled. His body, like Burns', was a mass of bites. He, too, had last been seen in a gay pub, the Prince of Wales, in Brixton.

On Thursday night, May 8th, 1986, as he was coming out of the Market Tavern, at Nine Elms, Battersea, David Cole (30) noticed a good-looking, dark-haired young man in a leather jacket and ripped jeans standing near the door.

His fancy taken, he got into conversation with him, and, both with similar sexual intent, they strolled together to a nearby large, open-air lorry park. There, sheltering behind the curtain of darkness, standing between the rows of articulated trailers, looming in the gloom like the skeletons of bulky prehistoric monsters, they sniffed 'poppers', mild drugs that enhance sexual pleasure. Suddenly, for Cole, the dalliance turned to terror.

The dark stranger's caressing arm about his neck was inexorably tightening. He felt a strip of some material pressing into his windpipe, his senses beginning to swim. Summoning up a panic-powered burst of strength, he managed to throw his assailant off. The dark stranger ran away to lose himself in the blackness of the night, leaving behind in his intended victim's grasp the silk sock with which he had been trying to strangle him.

Cole did a lot of hard thinking before finally deciding to go to the police. They persuaded him to trawl the gay night spots, with them in inconspicuous tow. At 9 p.m. on the evening of May 15th, 1986, Cole and his entourage set off. They visited the Market Tavern, the Royal Vauxhall Tavern, the nightclub called 'Heaven', near Charing Cross, and the Prince of Wales, where Connolly had met his murderer. And it was here that Cole recognised the man with whom he had had his near-fatal encounter. He was leaning languidly against the wall, his eyes scanning the crowded bar. Seconds later, the four plain clothes police officers who had been shadowing Cole moved swiftly in, grabbed the dark, slightly-built man, and hustled him out on to the street.

Michael Lupo, the man they christened the Silken Strangler, was in the net. He was an Italian, 33 years old. A former choirboy, he had served in the army in an élite commando unit, before taking up a career in hairdressing. He had come to London in 1975, working at first as a hairdresser. He had moved over into the rag trade.

Like Deacon Brodie of old, this man, the very model of a modern multi-murderer, led a double life. By day, he was the smooth, smiling, elegant, witty and charming manager of a high-class Knightsbridge fashion boutique. After dark, he became 'Rudi', the cruising gay gay-killer, who, like the wild animal whose name he bore – *Lupo* is the Italian word for 'wolf' – bit and savaged his victims horrifically.

When first arrested, he denied everything. It was just a token resistance. Later, at Brixton police station, he was soon singing his head off, making a full confession in his heavily-accented English. Having admitted the murders of Burns, whom he strangled with a silken scarf, and Connolly, strangled with a silk sock, and the attack on Cole, he talked of two further murders, committed between those of Burns and Connolly. He said that he had strangled Damien McClusky with a silk sock, and directed the police to an empty basement in Cromwell Road, Kensington, where the young Irishman's ravaged body had lain undiscovered for weeks. He had also strangled, this time with his bare hands and for no motive, a down-and-out whom he had encountered on Charing Cross Railway Bridge in the early hours of the morning. The poor man had asked him for a cigarette.

Lupo said that he had also worked as a male prostitute, advertising his services in gay contact magazines. He had a kink for black leather and sado-masochism. In his flat, in Roland Gardens, South Kensington, he had a sort of torture chamber. Iron chains were fixed into the ceiling above the bed, upon which clients were trussed up and whipped. He lived mostly at another flat in Sydney Mews, Chelsea.

Searching Lupo's home, police found diaries containing the names and telephone numbers of people in show business and high society. Among them were Freddie Mercury and Kenny Everett. According to Lupo's reckoning, during his years in London he had had sex with between 3,000 and 4,000 men. In March, 1986, he also discovered that he had acquired AIDS.

At his trial at the Old Bailey, in July, 1987, he pleaded guilty to four murders and two attempted murders. Sentencing him to life, Sir James Miskin, the Recorder of London, told him: 'For a man whose life has been such that he suffers from AIDS, whether your fault or not, it would be absurd to make a minimum recommendation on your sentence. In your case, life means life.'

PRIME SOURCE:
Contemporary newspapers.

Dr Jeffrey MacDonald

Guilty or Not Guilty?

MURDERER: Dr Jeffrey R. MacDonald.

VICTIMS: Colette S. MacDonald (26): wife. Kimberley K. MacDonald (5): daughter. Kristen J. MacDonald (2): daughter.

LOCUS: 544 Castle Drive, Corregidor Courts, Fort Bragg, Fayetteville, North Carolina.

DATE: February 17th, 1970.

MEANS: Stabbing 16 times with a knife and 21 times with an ice pick. Also six blows with a club (Colette). Three blows with a club and 8 to 10 stabbings with a knife (Kimberley). Thirty-three stabbings with a knife and an ice pick (Kristen).

MOTIVE: Uncontrollable rage, without premeditation. A matrimonial quarrel that flared into homicide, and was then compounded to mimic a Manson-like massacre.

CRIMEWATCH: Dr MacDonald, an achiever, aged 26, was a serving medical officer with the Green Berets. Joe McGinniss, in *Fatal Vision*, makes much of the doctor's ingestion of amphetamines before the tragedy, but MacDonald always claimed that four intruders, drug-crazed hippies, did the killings; they said 'Kill the pigs', and 'Acid is groovy.' MacDonald himself was found with minor injuries and a partially collapsed lung. Some people thought it significant that the 'drug-crazed hippies' attack came just six months after the Sharon Tate Manson Family murders. A drug-addicted girl, Helena Stoeckley, confessed and retracted. She died of liver disease in 1983. More than nine years after the killings, MacDonald was finally tried at Raleigh, North Carolina, and found guilty of second-degree murder of Colette and Kimberley, and of first-degree murder of Kristen. August 29th, 1979, given three life sentences. He appealed and his conviction was overturned by the Circuit Court of Appeals. He was released. In March, 1982, the Supreme court reinstated the conviction, and he was returned to prison. In August, 2002, he married 44-year-old Kathryn Kurichh. He is now 61.

PRIME SOURCES:

Fatal Vision. Joe McGinniss. G.P. Putnam's Sons, New York, 1983.

I Accuse: The Torturing of an American Hero. Melinda Stephens. American Ideal Publishing, 1987.

The Journalist and the Murderer. Janet Malcolm. Bloomsbury, London, 1991.

Fatal Justice: Reinvestigating the MacDonald Murders. Jerry Allen Porter and Fred Bost. W. W. Norton, New York, 1995.

Patrick Mackay

Lethal Psychopathy

MASS MURDERER

MURDERER: Patrick David Mackay.

VICTIMS: Isabella Griffiths (84): widow who had befriended MacKay. Adele Price (89): widow, a stranger, who offered him a glass of water. Father Anthony Crean (64): priest, a friend, from whom MacKay had stolen money.

LOCI: 19 Cheyne Walk, Chelsea, London (Griffiths). Lowndes Square, London (Price). The Malt House, St. Catherine's Convent, Shorne, Kent (Crean).

DATES: February 14th, 1974 (Griffiths). March 10th, 1975 (Price). March 21st, 1975 (Crean).

MEANS: Manual strangulation and stabbing with a 12-inch kitchen knife (Griffiths). Manual strangulation (Price). Axe and knife (Crean).

MOTIVE: No rational motive; psychopathic rage – frenzy – triggered by minor rejections, taunts, alcohol, drugs, despair and loneliness.

CRIMEWATCH: Bad case of gross personality disorder, diagnosed early. In and out of institutions. Dangerously out of control, and a heavy drinker. IQ 92. His father, violent, and an alcoholic. As a boy, Mackay tortured animals, and was preoccupied with Nazism, calling himself 'Franklin Bollvolt the First.' The root of his troubles seemed to lie with the drunken violence which his father had inflicted on his family, before he died, when Mackay was ten. His mother could not control his violent rages and was herself ambivalent in regard to having him confined. The authorities passed him about for years. He went for the vulnerable and unprotected, especially elderly women. If they tried to help him, so much the worse for them. He explained his impulse to kill: 'I felt hellish and very peculiar inside. This peculiar feeling I had for some days before and after each killing.' Sometimes he was suicidal. He obviously found some kind of release and revenge when he killed for no rational motive. At the Old Bailey on November 21st, 1975, he came easily under the umbrella of 'Diminished Responsibility'. Sentenced, aged 23, to life for manslaughter of three. Two killings left on file and 24 muggings.

PRIME SOURCES:
Psychopath. Tim Clark and John Penycate. Routledge and Kegan Paul, London, 1976.
Encyclopaedia of Modern Murder: 1962 – 1982. Colin Wilson and Donald Seaman. A Barker, London, 1983.

Charles Manson

The Family Man

MURDERER: Charles Milles Manson.

VICTIMS: Gary Hinman (34). Sharon Marie Tate or Polanski (26). Abigail Anne Folger (25). Wojiciech 'Voyteck' Frykowski (32). Jay Sebring (35). Steven Parent (18). Rosemary LaBianca (38). Leno LaBianca (44). Donald Jerome 'Shorty' Shea (36).

LOCI: 964 Old Topanga Road, Malibu (Hinman). 10050 Cielo Drive, Los Angeles. (Sharon Tate killings). 3301 Waverley Drive, Los Angeles (LaBianca Killings). Spahn Movie Ranch, 12000 Santa Susanna Pass Road, Los Angeles (Shea).

DATES: July 27th, 1969 (Hinman). August 9th, 1969 (Tate, Folger, Frykowski, Sebring, Parent). August 10th, 1969 (the LaBiancas). August 25th or 26th, 1969 (Shea).

MEANS: Multiple stabbings and shootings, sometimes in concert.

MOTIVE: Manson's followers, particularly the besotted, drop-out girls, sodden with drugs, acted at his behest and in fear of him and their peers. Manson pushed them as far as he could. This was mainly killing for pleasure. Otherwise, young Parent was in the way, and cowboy Shorty Shea knew too much. Although partly motivated by blood-lust in the cases of the transported executants, these were not serial murders, as the inciter, at a remove, had his own psychopathological, sociologic reasons, which had little to do with either sex or enjoyment.

CRIMEWATCH: Manson incited to murder. Apart from his 9 murder convictions, there were other killings by the Manson Family – the total may be about 35. From his free-range hippy commune in the desert, with its free-for-all of sex and drugs, and rattlesnakes, he sent forth his murder squads to 'off' representative pockets of the rich and privileged. His converts enjoyed the blood-release. An elaborate delusional system based on 'Helter-Skelter', from an interpretation of the Beatles' song, with the murders acting as a warning against a black uprising, was imputed to Manson, who was, indeed, diagnosed in prison as paranoid and schizophrenic, but, a shrewd old gaol bird (born November 12th, 1934), he later repudiated his apocalyptic ideas and his Satanic image. He serves life in San Quentin.

PRIME SOURCES:
Witness to Evil. George Bishop. Nash Publishing, Los Angeles, 1971.
The Family. Ed Sanders. Rupert Hart-Davis, London, 1971.
The Manson Murders. Victor Bugliosi & Curt Gentry. Bodley Head, London, 1974.
Without Conscience. Charles Manson & Nuel Emmons. Grafton Books, London, 1987.

Peter Manuel
Murder for Pleasure

MURDERER: Peter Thomas Anthony Manuel.

VICTIMS: Anne Knielands (17). Marion Watt (45). Vivienne Watt (16): daughter. Margaret Brown (41): sister. Isabelle Cooke (17). Peter Smart (45). Doris Smart: wife. Michael Smart (11): son.

LOCI: All the killings were restricted to a 24-square- mile expanse of Lowland Scotland situated to the east and south-east of Glasgow. Capelrig Copse, East Kilbride Golf Course (Knielands). 5 Fennsbank Avenue, High Burnside (The Watts). Ploughed field, Burntbroom Farm, Mount Vernon (Cooke). 38 Sheepburn Road, Uddingston (The Smarts).

DATES: January 2nd, 1956 (Knielands). September 16th, 1957 (The Watts). December 28th, 1957 (Cooke). January 1st, 1958 (The Smarts).

MEANS: Battering with iron bar (Knielands). Shooting with Webley .38 revolver (The Watts). Shooting with Beretta pistol (The Smarts). Strangling with brassière (Cooke).

MOTIVE: Manuel killed for pleasure and sexual gratification. He was a known sex offender with a history of indecent assaults and rapes.

CRIMEWATCH: Born on March 15th, 1927, in Manhattan, his parents having emigrated to America in search of work. He returned with them to Britain in 1932. After a youth dedicated to petty theft and burglarious enterprise and, in consequence, spent largely in approved schools and Borstals, he was, unmarried, living in 1956 with his father and mother at 32 Fourth Street, Birkenshaw, in the centre of the killing territory. A classic psychopath, boastful, a liar, and a loner who loved the dark, he was also clever and competitive. He liked to 'take on' and 'best' the police. It came to their ears that Manuel was spending recklessly. They searched his home and found burglary loot there. Arrested on January 14th, 1958, and charged with the Smart murders. He did all he could to impeach the Crown witness, William Watt, sole surviving member of the murdered family. Tried at Glasgow High Court, May 1958, before Lord Cameron, Manuel elected to conduct his own defence – which he did surprisingly adroitly. He was found guilty of 7 of the 8 charges. No corroborative evidence – as required in Scots law – was forthcoming in regard to the killing of Anne Knielands. Hanged at Barlinnie prison, July 11th, 1958. Before his execution he confessed to the murders, and those of Helen Carlin, prostitute, strangled in Pimlico, September 1954; Anne Steele (55) spinster, battered to death, Glasgow, January 11th, 1956; Ellen Petrie, stabbed, Glasgow, 15th June 1956. He is thought to have murdered also Sydney Dunn (37), c. December 6th/7th, 1957, a taxi driver, found shot and with gashed throat on the moors near Edmondbyers, County Durham.

PRIME SOURCES:
The Trial of Peter Manuel. John Gray Wilson. Secker & Warburg, London, 1959.
The Hunting Down of Peter Manuel. John Bingham. Macmillan, London, 1973.

Florence Elizabeth Maybrick

The Battlecrease House Poison Mystery

MURDERER: Florence Elizabeth Maybrick (26).

VICTIM: James Maybrick: husband (50).

LOCUS: Battlecrease House, 7 Riversdale Road, Aigburth, Liverpool.

DATE: May 11th, 1889.

MEANS: Arsenic.

MOTIVE: To be rid of a choleric, faithless husband.

CRIMEWATCH: Highly contentious Victorian *cause célèbre*. Not even proved that habitual drug and nostrum-swallowing James Maybrick did in fact die of arsenical poisoning. His American wife, Florence – born September 3rd, 1862, Mobile, Alabama – mother of two, James and Gladys, was condemned as much as anything for her discovered adultery with Maybrick's fellow cotton broker, Alfred Brierley. That James had a mistress and several illegitimate children did not count. Undeniably, the Maybricks, with a 24-year difference between their ages, did not have a happy marriage. It came to blows, he administering a black eye to her following a quarrel over Brierley at the Grand National racecourse on March 29th, 1889. Seen by a servant soaking flypapers in water, Florence said it was to obtain arsenic for a face lotion. Others put a more sinister interpretation on it when Maybrick died. Tried in St. George's Hall, Liverpool, she was convicted, sentenced to hang, and reprieved. After serving 15 years, she returned in 1904 to America, surviving to a poverty-stricken, eccentric old age, dying as Mrs. Chandler, the Cat Woman, in a tumbledown shack, near South Kent, Connecticut, on October 23rd, 1941. A deceitful, untruthful, light-fingered woman it is alleged, it later emerged that, in the last week of April, 1889, she had obtained from a Liverpool chemist, Richard Aspinall, of Leece Street, a quantity of 'Arsenic for Cats' without signing his Poisons Book.

PRIME SOURCES:

The Maybrick Case. Alexander William MacDougall. Baillière, Tindall and Cox, London, 1891.

The Necessity For Criminal Appeal as Illustrated by the Maybrick Case. J. H. Levy. P. S. King and Son, London, 1899.

My Fifteen Lost Years. Florence Elizabeth Maybrick. Funk & Wagnalls, New York, 1905.

Notable English Trial. Edited by H. B. Irving. William Hodge, Edinburgh, 1912.

This Friendless Lady. Nigel Morland. Frederick Muller, London, 1957.

Etched in Arsenic. Trevor L. Christie. Harrap, London, 1969.

The Poisoned Life of Mrs. Maybrick. Bernard Ryan with Sir Michael Havers, QC, MP. William Kimber, London, 1977.

The Last Victim. Anne E. Graham and Carol Emmas. Headline, London, 1999.

John Donald Merrett
Matricide and Uxoricide

MURDERER: John Donald Merrett alias Ronald John Chesney.

VICTIMS: Mrs. Bertha Merrett (56): mother. Isobel Veronica Chesney (42): wife. Mrs. Mary Bonnar aka Lady Menzies (68): mother-in-law.

LOCI: 31 Buckingham Terrace, Edinburgh (Bertha Merrett). 22 Montpelier Road, Ealing, London (Isobel Veronica Chesney, Lady Menzies).

DATES: March 17th, 1926 (Mrs. Bertha Merrett).February 11th, 1954 (Vera Chesney, Lady Menzies).

MEANS: Shot with .25 Spanish automatic pistol (Mrs. Bertha Merrett). Drowned in bath (Vera Chesney). Strangled with a stocking (Lady Menzies).

MOTIVE: All for his convenience.

CRIMEWATCH: As there are two names for this man, so are there two views as to his *persona*. There is John Donald Merrett, the cheating son who robbed his mother, first of her money, then of her life. And there is Ronald John Chesney, the flamboyant, fun-loving, swashbuckling buccaneer, who drowned his wife and strangled his mother-in-law. Both Merrett and Chesney died when, having reached the end of his hawser, the huge, 22-stone, bearded giant shot himself with his Colt .45 in a wood outside Cologne on February 16th, 1954, mourned only by his faithful German mistress, Gerda Schaller. Born in New Zealand on August 17th, 1908, his parents subsequently drifted apart. Came with his Manchester-raised mother, who doted on Donald, to Britain in 1924. Highly intelligent; highly undisciplined. Sent, first, to Malvern College, then, Edinburgh University. Got away with the murder of his mother. Imprisoned for forging her cheques. Became a naval officer, serving with courageous – but reckless – 'seamanship', which earned him the nickname 'Crasher' Chesney. Bully, braggart, glutton, vast drinker, gambler, smuggler, hot-blooded lover, cold-blooded killer, Merrett was a monumental self-indulger, the complete psychopath, prepared to sacrifice anyone or anything at the altar of his own sacred desires.

PRIME SOURCES:

Notable British Trial. Edited by William Roughead. William Hodge, Edinburgh, 1929.
Portrait of a Bad Man. Tom Tullett. Evans Brothers, London, 1956.
Chesney: The Fabulous Murderer. Hugh McLeave. Pinnacle Books, London, n.d.

Louisa Merrifield

Rat Poison in a Blackpool Bungalow

MURDERER: Louisa May Merrifield.

VICTIM: Sarah Ann Ricketts (79).

LOCUS: The Homestead, 339 Devonshire Road, North Shore, Blackpool.

DATE: April 14th, 1953.

MEANS: Phosphorus (Rodine rat poison).

MOTIVE: Gain.

CRIMEWATCH: The Merrifields, Alfred and Louisa, husband and wife, went in answer to an advertisement as live-in housekeepers to Mrs. Sarah Ann Ricketts. During the honeymoon period all was sweetness and light. That was when, after a mere twelve days, Mrs. Ricketts made her fatal mistake. She confided that she was going to bequeath the bungalow to them. But the Merrifields rapidly became disenchanted with their 'invalid lady'. She began to display tantrums. She showed herself as awkward, impatient, disagreeable, and an alcoholic into the bargain. Louisa May, strict Baptist and a Wigan miner's daughter, had married, aged 25, Joseph Ellison, and had had four children, who were taken into care because of her drinking and negligence. Ellison died in 1949. Three months after his death, she, then 42, had married 78-year-old Richard Weston. Ten weeks later he was dead. In 1950, she married Merrifield (67). She felt that they had landed on their feet at The Homestead – but couldn't wait to get their hands on their inheritance. Tried at Manchester, Mrs. Merrifield was hanged at Strangeways on September 18th, 1953. She was 46. The Attorney-General having entered a *nolle prosequi*, Alfred Merrifield was released. He died, aged 80, in 1962.

PRIME SOURCE:
Contemporary newspapers.

Ivan Milat

The Backpacker Murders

SERIAL KILLER

MURDERER: Ivan Robert Marko Milat.

VICTIMS: Joanne Walters (22). Caroline Clarke (21). Deborah Everist (19). James Gibson (19). Simone Schmidl (21). Anja Habschied (20). Gabor Neugebauer (21).

LOCUS: Belanglo State Forest, near Sydney, Australia.

DATES: 1989 – 1992.

MEANS: Shooting. Stabbing. Suffocation. Strangulation.

MOTIVE: A mixture of sexual gratification and killing for pleasure.

CRIMEWATCH: Keith Seily and Keith Caldwell, members of the Scrubrunners Orienteering Club of Campbelltown, were jogging through eucalyptus scrub in Belanglo State Forest, 60-odd miles south-west of Sydney. It was at 3.45 p.m. on the afternoon of Saturday, September 19th, 1992, that they saw a long, thin bone protruding from a leaf and twig covered mound. They had found the savaged body of 22-year-old Joanne Walters.

The girl had been gagged, and there were stab wounds to the chest and neck. They had been delivered with such wanton violence that pieces of the spinal cord had been cut off, ribs haphazardly sliced, and it looked as if the aorta had also been severed, She was wearing no underclothes, the fly of her trousers had been undone and her T-shirt and bra were pushed up, exposing her breasts.

She and another young woman, Caroline Clarke (21), were a pair of British backpackers, who had set out hitch-hiking from Sydney around the previous April, and neither hair nor hide of them had been seen since. The following morning – Sunday, the 20th – Police Constable Suzanne Roberts, approaching a fallen tree about 32 yards from where Joanne Walters' body had been found, noticed a pile of twigs and branches stacked against it, and there, sticking out, she saw a human leg. Now

Caroline Clarke had also been found.

She had been shot ten times. There were seven bullets in her head and shoulders, a stab wound in her back, and a round wound on the right side of her chest. The indications were that both young women had been sexually attacked.

A little over twelve months later, on October 5th, 1993, Bruce Pryor, a potter who lived in the area, was out in Belanglo Forest in quest of firewood. What he found was two more corpses.

The first was that of Deborah Everist. The second, that of her boyfriend, James Gibson. They were both nineteen years old. They were both skeletonised. They lay in shallow graves, 27 yards apart. The couple, native Australians, came from Victoria. They had been missing since December, 1989, when they had disappeared somewhere between Liverpool and Goulburn, while hitch-hiking to a conservation rally.

Deborah's skull had been fractured and her jaw broken. There was evidence of a single stab wound, together with a number of slicing-type injuries, such as could have been made by someone lashing out with a machete. James' injuries were quite appalling. A knife had been plunged numerous times into his chest and back. It had been driven in with such terrible force that it had chipped, cut, and gouged the bones. There was evidence that they had both been subjected to sexual assault. The zipper on James' jeans was in the down position. A pair of knotted tights found four or five yards from her body suggested that Deborah had been tied up.

The fifth body to surface was that of a 21-year-old German girl, identified by forensic dentistry as Simone Schmidl, from Regensburg, the eastern Bavarian port on the Danube. She had, against the good advice of friends, set off, on January 20th, 1991, to hitch-hike from Sydney to Melbourne, and had vanished from the Liverpool-Goulburn road. Her skeleton was found on November 1st, 1993.

Marks on the vertebrae and the ribs clearly showed that she had been stabbed, twice in the neck, four times in the back of the left chest, and twice at the back of the right chest. These multiple stab wounds were the cause of death. Simone Schmidl had ceased to be just another statistic in the missing persons files of the New South Wales and Victorian police forces.

The authorities were by now certain that they had a serial killer on their hands. Or, possibly, serial killers, for while Joanne Walters had been stabbed to death, Caroline Clarke had been shot. Two weapons; two killers? Similarly, Deborah Everist had been cut to pieces with something like a machete. James Gibson had been stabbed with a knife. The detectives also considered that 'the fact that both pairs of victims were not found side by side suggests that they had been led or forced to separate areas by two or more people.'

The last two bodies of the series to be discovered were those of two Munich University students, Gabor Neugebauer (21) and his 20-year-old girlfriend, Anja Habschied. They had last been seen alive on December 26th, 1991, when they set out from Kings Cross, Sydney, to hitch-hike to Darwin. On November 4th, 1993, Belanglo Forest once again gave up its dead to the searching policemen. Like a one-word threnody, the cry 'Find!' rang out, a resounding tocsin echoing through the eucalyptus.

Sergeant Nail Smith, one of the team raking the woodland for fresh cadavers, had found, stretched under a mortuary roof of small logs, the skeleton that was once the lovely, lively Anja Habschied. But there was no skull; nor was it ever found. Chillingly, she had been beheaded. Some weapon, large and sharp, had done it with a single blow. Her lover, Gabor Neugebauer, a skeleton too, lay in his twigs-and-fern-leaf mausoleum a few yards to the south-west of Anja. He had ben shot six times in the head.

A curious feature which linked the Belanglo Forest killings was that all the victims had been placed face downwards with their hands arranged behind their backs alongside a fallen tree-trunk, and a triangular canopy of sticks and ferns erected over the corpses. The realisation that they had a serial killer on the loose in their community brought alarmed calls from the public pouring in to the police, who were now publishing photographs of the unknown killer's victims.

The one call of real significance came in February, 1994. It was from a British subject, a 25-year-old former sailor, Paul Onions, who had been over in Australia backpacking in 1990. Telephoning from London, he told them that he had been thumbing rides in January, 1990, and was picked up by a big man with a handlebar moustache, driving a silver Nissan four-wheel-drive truck.

The man had said his name was Bill. They were just north of Belanglo Forest, when Bill had suddenly stopped the truck, brandished a gun, and told his startled passenger, 'This is a robbery!' Onions had leapt out of the truck and run for his life through the bush, bullets zipping past his head. He had succeeded in getting away, after a hectic chase. Onions was able to identify Milat from his mugshot and could also recognise his silver car.

Reviewing their records of known sex offenders, investigators pulled out the allegation of a December, 1974, rape, filed against a man named Milat. Ivan Milat, the son of a Croatian immigrant, had been born in Australia on December 27th, 1944. He neither drank nor smoked. His known hobbies were motor-biking, off-road touring in his four-wheel-drive vehicle, and hunting. He answered to the nickname 'Bill'. Since his name had also cropped up several times in recent public phone-ins about the crimes, it was decided to pay him a surprise dawn visit at his home in the Sydney suburb of Eagle Vale, where he lived with a girlfriend. They discovered there firearms which proved to have been connected with the murders. In particular, there was an unusual .22-calibre Ruger, which was of the type which fired cartridges lying near the body of Caroline Clarke. They also found camping gear stolen from the victims, and a fearsome-looking sword, which it was thought that he had used to behead Anja Habschied.

The detectives believed it likely that Milat, a gun freak, had used his victims' heads for target practice. That would account for the multiple head wounds, as in the case of Caroline Clarke. He was known to be a violent and sadistic man, who beat up his women, and who would go out shooting birds, taking care not to kill them, but just to wound them, so that he could enjoy watching their agony.

Put on trial in 1996, Milat's defence included the offering up of two of his brothers, Richard and Walter Milat, as alternative suspects. It was a ploy that failed. He was found guilty of all seven murders, and given six life sentences, plus an additional six years for the attempted murder of Paul Onions. The New South Wales authorities felt very sure that Milat had committed many more homicides; maybe as many as 12 or 13 murders, stretching back to the late 1970s. A 41-year-old woman from Newcastle, New South Wales, told of being abducted and raped by him in 1978.

PRIME SOURCES:
Highway to Nowhere. Richard Shears. HarperCollins, Australia, 1996.
Sins of the Brother: The Definitive Story of Ivan Milat and the Backpacker Murders. Mark Whittaker and Les Kennedy. Macmillan, Australia, 1998.

Jessie M'Lachlan
The Sandyford Mystery

MURDERER: Jessie M'Lachlan.

VICTIM: Jessie M'Pherson (*c.* 38).

LOCUS: The basement of 17 Sandyford Place, Glasgow.

DATE: July 4th–5th, 1862.

MEANS: Ferocious attack with a butcher's cleaver.

MOTIVE: According to the prosecution of M'Lachlan, financial gain. But all very dubious.

CRIMEWATCH: While 78-year-old James Fleming's widowed son and grandson went away to Dunoon for the weekend, he was left with the young maid, Jessie M'Pherson. On the family's return, Jessie was found near-naked and dead in her bedroom. On the floorboards were imprints in blood of a naked foot. There were signs of a severe struggle in the kitchen. Some silver spoons were missing. Also garments from the dead servant's box. M'Pherson's friend, Jessie M'Lachlan (29), who had called on her that fatal Friday night, was arrested. She had pawned the missing spoons. She had had possession of M'Pherson's clothes. Her foot matched the bloody imprint. Tried at Glasgow, she entered the special defence that the chief Crown witness, Auld Fleming, who had an unsavoury reputation with women and who had originally been arrested, had committed the crime. He had, she said, been forcing his attentions on M'Pherson. There was a quarrel, and he killed her. M'Lachlan had been there and seen it all. She was not believed. Found guilty and sentenced to death, she was reprieved. Her 15 years in Perth prison were most likely a miscarriage of justice. Released, she went to America, dying in 1899, at Port Huron, Michigan.

PRIME SOURCES:
The Sandyford Murder Case. J. H. Hastings. Glasgow, 1862.
The Sandyford Murder: A Plea For Mrs. M'Lachlan. A Clergyman of the Church of Scotland. Thomas Murray & Son, Glasgow, 1862.
Notable Scottish Trial. Edited by William Roughead. William Hodge, Edinburgh, 1911.
Heaven Knows Who. Christianna Brand. Michael Joseph, London, 1960.

Raymond Morris

The Corpses in Cannock Chase

MURDERER: Raymond Leslie Morris.

VICTIM: Christine Anne Darby (7).

LOCUS: Cannock Chase, Staffordshire.

DATE: August 19th, 1967.

MEANS: Suffocation.

MOTIVE: To expedite sexual violation and/or to prevent identification.

CRIMEWATCH: The bodies of three little girls were found in Cannock Chase in 1966-7, but Raymond Morris was indicted and convicted for killing only the third child, Christine Darby, because the police could not find evidence to link him to the previous two murders. The enquiry was closed, and the murders ceased.

Margaret Reynolds, aged six, disappeared from the streets of Aston on September 8th, 1965, while walking back to school after her lunch hour. She never arrived.

Diane Tift, aged five, vanished in Bloxwich on 30th December 1965, while walking home from her grandmother's house. She never arrived. Diane's body was found in a ditch on January 12th, 1966, by a man who was looking for rabbits: beneath her were the skeletal remains of Margaret Reynolds, and the skull had been washed downstream.

Christine Darby lived in Walsall, 14 miles from Cannock, along the A34. On Saturday, August 19th, 1967, in the afternoon, she was abducted from her own street by her killer in a grey car. Her friend, Nicholas Baldry (8) was too young to note the registration number, but not too young to notice his local accent, and the appearance of the car.

Cannock Chase, north of Birmingham is a large, green beauty spot, afforested with plantations and heaths. Search parties beating through bracken, found the body on August 22nd, 1967, in Plantation 110. It later appeared that Raymond Morris' name had come up five times in the investigation, just as the Yorkshire Ripper's was to come up nine times. In both cases, the problem was the sheer weight of files, before the advent of computerisation. Additionally, there was a failure to grade alibis according to their convincingness.

Morris' wife, Carole Dianne, gave him an alibi, saying that he had returned from work on the Saturday afternoon, when she knew that he had not done so, because at that time she thought him incapable of such a crime. Later, full realisation came to her, and she gave evidence against him, although a wife, by law, is not compellable to do so. Earlier in the investigation, it was noted that Morris' own brother had gone in to state that he had an interest in young girls and was capable of such a crime.

The grey car, a 1960 Grampian A55 was traced to Morris, although, of course, he had passed it on. By a strange twist, he lived at 20 Regent House, Green Lane, Walsall, a tower block opposite Walsall police station – the heart of the massive man-hunt since Margaret Reynolds had disappeared.

A coloured Identikit picture had been prepared from information supplied by eye-witnesses who were in the Chase on the afternoon of August 19th: Victor Whitehouse, who saw a man standing by his grey car, and Mrs Jeanne Rawlings, who held her retriever dog to one side as a man drove past her. There certainly was a resemblance to Morris.

Near the end, on November 4th, 1968, Morris made the mistake of trying to entice Margaret Aulton (10) into his car with a promise of fireworks, as she was building a bonfire on wasteland, in front of a witness, Mrs Wendy Lane, who was able to identify Morris' current car as a green and white Ford Corsair. She also got the registration number nearly right.

When Morris' flat was searched, some damning photographs were found in a cardboard box. They showed a little girl, aged five, who turned out to be his wife's niece, lying half-naked on a bed, arranged in an indecent position.

Much was made of this position at the trial, when it was suggested that it mimicked that in which the body of Christine Darby was found, and that Morris derived perverted pleasure from this re-enactment. A watch, which showed up in the photographs, was proved to belong to Morris: realising the incriminating connection, he had hidden it around his ankle before being searched.

At Staffordshire Assizes on February 10th 1969, Raymond Morris, a 39-year-old foreman engineer, was tried on three charges: the murder of Christine Darby, the attempted abduction of Margaret Aulton, and the indecent assault on the five-year-old girl at his flat in August, 1968. A previous assault on her, aged four, in 1967, was left to lie on the file.

The defence tried unsuccessfully to separate the charges: the judge ruled that all three should be tried together – a great victory for the Crown. Morris pleaded guilty to the indecent assault, but not to the two more serious charges. The jury convicted and he was sentenced to imprisonment for life for the murder, three years' imprisonment for the attempted abduction, and 12 months' imprisonment for the indecent assault, the last two sentences to run concurrently with the first.

It was said that he glared at his wife in the gallery before being removed from court. The grey car that carried Christine Darby on her last journey to Cannock Chase was bought up by a dealer who ceremonially torched it. They called it 'the car that died of shame'.

PRIME SOURCES:
Murder on the A34. Harry Hawkes. John Long, 1970.
Squad Man. Ian Forbes. W.H Allen, 1973.
Not the Moors Murders. Pat Molloy. Gomer, 1988.

Herman Webster Mudgett
The Bluebeard of Holmes' Castle

MURDERER: Herman Webster Mudgett aka H. H. Holmes.

VICTIMS: Admitted to killing 27 people. Then retracted, claiming two deaths only – resultant upon illegal operations. Thought to have murdered 150-200, mainly women and children.

LOCI: 701-703 Sixty-Third Street, Englewood, Chicago. (Scene of the mass murders.) Momence, Illinois (Minnie Williams). Leadville, Colorado (Baldwin Williams). 1316 Callowhill Street, Philadelphia (Benjamin Fuller Pitezel). Irvington, Indiana (Howard Pitezel). 16 Vincent Street, Toronto, Canada (Alice and Nellie Pitezel).

DATES: *c.* 1891-94.

MEANS: Varied: merciful chloroforming in sleep, savage butchery, gloating poison-gassing.

MOTIVE: Financial profit – admixed with sexual advantages.

CRIMEWATCH: Described as America's 'arch-fiend of murder', Mudgett was essentially a swindler, but he was also a sadist who enjoyed murdering and torturing. An escalating career of fraud began with the theft of cadavers from his medical school – Ann Arbor, Michigan – and climaxed with his gothic 'murder factory', the Englewood 'hotel' nicknamed 'Holmes' Castle'. This was a maze of nearly 100 rooms, many hidden, with concealed staircases, trap-doors, torture chambers, a chute for bodies to slide down to a dissecting table, quick-lime pits, acid vats, and a stove-cremator in the basement. For murdering his crooked associate, Benjamin F. Pitezel (whose three children he had also slaughtered) Mudgett was hanged at Moyamensing Prison, Philadelphia, on May 7th, 1896, nine days before his 36th birthday.

PRIME SOURCES:
The Holmes–Pitezel Case. Frank P. Geyer. Publishers' Union, Philadelphia, 1896.
The Trial of Herman W Mudgett. George T. Bisel. Philadelphia, 1897.
The Girls in Nightmare House. Charles Boswell & Lewis Thompson. Gold Medal Books, Fawcett Publications, Greenwich, Connecticut, 1955.
The Torture Doctor.. David Franke. Hawthorn Books, New York, 1975.

Herbert William Mullin

The Voices Said 'Kill'

MASS MURDERER

MURDERER: Herbert William Mullin.

VICTIMS: Lawrence White (55). Mary Margaret Guilfoyle (24). Father Henri Tomei (65). James Ralph Gianera. Joan Gianera (21). Kathy Francis (29). Daemon Francis (4). David Hughes (9). David Allan Oliker (18). Robert Michael Spector (18). Brian Scott Card (19). Mark John Dreibelbis (15). Fred Abbie Perez (72).

LOCI: Highway 9, Henry Cowell State Park, Canada del Rincon en el Rio section (White). Smith Grade junction with Empire Grade, mountain road north-east of Santa Cruz (Guilfoyle). St. Mary's Catholic Church, Los Gatos (Tomei). 520 Western Drive Santa Cruz (the Gianeras). Branciforte Drive, Santa Cruz (the Francis family). Henry Cowell State Park, Santa Cruz (Oliker, Spector, Card, Dreibelbis). Lighthouse Avenue, near Gharkey Street, Santa Cruz (Perez).

DATES: October 13th, 1972 (White). October 24th, 1972 (Guilfoyle). November 2nd, 1972 (Tomei). January 25th, 1973 (the Gianeras, the Francis family). February 6th, 1973 (Oliker, Spector, Card, Dreilbelbis). February 13th, 1973 (Perez).

MEANS: Beating to death with a baseball bat (White). Stabbing with hunting knife (Guilfoyle, Tomei). Shooting (the Gianeras, the Francis family, Oliker, Spector, Card, Dreibelbis, Perez).

MOTIVE: An absolutely typical paranoid schizophrenic, he believed in the voices which commanded him to offer human sacrifices to save California from impending earthquake disasters and also required him to kill for other, more arbitrary, reasons.

CRIMEWATCH: Born April 18th, 1947. Oppressive Roman Catholic upbringing. Normal boyhood. Voted 'most likely to succeed' by his high school class. At 17, engaged to Loretta Ricketts. Close male friend, Dean Richardson, died in 1965 motor accident. Grief-stricken, Herb set up a shrine round Dean's photograph in his bedroom, and told Loretta he was afraid he was homosexual. When he further announced himself a conscientious objector and went off to study religion in India, Loretta broke with him. By age 21, he was undergoing pronounced personality changes. He had smoked marijuana and taken LSD for years. He was hearing voices. They told him to shave his head and burn his genitals with a lighted cigarette. After hospital treatment, discharged early in 1970, he was back in hospital in Hawaii by the summer. Returned home – 1541 McLellan Road, Felton, California – in a disturbed state. He killed 13 times in Santa Cruz mountain country. Arrested – February 13th, 1973 – pleaded not guilty by reason of insanity. But the jury found him responsible. He is locked away until 2025. The case is held to demonstrate foolishness of state legislation which closed mental hospitals on grounds of economy and left psychotic time bombs like Mullin perilously at large.

PRIME SOURCE:
The Die Song. Donald T. Lunde and Jefferson Morgan. W. W. Norton, New York, 1980.

Donald Neilson

The Black Panther

MURDERER: Donald Neilson (born Donald Nappey).

VICTIMS: Donald Lawson Skepper (54). Derek Astin (43). Sidney James Grayland (56). Lesley Whittle (17).

LOCI: Sub-post office, Skipton Road, New Park, Harrogate, Yorkshire (Skepper). Sub-post office, Higher Baxenden, Accrington, Lancashire (Astin). Sub-post office, High Street, Langley, West Midlands (Grayland). Main shaft, Bathpool Park underground drainage system, Kidsgrove, Staffordshire (Whittle).

DATES: February 15th, 1974 (Skepper). September 6th, 1974 (Astin). November 11th, 1974 (Grayland). On a date unknown between January 13th and March 7th, 1975 (Whittle).

MEANS: Sawn-off shotgun (Skepper). Sawn-off shotgun and .22 pistol (Astin). .22 pistol (Grayland). Vagal inhibition caused by suspension from a wire attached to the neck (Whittle).

MOTIVE: Financial gain - the pursuit of robbery (the three shootings). Elimination of kidnap victim who could identify him (Whittle).

CRIMEWATCH: Did Lesley Whittle fall from the narrow ledge in the shaft, or did Neilson push her off when his kidnap plan went wrong? He said it was an accident, that he saw her slip, and she was dead when he left her. But then he said the post office shootings were all accidents. The Defence well argued that if the tethering wire had not snagged, the girl's feet would have touched the ground. The wire was padded with Elastoplast. Neilson claimed that he always wore his panther hood and Lesley never saw his face. Horribly, the post-mortem showed empty stomach and intestines. Did he just abandon her? Psychopath with paranoid and obsessional features, who forced his wife and daughter to play war-games, the Black Panther, aged 39, was caged for life.

PRIME SOURCES:
The Black Panther Story. Steven Valentine. New English Library, London, 1976.
The Capture of the Black Panther. Harry Hawkes. Harrap, London, 1978.

Earle Nelson

The Human Gorilla

SERIAL KILLER

MURDERER: Earle Leonard Nelson

VICTIMS: Miss Clara Newman (60). Mrs Laura Beale (60). Mrs Lilian St Mary (63). Mrs Anna Russell (58). Mrs Mary Nisbit (52). Mrs Beatrice Withers (35). Mrs Mabel Fluke. Mrs Virginia Grant (59). Mrs Wilhelmina Edmonds (56). Mrs Florence Monks. Mrs Blanche Myers (48). Mrs John Beard (49). Mrs Bonnie Pace (23). Mrs Germania Harpin (28) and her 8-month-old daughter. Mrs Mary McConnell (60). Mrs Jennie Randolph (35). Mrs Minnie May (53) and Mrs M.C. Athory (sisters). Mrs Mary Sietsema (27). Lola Cowan (14). Mrs Emily Patterson.

LOCI: San Francisco; Santa Barbara; Oakland, California; Portland, Oregon; Seattle; Council Bluffs, Iowa; Kansas City; Philadelphia; Buffalo N.Y.; Detroit; Chicago; Winnipeg, Manitoba.

DATES: A period from February 20th, 1926–June 12th, 1927.

MEANS: Strangulation (usually manual) and rape. Not necessarily in that order.

MOTIVE: Sexual gratification, obviously.

CRIMEWATCH: The saga of Earle Nelson provides a cautionary tale: if you are a landlady be very, very careful about taking in a male lodger, bearing a Bible and quoting the text, like Bible John. Nelson practised a clearly defined criminal system: he would search the streets for a card showing a room to let, be allowed entrance, and then, indecently soon, fall upon the woman, strangle her, and ravage her body. Landladies tended to be in the 60s age-bracket, but none the worse as prey for Nelson. There was the odd exception – even a baby girl of 18 months.

They began to call him the 'Gorilla', like some creature in a story by Edgar Allan Poe – and he was a greatly feared apparition. He was stocky, aged 30, with long, strong arms, huge hands, simian brow and lips, and piercing eyes without mercy. He was said to have webbed fingers, and to have claimed that he could use reptilian hands as suction cups to scale the sides of buildings – like a Spider Man.

The term for webbing is syndactilism, and it can occur in cases of congenital syphilis, which is precisely what Nelson was suffering from. He knew it himself, because his kind aunt had told him about it: 'I have been most unfortunate since the day of my birth, and have been sadly handicapped by the sins of one of my parents, who left a taint in my blood which has caused me an agony of my mind and body.'

The facts that are known – and it is perhaps surprising that there was such a measure of frankness – are that his mother died aged 20, nine or ten months after giving birth to him, 'as a result of a disease contracted from her husband', who followed her to his grave seven months later. Earle was born on May 12th, 1897, and his aunt, Mrs Lilian Fabia, adopted him, bearing away the orphan boy with a terrible future. As if to punish him for his 'taint' and to scour out any potential for familial sin, the aunt brought him up repressively, and enforced long Bible studies.

It is doubtful if he was ever mentally normal. A photograph taken when he was three showed a 'loose-mouthed degenerate infant with the abstracted vacancy of expression of a handicapped child.' Severe symptoms of congenital syphilis used, in the days before effective treatment, to show up at puberty, supposing that the child was not already feeble, mentally or physically, even to the point of early death.

By a double whammy, Earle suffered a brain injury at the age of 10. He was running for a ball in the road near his home in Philadelphia when his clothing became entangled in the cow-catcher of a passing street-car. He was dragged for yards, and was left with a hole in his temple and concussion, and was unconscious for days.

Always a loner and moody, he deteriorated, and scanned the Bible for cruel and sexual deeds, ruminating upon them pleasurably. As he grew up and was physically strong, his aunt became afraid of him. She noticed how he stared at her daughters, and sometimes used to send him away to sleep at a hotel. Perhaps there he watched the female guests.

Trouble came on his 21st birthday, when he raped a girl in a basement. The Court heard that he had already been pronounced insane by a Naval Hospital Board when called up for service, and he was now committed to the Napa State Hospital for the insane, where he pulled out all his eyebrows and was confined in a straightjacket. He escaped five times from confinement – he was always a great escapologist, an insane Houdini.

In the interstices of his admissions, he met and married, on August 12th, 1919, a school matron who deeply regretted her choice. She found him impossible to live with: he suffered from morbid jealousy, possibly of morbid delusional origin. When she was in hospital suffering with stress, he barged in and raped her before running away.

His libido was unstoppable, and in 1926 he began his tour of terror, moving from state to state when things became too hot to linger. His method was to leave the bodies in the house where he found the vulnerable women, concealing them roughly in order to gain a few hours to leave the area or the town. A favourite place to stow the remains, often bloodied by mutilation, was under the bed, rolled in a carpet. That was the sight that met the eyes of William Paterson, a pious man, of 100 Riverton Avenue, Winnipeg, when he sank to his knees to ask for the help of God in finding his missing wife.

Nelson took to stealing clothes, jewels, and money from the scene of his crimes – more to finance his motive-full wanderings than as trophies of the true serial killer. The move to Canada was unwise. His considerable store of cunning was running out. He was more conspicuous and he was recognised from photographs and his description in the Winnipeg newspapers, in a post office and store at Wakopa.

He was captured, but escaped from his jail-cell in Killarney. Such was the panic, the fear of the Gorilla, that the women and children of the town were herded into a hall and guarded by their menfolk with guns and pitchforks. They caught him again, by the railway. He was tried at Winnipeg, and the defence of insanity was put up. That seems fair enough, but the judge would have none of it.

The careful, sonorous phrases of our old McNaughton Rules rolled out in the courtroom, but it was thought that because Nelson repeatedly escaped and kept changing his clothing for purposes of disguise, he obviously knew the nature and quality of his acts, and that they were wrong. As a matter of fact, his aunt had testified that one of his strange rituals, from a very early age, was to go out, dispose of his clothes, and return with inferior items. Casting off his sins, perhaps?

Many and bizarre were his actions as described by his aunt: he always walked with his head in the air as if looking up to Heaven, used to pick up heavy oak chairs with his teeth, and walk on his hands. His wife, also called, said that he would sit for two or three hours in a kind of daze. His eyes seemed to take on a different colour. They were wide and staring and very dilated, or you could see nothing except the whites.

It was all no use and he was hanged on January 13th, 1928. He showed no remorse or concern and denied everything. The Gorilla was dead.

PRIME SOURCES:
Mass Murder. L C Douthwaite. John Long, 1928.
Bloodletters and Badmen. Jay Robert Nash. M Evans, 1993.
Encyclopaedia of World Crime. Jay Robert Nash. Crimebooks Inc, Wilmette, Illinois, 1990.

Dennis Nilsen

The Lonely Necrophile

SERIAL KILLER

MURDERER: Dennis Andrew Nilsen.

VICTIMS: Admitted slaying 15 or 16 young men. Convicted of six murders. Kenneth James Ockendon (23). Malcolm Barlow (23). Martyn Duffey (16). John Peter Howlett. Billy Sutherland (27). Stephen Sinclair (20). Archibald Graham Allen (28) was identified too late to be included on the indictment. Nilsen did not know the names of all his victims; most, not all, were homosexual drifters. There were also seven attempted murders.

LOCI: Twelve or thirteen men were killed at 195 Melrose Avenue, Cricklewood, North London, and three at his attic flat, 23 Cranley Gardens, Muswell Hill, North London.

DATES: December 31st, 1978 - January 27th, 1983.

MEANS: Strangulation, sometimes in combination with drowning.

MOTIVE: Very murky psychopathology here. The actual killing was important to Nilsen, but so, too, was his contact with the freshly dead body: lying beside and masturbating over it, and carrying out a ritual of washing, drying and powdering. Any necrophilic sexual connection was, said Nilsen, not penetrative, but intercrural. The psychiatrists had a field day.

CRIMEWATCH: Lonely civil servant, frightening fantasist, half in love with easeful death, Nilsen took young men home from casual encounters in pubs. Alcohol and music contributed to his mood. Disposal of corpses was a problem. There was a useful garden at Melrose Avenue. Bodies were stored under floorboards, buried outside, stowed in suitcases in a shed, and burnt on a bonfire. Cranley Gardens was more difficult, but not insurmountable. Bodies were dismembered in the bath, put out with garbage, dumped any old where, and flushed down the lavatory. The resultant blockage and the calling in of the man from Dyno-rod led to Nilsen's arrest. Police found, in a wardrobe, two plastic bags with mixed human remains, including two torsos, a boiled skull and another partially boiled head. Nilsen had used a large cooking-pot. In a tea-chest, another torso and skull. In a bag in the bathroom the lower half of Stephen Sinclair. At the Old Bailey, on November 4th, 1983, a jury rejected a plea of diminished responsibility and Nilsen was sentenced, aged 37, to life imprisonment.

PRIME SOURCES:
The Nilsen File. Brian McConnell and Douglas Bence. Futura, Macdonald & Co., London, 1983.
House of Horrors. John Lisners. Corgi Books, London, 1983.
Killing For Company. Brian Masters. Jonathan Cape, London, 1985.

Pietro Pacciani

The Monster of Florence

Serial Killer

Murderer: Pietro Pacciani (?).

Victims: Antonio Lo Bianco (29), Barbara Locci (32), PasqualeGentilcore (18), Stefania Pettini (18), Giovanni Foggi (30), Carmela De Nuccio (21), Stefano Baldi (26), Susanna Cambi (24), Paolo Mainardi (22), Antonella Migliorini (20), Horst Meyer (24), Uwe Rusch Sens (24), Claudio Stefanacci (20), Pia Rontini (18), Jean-Michel Kraveichvili (25), Nadine Mauriot (36).

Loci: Near the cemetery at Campi Bisenzio, 15 miles west of Florence; Borgo san Lorenzo, 20 miles north of Florence; Scandicci, a suburb south-west of Florence; near Calenzano; a suburb of Prato, 12 miles north-west of Florence; near Baccaiano, 15 miles south-west of Florence; Galluzzo, near Scandicci; near Vicchio, to the east of Borgo san Lorenzo; Sant' Andrea, in Percussina, 15 miles south of Florence.

Dates: August 21st, 1968. September 17th, 1974. June 6th, 1981. October 22nd, 1981. June 19th, 1982. September 9th, 1983. July 29th, 1984. September 8th, 1985.

Means: Shooting. Stabbing.

Motive: Sexual – with mutilation.

Crimewatch: It was the Italian newspapers that christened the faceless, nameless serial killer stalking the suburbs of the city and killing copulating couples in parked cars 'Il Mostro di Firenze', the Monster of Florence. And the name struck fear in the hearts of the Florentine citizenry, who stayed home at nights behind locked doors. Whoever he was, the Monster was ringing the city with a circle of fear. Signs were posted around Florence warning children and lovers not to stop or linger in isolated spots.

The Monster's first attack was on the night of August 21st, 1968. Antonio Lo Bianco was a married man with children, and his mistress, Barbara Locci, from Lastra a Signa, eight miles west of Florence, was also married, and her six-year-old son was asleep in the back of the car. They parked near a disued cemetery, at Campi Bisenzio, 15 miles west of the centre of Florence, and were making love when a dark figure suddenly materialised out of the blackness of the night and fired eight shots into the heaving couple, killing them both.

The murder weapon was a .22-calibre automatic. Locci's husband, Stefano Mele, was suspected. He had suffered through his wife's serial infidelities. The cuckold supreme, he had even been known to serve her lovers breakfast in bed. Interviewed, he implicated four of Barbara's lovers – the brothers Francesco, Giovanni, and Salvatore Vinci, and Carmelo Cultrano. But, in March 1970, he himself was found guilty of the murders and sentenced to 14 years. The Monster's second killing was on September 14th, 1974. It took place in the Borgo san Lorenzo area, 20 miles north of Florence. Pasquale Gentilcore and Stefania Pettini had both been shot – by a .22-calibre Beretta. The young man's body, half-naked, was in the driver's seat of the Fiat 127. The completely naked corpse of the young woman lay spread-eagled on the ground, a vine stalk protruding from her vagina. Although shot three times, her death was the result of some 96 stab wounds.

Double killing No.3 was that of Giovanni

Foggi and Carmela De Nuccio, in a parked car in the south-west Florentine suburb of Scandicci. Two shots had been fired from a .22-calibre automatic pistol; one killed Foggi instantly, the other had merely grazed Carmela, who ran off into a field, and fell into a ditch. The killer fired three shots into the back of her neck. He then took a scalpel or razor-sharp knife and cut out her vagina. The size and depths of some footprints found at the murder scene indicated that the Monster was most likely a large man. Enzo Spalletti, known as an occasional voyeur, was arrested and tucked away behind bars to await trial.

On October 23rd, 1981, there was a fourth double killing – that of Stefano Baldi and Susanna Cambi. They had parked in a vineyard at Calenzano, 12 miles north-west of Florence. Both had been shot and stabbed, and the woman's body had been genitally mutilated. Again, the firearm used proved to have been a .22-calibre Beretta. Since he had been securely locked up in jail at the time of these killings, charges against Enzo Spalletti were dropped, and he was released.

June 19th, 1982, saw the shooting of Paolo Mainardi and Antonella Migliorini, who were at the time making love in a parked car at Baccaiano, 15 miles south-west of Florence. Apparently, Mainardi had caught sight of the Monster approaching. He had started the car and reversed into a ditch. The Monster shot out the headlights and fired two bullets through the windscreen which also went through the heads of the couple. His routine put out of joint, the Monster quit the scene without carrying out his usual ritual mutilation.

Nearly a year went by before the killer struck again on September 9th, 1983. His victims were a brace of West German homosexual boys, Horst Meyer and Uwe Rusch Sens. They were shot while sleeping in a Volkswagen camper, in a grassy clearing just 19 miles south of Florence. One of the victims had very long blond hair, and it is just possible that he was initially mistaken for a woman by the killer. There was no mutilation of the bodies. Ballistic tests subsequently showed that the murder weapon was a .22-calibre Beretta.

The seventh killing was that of Claudio Stefanacci and Pia Rontini. They were shot and stabbed on July 29th, 1984, near Vicchio, 14 miles north-east of Florence. The woman was found, totally naked, spread-eagled on the ground behind some bushes. Her genitalia and left breast had been removed. The corpse of the man, wearing only underpants and a vest, was in the back seat of the car. He had been slashed more than a hundred times.

The Monster of Florence struck for the last time on September 8th, 1985. His victims were French tourists Jean-Michel Kraveichvili and Nadine Mauriot. They were camping in the San Casciano area, just outside Florence. Both had been shot while making love in their tent. The woman received the first four bullets, three through the skull and one through the throat. The man was probably lying on his back with the woman on top of him. The woman's vagina was removed, as was her left breast.

In the course of the next eight years, more than 100,000 people were questioned, but no solid, convincing suspect emerged. Then, in November 1993, the newspapers triumphantly announced that the Monster had at last been caged. His name was Pietro Pacciani. He was a 68-year-old, semi-literate farmer who worked a smallholding at Vicchio, and enjoyed hunting and taxidermy. The police had, in fact, had their eyes on him since the early 1990s. He had a record.

He had been arrested for murder in 1951. He had caught a travelling salesman sleeping with his girlfriend, Miranda. After frenziedly stabbing him and stamping him to death, he had raped his still warm body, and then forced Miranda to make love with him beside the corpse. Pacciani was later to say: 'I saw Miranda's left breast uncovered, and that sparked my jealousy.' In the light of this, the removal of the left breast in the cases of Pia Rontini and Nadine Mauriot takes on a putatively revelatory significance, becomes a clue. Duly convicted, Pacciani served 13 years in prison. Following his release, he married, but was jailed again in 1987 for four years for beating his wife and sexually molesting his two young daughters.

He was also reported to be involved with three men – Mario Vanni, Giovanni Faggi, and

Giancarlo Lotti – who were all known as nocturnal, rambling, peeping Toms. Arrested on January 17th, 1993, he was brought to trial in November, 1994. The evidence against him was not strong, and was largely circumstantial. But he was pronounced guilty of seven of the double murders, sentenced to life, and dragged howling his innocence from the court.

However, on February 16th, 1996, his conviction was overturned on appeal, and Pacciani, now 71, was released. As he walked free, the police, acting on new information, arrested Mario Vanni (70), Giovanni Faggi (77), and Giancarlo Lotti (54). And on December 12th, 1996, the Italian Supreme Court ordered Pacciani to undergo a re-trial. Vanni and Lotti, tried in May 1997, were sentenced to life and 26 years respectively, for involvement in five of the double murders. Pietro Pacciani was never brought back for trial. On February 23rd, 1998, he was found lying face-down on the floor of his home, his shirt up around his neck, his trousers down to his ankles, and his face blue and distorted. He had taken a fatal dose of mixed drugs. There is reason to think that the 16 murders were the work of not one man, but of a group of sexual deviants, but that Pacciani was the leader, their chief inspiration and motivator . . . and, to that extent, it was he who truly was the Monster of Florence.

PRIME SOURCE:
Contemporary newspapers.

The Pageant Beauty Queen Murder

MURDERER: Unknown.

VICTIM: JonBenét Ramsey.

LOCUS: 755 Fifteenth Street, Boulder, Colorado.

DATE: December 25th-26th, 1996.

MEANS: Ligature strangulation.

JonBenét Ramsey (victim)

MOTIVE: The indications are that it was very likely sexual.

CRIMEWATCH: From early blue-rimmed dusk to velvet black, smoothly and silently night glided down over the city of Boulder, Colorado, in a gentle flutter of seasonal snowflakes, borne on the keen, rinsing wind blowing off the towering Flatiron and the Front Range of the Rocky Mountains. Christmas, 1996, was just dead, but the multicoloured bulbs still shone and sparkled, reflected in the light spattering of snow around the fine old stately houses in the select area of University Hill.

The imposing Tudoreque house – No.755 Fifteenth Street – with a tinsel and spun glass bauble laden Christmas tree flashing in every room, was the Ramsey residence. Here, cushioned by a millionaire's wealth, yielded by his computer business, Access Graphics – just passed the billion-dollar annual profit mark this year – lived John Ramsey, his wife, Patsy, their nine-year-old son, Burke, and six-year-old daughter, JonBenét. But, on this Boxing Day, 1996, every ultimate iota of festivity had drained away from the Ramsey household. Just after a quarter to six that morning, Patsy Ramsey had come downstairs to discover a ransom note demanding $118,000 for the safe return of her daughter, JonBenét, whom they, signing themselves 'Victory, SBTC' – 'We are a group of individuals that represents a foreign faction' – claimed to have in their possession. Rushing upstairs to her daughter's room, she found the bed empty, and the little girl vanished.

At 5.52 a.m. Patsy Ramsey called the Boulder City police. Incredibly, it was not until eight hours later, just after 1 p.m., when John Ramsey and his friend, Fleet White, made a further search of the basement, already searched by the police, that JonBenét was discovered. She was lying, partially covered by a white blanket, in a small room behind the boiler. Her hands, extended above her head, were tied together. Masking tape was plastered across her mouth. There was a ligature around her neck. A small wooden stick was attached to it, forming a garrotte.

JonBenét had been a very special little girl. Following in the competitive, parade strolling footsteps of her mother, a former Miss West Virginia, and her Aunt Pam (Paugh), also once crowned Miss West Virginia, she had already achieved great things in the juvenile beauty stakes, including her election as Little Miss Charlevoix (Michigan) in 1994, Little Miss Colorado Sunburst and America's Royale Tiny Miss in 1995, and had been tilting her pretty head very realistically in the direction of the Little Miss America boardwalk, its sash, trophy, and tiara.

But now, for little JonBenét, the masquerade was over. Even before this, the final curtain, there had been problems. JonBenét had been a bed-wetter, and she had been observed nervously massaging herself in a way suggestive of masturbation, both symptoms commonly – but not necessarily exclusively – seen in sexually abused children. To add fuel to the flickering flame of suspicion, autopsy revealed a residue on her upper thighs that could have been semen.

Blood traces and black fibres found in the vaginal area indicated that those surfaces had been wiped clean by someone. The hymen was broken, having only a rim of tissue running from the upper left at about ten o'clock to the two o'clock position. There was dried and semi-dried blood in small amounts at the entrance to the vagina, and a reddening in the vaginal walls.

The pathological conclusion from examination of the genital area was that the child could have suffered vaginal penetration, consistent with a sexual assault. Apart from the death causative strangulation, the child's skull displayed a dextral linear fracture, running approximately eight and a half inches from the front of the head to above the right ear. And at the back of the head there was a displaced rectangular section of the skull, three quarters by half an inch in length.

These findings pointed to the victim's having sustained a very heavy blow to the head. For a number of extremely sound reasons, the ransom note was held to be bogus, the foreign kidnappers non-existent. Over the years, a plethora of theoretical accusations have been formulated – and dismissed.

Initially, JonBenét's parents were put in the frame. It was hazarded that their daughter's bed-wetting had angered her mother, and that she had accidentally killed JonBenét while reprimanding her physically too severely, and then written the ransom note herself to deflect suspicion.

Another suggestion, unsupported by any legally acceptable proof, was that JonBenét's brother, Burke, had killed her out of sibling rivalry. It has been reported that when she, as she thought, hung up after calling the police that early morning of December 26th, Patsy Ramsey somehow failed in her state of panic to replace the telephone receiver properly, and the police heard background noises which they were unable to understand. They sent the tape of the telephone call to an expert electronics company, who were able to bring the sounds up, clarified. Burke could be heard saying: 'Please, what do I do?' John Ramsey replies: 'We're not speaking to you.' Then Burke is heard saying: 'What did you find?'

But Pat Ramsey had testified that her son had slept all through the discovery of the ransom note and the further discovery of JonBenét's absence from her room. Both she and the boy had clearly lied about this. Why? Had Burke killed his little sister, and had his distraught parents created the ransom note to take the focus of attention away from him?

Other vaunted possibilities include some kind of horrific domestic disaster, such as that she fell, or was pushed, down the stairs, striking her head against some hard object, like the banisters; accidentally killed during rough horseplay; injured in the course of an argument that turned violent.

But most likely is that she fell into the hands of a sexual predator. Of possible vital significance is the following. On the evening of December 23rd, the Ramseys gave a Christmas party for their friends, among whom was Bill Reynolds, a retired professor from the University of Colorado. Entering into the spirit of the thing, he came dressed as Santa Claus, and lent a decided touch of welcome colour to the occasion.

The following day, JonBenét went to another party at the home of one of her young friends, and she told this friend that she had already seen and actually talked to Santa, who had been at her family's party the previous evening, and he had promised her that he would be coming over to her house late on Christmas night, when he would be giving her a very special present.

The mother of JonBenét's friend, happening to overhear this, thought that JonBenét must have meant that Santa had said that he would be coming on Christmas Eve, not Christmas night, but no, absolutely no, JonBenét insisted that he had said Christmas night.

Oddly, Bill Reynolds, the man who had played Santa Claus, and who had said that he would come down JonBenét's chimney on Christmas night, had a nine-year-old daughter who was abducted on Boxing Day, 1974. She was never seen again. In 1976, the girl's mother wrote an award-winning play about the death of a girl who was sexually abused and tortured in a basement.

PRIME SOURCES:

Perfect Murder: Perfect Town. Lawrence Schiller. HarperCollins, 1998.

JonBenét: Inside the Ramsey Murder Investigation. Steve Thomas with Don Davis. St. Martin's Press, New York, 2000.

The Death of Innocence. John and Patsy Ramsey. Thomas Nelson, Nashville, 2000.

Cracking More Cases. Dr Henry C. Lee with Thomas W. O'Neil. Prometheus Books, Amherst, New York, 2004.

Christine Papin & Léa Papin
The Fiendish Housemaids of Le Mans

MURDERERS: Christine Papin and Léa Papin.

VICTIMS: Madame Marie Lancelin. Geneviève Lancelin (27): Daughter.

LOCUS: Le Mans, Sarthe Department, Western France.

DATE: February 2nd, 1933.

MEANS: Extreme violence. Gouging out of victims' eyes, battering with pewter pot and hammer, attack with knives.

MOTIVE: Never satisfactorily established. Speculation postulates revenge, resentment, sheer bad temper; an *acte gratuit*. But for some time an atmosphere had been building in that house. Incidents, small in themselves, had been piling up. Mme. Lancelin, haughty, distant, speaking only to scold, was always spying, counting the sugar lumps, running a white-gloved finger along the furniture to check if the dusting had been done properly. The slightest damage was taken out of the Papin sisters' wages. The heaviness became heavier; the stillness stiller, like the air before a storm. What may have been the spark in that *huis clos* was the blowing of the fuses by the iron. The iron had gone wrong in January. It had been repaired – 5 francs out of the maids' wages on February 1st. The iron went wrong again on February 2nd, plunging the house in darkness. When Madame Lancelin and her daughter returned about 5 p.m. there was a scene. It escalated. Terrible bloodshed.

CRIMEWATCH: When lawyer René Lancelin's wife and daughter did not arrive for dinner with him at a friend's, he hurried home to investigate. Finding his house dark and locked against him, he summoned the police. The first clue was a human eyeball caught in torchlight on the stair. On the first-floor landing lay the dead and mutilated bodies. The maids, cowering naked upstairs, admitted guilt. Christine (28) and Lea (21) were the products of a harsh background. They and their elder sister, Emilie, now a nun, had all been interfered with by a brutal drunkard father, from whom their mother separated in 1913. Brought up in convents and orphanages, the younger sisters went into service. In 1926, they came to work together at the Lancelins'. There were strong indications of a fierce lesbian relationship between them, but, specifically questioned by the judge, Christine, the dominant sister, flatly denied it. Tried in September, 1933, at the Le Mans Palais de Justice, pleas of insanity failed. Both were found guilty. Léa was given 10 years' hard labour. Christine, sentenced to death, was reprieved. She died in Rennes asylum in 1937. Léa, released in 1942, went back to work – as a chambermaid in good class French hotels.

PRIME SOURCES:
The Papin Sisters. Rachel Edwards and Keith Reader. Oxford University Press, 2001.
Contemporary newspapers.

Gordon Park

The Lady of the Lake

MURDERER: Gordon Park.

VICTIM: Carol Park (30).

LOCUS: 'Bluestones', Leece, Nr Barrow-in-Furness, Cumbria.

DATE: July 17th, 1976.

MEANS: Battering with an ice-axe.

MOTIVE: A pure domestic murder: elimination of wife.

CRIMEWATCH: They called her the Lady of the Lake when they brought her up from the waters of Coniston. There she had lain for 21 years, dwelling, like Tennyson's Fairy Lady, 70 feet down 'in a deep, calm, whatsoever storms may shake the world.' If Gordon Park had taken his dinghy further out, the weighted bundle would have sunk lower, beyond trace.

Restless lies the head that holds the memory. How did he manage to sleep, to lead an apparently normal life, look after his three children, marry twice more, teach at his school, while all the time, the lake lapped at its shores and the tethered bundle swayed and shifted beneath? The censor in the brain, which suppresses bad thoughts and dreams, must have been at full throttle.

His personality was controlling, rigid, regimental, and obsessional, and he made Carol Park very unhappy. She was warm, vivacious, and spontaneous. If there had been an attraction of opposites, it had soon waned. She was a life-enhancer: he was a life-despoiler. Twice she had left him for a more romantic relationship, but the Magistrates' Court awarded custody of the children to the husband, and she pined for them, and eventually returned to the matrimonial home.

How forgiving was he really? She took the anti-depressant, Tryptizol. He brooded that a divorce might deprive him of custody of the children and his cherished bungalow, 'Bluestones', which he built himself. There is a strong suggestion of premeditation about the murder, because it took place in July, 1976,

at the beginning of a summer holiday, when Carol, a deputy headmistress, would not be generally missed.

After six weeks, he calmly reported his wife as missing, and since she had left home before, on the whole he was believed or, let us say, there was a lack of evidence to the contrary. Time passed. Then, on August 13th, 1997, divers from the Kendal and Lakes Sub-Aqua Club discovered the suspicious bundle. Identification of Carol Park was absolute, if a little delayed, once her dental records had been traced, stowed away in a garage.

Gordon Parks was on a cycling or caravanning holiday in France. They let him come home, and then, on August 25th, they arrested him, but he was as always, defiant, uncooperative, challenging even, and eventually the Crown Prosecution Service decided that there was insufficient evidence to proceed against him. He was triumphant, and he gave a sanctimonious interview to the Mail on Sunday, for which he was paid £50,000. However, the investigation continued, and he was re-arrested on January 13th, 2004.

His trial began at Manchester Crown Court on November 22nd, 2004. A couple who had been sitting in a car beside the lake at the relevant spot on July 17th, 1976, remembered seeing a slim, bespectacled man in a wetsuit tipping a sizeable bundle over the side of his dinghy. 'I hope that isn't his wife!' Mrs Joan Young had joked. Clever Park had not counted on eye-witnesses.

He was said to have shown guilty knowledge

while on remand in Preston prison, and where he spoke to two inmates on separate occasions. The police thought that Park had drugged his wife with her own Tryptizol, and bludgeoned her to death with an ice-axe, smashing in the bones of her face. Such an act speaks of the way in which he thought about his wife. It was theorised that this horrible attack was to render her unrecognisable, but a man of his education would have known about dental identification. Activity to render a body difficult to identify usually *follows* the means of murder. Worse, Carol was without doubt conscious at some stage, because the bones in her hand were smashed to pieces as she was defending herself.

He taped her eyes with plaster, in order to hide them as they stared at him after death when he handled her body. Or did he tape her eyes first, before he fell on her, so that she was blind as she tried to fight him off? Park kept the corpse for a week, again it is thought, in the freezer chest in his garage.

Carol was small, only size 10. She was still wearing her blue Baby Doll nightdress when she was found two decades later. He occupied the waiting time by carefully fashioning a shroud out of a pinafore dress and a rucksack. It is typical of his obsessional personality that he punched 14 regular holes in the stout material before sewing it up with a sailmaker's needle and twine. He tied the parcel with 100 feet of rope fastened with special nautical and climbing knots – both areas of Park's expertise.

Secretly then, he drove the 20 miles from Barrow to Coniston, where he continued for all those years to sail over Carol's watery grave, and dumped her, weighted down with lead piping. A defining moment at the trial was the revelation that police divers using sonar equipment had found, on the lake bed, an alien piece of Westmorland green slate of the same type as that which Park used in the building of his bungalow. Additionally, a rock, which matched rocks in the wall at 'Bluestones', was discovered.

The jury took seven and a half hours to convict Gordon Park, by now aged 61, of the murder of his wife. Although he was otherwise of unblemished character, Mr Justice McCombe, sentencing him to life imprisonment, recommended that because of aggravating circumstance he would serve a minimum of 15 years: 'There was considerable physical suffering. Her eyes were taped. She inhaled blood and suffered disfiguring wounds. She also tried to defend herself from the brutal blows inflicted. The terrible concealment of the body has led to so much suffering inflicted on so many people over such a long period of time.'

It was especially painful for Carol's adopted daughter, Veronica, whose birth mother, Carol's sister, Christine, had been murdered by her boyfriend when Veronica was 18-months-old. Gordon Park, a family man at heart, had simply compounded the tragedy.

PRIME SOURCE:
Contemporary newspapers.

Colin Pitchfork
The Black Pad Murderer

MURDERER: Colin Pitchfork.

VICTIMS: Lynda Mann (15). Dawn Ashworth (15).

LOCI: In the grounds of Carlton Hayes Psychiatric Hospital, beside the Black Pad footpath, Narborough, Leicestershire. Beside Ten Pound Lane, five fields away, Narborough.

DATES: November 21st, 1983. 31st July, 1986.

MEANS: Strangling, in both cases.

MOTIVE: Sexual.

CRIMEWATCH: There is a treasured psychiatric concept that a 'flasher' is not really dangerous because the mere gross act, as long as the target is aware of it, and, preferably, reacts, provides total immediate satisfaction. When the early deviancy of serial killers is prised out of their family members, flashing is not usually a feature. This case provides what might be called 'Pitchfork's Warning'.

Colin Pitchfork, married with two children, a baker, with a special skill at creative cake-making, had a long history of flashing, and many were the solemn hours of psychotherapy which had been expended on 'curing' him. The escalation to violent rape and murder came about, according to his own cool confession, when both victims reacted in an unusual way, which inflamed him. They were supposed to walk on by, with a scream or two perhaps, but they fled back, into lonely places.

Lynda Mann left the main road and actually ran down The Black Pad footpath. As for Dawn Ashworth, he spotted her entering Ten Pound Lane, another dangerous footpath, and as he exposed himself, she jumped into a gateway, and he pushed her into the open field beyond. The murders, which swiftly followed the rapes, were, he said, to prevent them from identifying him as a rapist. When he was destroying Lynda Mann, his car was parked nearby, with his baby son safely strapped in a carrycot. Dawn Ashworth was much more fundamentally attacked, but here the confession became vague.

The young women of the three Leicestershire villages, Narborough, Littlethorpe, and Enderby, were on notice, after the first fatal attack, not to use the footpaths as a short cut. The brick-dark tower of the old psychiatric hospital loomed over the scene, but the case illustrates the truism that just because two bodies are found close to such a place, it is not safe to assume that the killer must be an inmate.

Enshrined, too, within the investigation, is a prime example of a false confessor. Richard Buckland (17), a kitchen porter at the very same hospital, went to pieces when he was interrogated, and wrongfully admitted raping and killing Dawn Ashworth, but not adamantly, Lynda Mann. His conscience was not entirely clear, since he was very interested in sex, and had been experimenting in a manner not to be proud of, indeed.

The date for his trial had even been fixed, but he was saved, exonerated, by the application of genetic fingerprinting, pioneered by Dr Alec Jeffreys, a geneticist, who coincidentally was working in the county at Leicester University. It was he who first analysed miniature particles of genetic material, matched those samples with specific individuals, and saw those distinctive grey and black bands, which look like supermarket bar-codes.

Dr Jeffreys was able to say that there was no match between genetic material from the two murdered girls and blood from Richard Buckland, the false confessor. The samples showed that one and the same man had committed the crimes. The decision was made to blood-test all male residents in the village, between the ages of 17 and 34 years. Doctors performed the task. Even those with needle phobias were persuaded, one way or another. Soon, the trawl was widened to include men who lived, worked, or had a recreational interest in the area. Then they turned to *alibied* young males, with figures eventually reaching some 6,000 individuals.

Colin Pitchfork, who was 27-years-old, was called, but never actually attended the sessions, although they thought he had. He had manipulated and intimidated a fellow-baker, 24-year-old Ian Kelly, into taking the test for him, presenting Pitchfork's passport with his own photograph inserted as evidence for the identification. No money changed hands.

It later transpired that Pitchfork had approached two other bakers and offered money for the impersonation, but they had refused. Discovery came when Ian Kelly blurted out to a group of friends what he had done. A baker's manageress, Mrs Jackie Foggin, agonised for six weeks before informing the police. The genuine Pitchfork blood matched.

Tried at Leicester, Colin Pitchfork pleaded guilty and was sentenced to life imprisonment with no recommendation for a minimum term. Ian Kelly was given an 18-months' term of imprisonment, suspended for two years, for the serious offence of conspiracy to pervert the course of justice. This was the first murder case in which DNA fingerprinting was used as an effective part of the investigation – exonerating an innocent suspect, flushing out the real criminal, and, finally confirming his guilt.

PRIME SOURCE:
The Blooding. Joseph Wambaugh. Bantam, 1989.

Heinrich Pommerencke

The Beast of the Black Forest

SERIAL KILLER

MURDERER: Heinrich Pommerencke.

VICTIMS: Hilda Konther (34). Karin Wälde (18). Rita Walterspacher (18). Dagmar Klimek (21). And almost certainly many others.

LOCI: Karlsruhe. Hornberg. Rastatt. Freiburg.

DATES: February 28th, 1959. March 26th, 1959. May 30th, 1959. June 4th, 1959. June 8th, 1959.

MEANS: Stabbing. Strangling. Throat-cutting. Battering to death.

MOTIVE: Sexual.

CRIMEWATCH: The beginning of the end of the blood-lusty career of the Beast of the Black Forest was heralded by the arrival, on June 9th, 1959, in Johann Kohler's modest tailor's shop in Hornberg, South Baden, of a tall, fair-haired young man, wearing a baggy grey suit, and carrying a bulging briefcase. Herr Kohler was both pleased and relieved to see him, as it had been several weeks since he had ordered a sports jacket and a pair of trousers, and there had been no sign of his coming back to pay for and collect them. He had known the young man well enough to allow him credit.

His name was Heinrich Pommerencke, and he was a waiter who worked at the Hotel Baren. Young Pommerencke explained that he had been unable to come earlier because he had been sent off to Frankfurt as a relief waiter at very short notice. Now, he tried on his new clothes. Evidently pleased with them, he handed his old grey suit to the tailor and asked him to parcel it up for him. Then, having paid for the coat and trousers, he said that he was going for a haircut, and would Herr Kohler be so kind as to look after his briefcase and the parcelled-up suit for half an hour or so.

After the young man's departure, Kohler picked up the briefcase. It was extraordinarily heavy. He moved it from the chair, where Pommerencke had left it, on to the floor. As he did so, the strained and defective catch burst open, and a sawn-off rifle came clattering out.

The briefcase also contained an automatic pistol, a box of ammunition, two knives, some cash, some soiled clothing, several pornographic magazines, and a bottle of pink liquid labelled 'Love Cocktail'.

Kohler, knowing that there had recently been an interrupted robbery at Durlach station, in the eastern district of Karlsruhe, in the course of which the thief had threatened a railway employee with a sawn-off rifle, immediately telephoned the police. They were waiting for Pommerencke when he returned to the tailor's shop.

Born in 1937 in the village of Bentwisch, near Rostock, in East Germany, Heinrich Pommerencke was an only child, and the product of a broken home. He endured an abnormally lonely childhood, and developed compulsive sexual urges at an early age. By the time he was fifteen, he was hanging about outside the local dance-hall, trying his luck with the young women as they emerged. According to his own story, those girls he molested who were unwilling to let him make love to them, he knocked down and raped.

In 1953, aged 16, fearing that he would be prosecuted for a sexual offence he had committed, he ran away to Switzerland, where he got jobs as a waiter and a handyman. Two years later, he was arrested for burglary, served a short prison sentence, and was deported. He arrived home in Germany in 1955, and lived in

Hamburg, Heidelberg, Düsseldorf, Frankfurt, and Hornberg. In 1957, he was sent back to jail for a year, not for the seven rapes he had carried out since his return, but for robbery.

A young waitress, Elke Braun, walking home from work in Karlsruhe on Friday, February 27th, 1959, was suddenly grabbed from behind. A man with a knife flung her to the ground and began to rip at her clothes. Screaming at the top of her lungs, she gamely tried to fight him off. Fortunately, a passing taxi driver heard her cries, stopped his cab and ran over to investigate. Her attacker sprinted off. The girl described the man as young, tall, slim, fair-haired, and baby-faced.

Pommerencke was later to say that what had turned him to murder, was a visit to the cinema. On February 28th, 1959, he went to see the Hollywood epic, *The Ten Commandments*. He watched transfixed as half-naked women danced round the golden calf – 'I thought they were a fickle lot. I knew I would have to kill.' And he did just that. Came out of the pictures and broke the fifth commandment.

The victim of that first murder was a 34-year-old cleaning woman, Hilda Konther. She was found in bushes in a park near her home in Karlsruhe. She had been brutally beaten, raped, and had her throat cut.

On March 26th, 1959, Karin Wälde, an 18-year-old beautician, failed to return from work to her home in Hornberg. Her body was found by her parents next morning in a clump of bushes close to her home. She had been raped, and battered to death with a heavy stone.

Shortly after midnight on June 3rd, 1959, as the Riviera Express was steaming out of Freiburg-Im-Breisgau railway station, a fair-haired young man in a baggy grey suit, clutching a platform ticket in his hand, had slipped on to the train. Pommerencke had once worked as a steward on holiday trains, and knew they were 'good places for doing the job.' Aboard the train was a party of 30 student-teachers from Heidelberg, bound for a summer holiday by the Italian Lakes.

One of the students was 21-year-old Dagmar Klimek. Pommerencke was waiting in the darkness of the corridor, from which he had removed the electric bulb, when she emerged from the lavatory. He seized her, opened a carriage door, and flung her bodily out on to the line, then, after a brief pause, pulled the communication cord. As the train slowed, he leapt out and ran back along the track. It took him half an hour to reach the injured girl. He fell upon her, raped her, and stabbed her to death.

Pommerencke's final rape-murder had been committed on the evening of June 8th, 1959. His victim was Rita Walterspacher. She was just eighteen years old, lived with her parents in Rastatt, worked as a clerk, and commuted daily to her office job at Baden-Baden. That Monday, she had telephoned her mother, warning her that she would be late home from work. When, however, there was no sign of her by the following morning, her worried parents went to the police.

Within an hour of a local radio appeal, a woman came forward with information. She had been a passenger on the train which ran a few minutes after that caught by Rita at 6.06 p.m., and as, at about 6.15 p.m., the witness' train was running into Rastatt, she had seen through the carriage window a young woman racing along the road which ran parallel with the railway track. She was being chased by a tall young man with fair hair, wearing a baggy grey suit. He had caught up with her and dragged her into the woods. At the time, witness had assumed they were a frolicking courting couple.

A search revealed Rita's corpse under a pile of branches, not far from the railway line. She had been strangled, stripped, and raped. In fact, her killer was already under arrest at Hornberg police station, but charged, so far, only with armed robbery. Pommerencke was transferred to Freiburg, where Police Commissioner Karl Gut, of the Freiburg Murder Squad, who was leading the investigation into the Black Forest murders, was waiting for him. He had decided to play a hunch.

He had two witnesses in the Dagmar Kilmek murder. One was a salesman who had seen a tall, gaunt, somehow furtive-looking young man with fair hair, wearing a shabby grey suit, clambering on to the small open platform at the rear end of coach 405, just as the train was leaving Freiburg station. The other was a man who, glancing out of the train window after the communication cord had been pulled, had caught a fleeting glimpse of a tall, slim figure, dressed in a baggy grey suit that made him look like a scarecrow, running back along the line towards the station. Gut played his hunch. He told Pommerencke that his baggy grey suit, just back from being forensically examined, provided irrefutable evidence linking him with Hilda Konther, Karin Wälde, and Dagmar Klimek. It was a lie: but this piece of Jesuitry did its end-justifying work. Pommerencke called for pencil and paper, and 'coughed' the lot. His trial opened at Freiburg on October 3rd, 1959. It lasted for five days. The appearance in the dock of the killer, who had been nicknamed by the press 'The Beast of the Black Forest', was that of a slender, girlish-looking young man, with bright blue eyes, and markedly Nordic colouring. He looked younger than his 23 years. He was charged with 4 murders, 12 attempted murders, 21 rapes and sexual assaults, and dozens of counts of robbery with violence, larceny, and blackmail. The charge sheet was 137 pages long. He told the Court that he had wanted to kill seven women, as seven was his lucky number. The explanation offered for his behaviour was that he suffered from an inferiority complex! Judge Friedrich Kaufmann sentenced him to eight terms of life imprisonment, plus another 156 years, with hard labour.

Prime Sources:
Contemporary newspapers and magazine translations.

Dr Edward William Pritchard

The Hypocritic Oath

MURDERER: Dr Edward William Pritchard.

VICTIMS: Jane Taylor (70): mother-in-law.
Mary Jane Pritchard (38): wife.

LOCUS: 131 Sauchiehall Street, Glasgow.

DATES: February 25th, 1865 (Taylor). March 18th, 1865 (Pritchard).

MEANS: Poisoning by a combination of antimony, aconite, and opium.

MOTIVE: Clearly to be rid of his wife. Mother-in-law had to go because she knew – or guessed – too much.

CRIMEWATCH: Pritchard the poisoner was the very type specimen of the hypocrite, the weeper of crocodile tears. He shed them copiously over the open coffin of 'Mary Jane, my own beloved wife', whom he had been mercilessly slow-poisoning through endless weeks of agony. 'No torment surrounded her bedside,' he wrote in his diary, 'but, like a calm, peaceful lamb of God, passed Minnie away.' A liar as well as a lecher. Crafty, cruel, inordinately vain. But Pritchard is an enigma. Why did he elect to poison the wife and mother-in-law who worshipped him? Was it out of pure selfish boredom? Had he grown tired of his wife? Had his wandering eye fixed upon some possible future partner who might import wealth or social distinction? We can only speculate. There is not a speck of evidence. He was not a sadist. He would not kill for killing's sake. Only for his convenience. There is small doubt that, although he was never so charged, he was responsible for the death of Elizabeth M'Gim, the young servant-girl who perished in the fire he raised in his house at 11 Berkeley Terrace, Glasgow, on May 5th-6th, 1863. He also did his despicable best to cast suspicion of the poisonings of his wife and mother-in-law on 16-year-old Mary M'Leod, his maid-servant and his mistress. Mrs Taylor and Mrs Pritchard are buried in the Grange Cemetery in Edinburgh. A very gallant gentleman, the good Doctor was none the worse for a hanging – the last public execution in Glasgow, on the Green – on July 28th, 1865.

PRIME SOURCES:
A Complete Report of the Trial of Dr E. W Pritchard, Reprinted by Special Permission, from *The Scotsman*, Carefully Revised by An Eminent Lawyer. William Kay, Edinburgh, 1865.
Notable Scottish Trial. Edited by William Roughead. William Hodge, Edinburgh, 1906.

Dorothea Puente

The Rest Home Murders

MASS MURDERER

MURDERER: Dorothea Johansson Montalvo Puente.

VICTIMS: Ruth Munroe (61), Alvaro José Rafael Gonzáles Montoya (52), Leona Carpenter (78), Dorothy Miller (65), Benjamin Fink (55), James Gallop (64), Vera Faye Martin (65), Betty Palmer (79), Everson Gillmouth (77).

LOCUS: In the garden of 1426 F Street, Sacramento, California.

DATES: 1982 – 1989.

MEANS: In all cases cause of death indeterminate, but hazarded as being either by pills or pillows – poisoning or smothering. Perhaps a preliminary drug-induced passivity, followed by asphyxiation under a smothering soft pillow.

MOTIVE: Financial gain.

CRIMEWATCH: She was a little old lady with a halo of white hair – and a black heart. She posed as a sweet, grandmotherly seventy-year-old. She was actually a 59-year-old con woman, a congenital liar, and a control freak. The fact is that since her descent from milkshake parlour waitress to prostitute and brothel keeper, Dorothea Puente had planted her feet irrevocably on the road that was to lead her to mass murder.

Her entry upon the stage of life at Redlands, California, on January 9th, 1929, had not been auspicious. Her father, Missouri-born ex-serviceman Jesse James Gray, had died when she was eight years old, and her mother, Trudy Mae Gates, had followed him into the grave within a twelvemonth. Like Wordsworth's Lucy, little Dorothea could say of herself and her siblings, 'We are seven.'

But their parents' deaths separated the children, and Dorothea Helen Gray went off, aged nine in 1938, to live with an uncle and aunt in the railroad hub city of Fresno, central California. Her first paid work had been, according to her, at the age of three, 'picking cotton, potatoes, cucumbers, and chillis.' Later, she went up in the world, literally, climbing into trees to pick fruit

When she was sixteen, she married Frederick McFaul, in Riverside, the citrus-fruit city of California. Between 1946 and 1948, she gave birth to two daughters. The first was shipped off to live with relatives, the second, Linda, was immediately put up for adoption. The couple later divorced.

In 1948, aged 19, Dorothea earned her first taste of life behind bars. She was sent to prison for a year for forging signatures on a number of stolen Social Security cheques. She married again in 1952, a burly Swede, Axel Bernt Johansson. There were miscarriages, but no offspring. The marriage survived, on paper, until 1966. Half way through the Johansson union, Dorothea was charged with being in a house of ill-repute. Her claim that she had been visiting a friend there when the deputies arrived on the scene failed. She was given 90 days in the county jail.

Later in 1966, she met and married Roberto José Puente. He was 21: she was 39. Three years saw an end to that coupling. In 1969, she tried again. The bridegroom was Pedro Angel Montalvo. They married at Reno, Nevada. After two bitter weeks, Pedro packed his bags. It was her fourth and last marriage. Thereafter, eschewing partnerships, she took exclusively to self-help, which is to say helping herself to other people's Social Security monies for her support, which, apart from another stay in jail from 1982 to 1985, was all very well – until she contracted the habit of murder.

Shortly after her release from the California

Institute for Women, in Frontera, she rented, for $600 a month, a fine blue and white, 'gingerbread' Victorian house, No.1426 F Street, in downtown Sacramento. Here, she set up a boarding-house, specialising in a curious tenantry of elderly alcoholics, displaced, dysfunctional persons, down-and-outs – life's latter-day sinners and losers. The sole irrefragable requirement was that he or she, the elected one, should be in receipt of a Social Security income, by cheque or voucher.

Sometimes, these desirable undesirables were directed to her by the referrals of blissfully ignorant, and innocent, social workers. Sometimes, she would, as predator, personally rake the skid-row bars, herself downing vodka-and-grapefruit-juices, and, after distributing alcoholic largesse broadcast, bear off her quarry to the, oft times as it proved temporary, solace of fine food, warmth, and comfort of her very special rooming-house.

Some twenty-five different professional staff, from at least ten separate public and private agencies were hoodwinked by this grandmotherly woman, and they failed lamentably to extend the safety net, to provide a measure of protection, to those vulnerable, isolated, dependent people upon whose behalf they were employed. It was the disappearance of Alvaro José Rafael Gonzáles Montoya, generally known as 'Bert', a genial 52-year-old living on Social Security at Mrs. Puente's, that finally set the alarm bells clanging. No one had clapped eyes on him for months, but his Social Security cheques, sent to the boarding-house, had been regularly signed and cashed. Worried social workers reported their tardy suspicions to the police, who consulted the oracle of their computers, which duly brought forth the wide-ranging criminal history of the lady of the house.

Mrs. Puente's neighbours, while assuredly envious of the beautiful garden which she had created in her front, back, and side yards, had for a long time been less than enthusiastic as regards the foul-smelling manure – an all-pervading odour as of a dead and decaying animal – which she seemed habitually to use. They were, moreover, puzzled by her gardening habits, for she would usually be out there,

gardening away unobserved, well before dawn, and had vanished indoors at first light, to cook her lodgers' 5 a.m. breakfasts.

On November 11th, 1988, the first well-packaged corpse was resurrected by parole agent Jim Wilson, who took a spade and cut the first turf in Dorothea's garden of graves. Between Friday morning, November 11th, and Monday afternoon, November 14th, Veterans' Day, seven bodies were resurrected from their graves below the bright flower-bed, lovingly tended lawn, gazebo, garden shed, and religious shrine, in Dorothea's well-stocked yard. All were meticulously wrapped, mummy-like, and lodged in the ground in foetal position. They were 'like large larvæ – curled up, spun into cocoons of plastic and cloth, then deposited in the dark soil.'

The coroner, Charles Simmons, was faced with the formidable task of determining with which, if any, of the twenty-five boarders known to have passed through Dorothea Puente's helping hands the seven innominate bundles of human flesh and bone could be matched.

The first body found – on November 11th – proved to be that of Leona Carpenter, a septuagenarian lodger at Mrs. Puente's rooming house who had been dead for some considerable time, but whose Social Security monies Puente was still pocketing. In the case of Dorothy Miller, another Puentean lodger, the second body, dug up on November 12th, it was a lengthy fingerprint analysis that yielded her ID.

Body No.3, also found on November 12th, was again proved by fingerprint evidence to be that of 'Bert' Montoya. Tattoos above the right knee and on the left shoulder identified Body No. 4, found on November 13th, as that of Benjamin Fink.

Also excavated on November 13th, was Body No.5, shown by X-ray evidence to have been that of James Gallop. The last two corpses to emerge from the fertile soil of Dorothea's cultivated patch of Sacramento earth, both on November 14th, were Body No.6, confirmed by X-ray to be that of Vera Faye Martin – the plates revealing evidence of the presence of a number of recorded old bone injuries which had been sustained by her in life – and Body No.7, Betty Palmer, whose head, hands, and feet were missing, never found, was a triumph of scientific identification work.

The horripilant Dorothea Puente was to be charged with two further murders, more remote in time: the death, in 1982, of her fleeced business partner, Ruth Munroe, who perished from an overdose of codeine and acetaminophen, said then to have been self-administered, and that of the man in the box. Found in this crudely knocked-up coffin on the banks of the Sacramento River, on New Year's Day, 1986, he turned out to be Everson Gillmouth, a 77-year-old gentleman who had aspired to the hand of the seductive Dorothea. He was identified by, among other things, an X-ray, revealing that the corpse in the box had lost the tip of its right thumb. So had the long vanished Everson Gillmouth. Finally brought to justice, Dorothea Johansson Montalvo Puente was sentenced, on December 10th, 1993, to prison for life, without possibility of parole.

PRIME SOURCES:
Human Harvest: The Sacramento Murder Story. Daniel J. Blackburn. Knightsbridge Publishing Company, New York, 1990.
The Bone Garden: The Sacramento Boardinghouse Murders. William P. Wood. Pocket Books, New York, 1994.
Disturbed Ground. Carla Norton. William Morrow, New York, 1994.

Richard Ramirez
The Night Prowler

SERIAL KILLER

MURDERER: Richard Leyva Ramirez.

VICTIMS: Jennie Vincow (79). Dayle Okazaki (34). Tsai-Lian Yu (30). Vincent Zazzara (64). Maxine Zazzara (44): wife. Harold Wu aka William Doi (66). Malvia Keller aka Mabel Bell (83). Patty Elaine Higgins (32). Mary Louise Cannon (75). Joyce Lucille Nelson (61). Maxson Kneiding (66). Lela Kneiding (64): wife. Chitat Assawahem aka Charnarong Khovanath (32). Ahmed Zia aka Elyas Abowath (35). Peter Pan (66) and wife, Barbara (64).

LOCI: Glassell Park, Eagle Rock, LA (Vincow). Rosemead, LA (Okazaki). North Alhambra Drive, Monterey Park, LA (Yu). Whittier, LA (Zazzara). Monterey Park, LA (Wu, Nelson). Monrovia, LA (Keller). Arcadia, LA (Higgins, Cannon). Stanley Avenue, Glendale, LA (Kneiding). Sun Valley, IA (Assawahem). Diamond Bar, San Gabriel Valley (Zia). Lake Merced, San Francisco (Pan).

DATES: June, 1984 – August, 1985.

MEANS: Shooting (Okazaki, Yu, Wu, Kneiding, Assawahem, Zia). Stabbing (Zazzara). Bludgeoning (Keller). Throat-cutting (Vincow, Higgins, Cannon). Beating to death (Nelson).

MOTIVE: Sadistic sexual satisfaction expediently linked with robbery.

CRIMEWATCH: Light-fingered Hispanic sneak thief, born in El Paso, Texas, February 28th, 1960. Thumbnail-sketched as 'a confused, angry loner who sought refuge in thievery, drugs, the dark side of rock music – and, finally murder and rape.' Self-proclaimed Satanist, living a street life of drugs and junk food, was obsessed with 'Night Prowler', recorded by mock-Satanic 'heavy metal' group AC/DC. Unlike the majority of serial killers, who target drifters, prostitutes, and alcoholics, he selected middle-class rich, or at least well-heeled, victims. He would break into random houses by night to steal, would shoot or stab men as they slept, and beat, rape, sexually abuse, and, often, murder women, regardless of age. He would also sexually abuse, but not kill, children of both sexes. Used to draw occult signs, such as pentagrams, on the victim's body or the wall above it. The extreme savagery of his attacks led to a reign of terror in LA. He gouged out one victim's eyes and took them away with him. They were never found. Identified by a smudged fingerprint lifted from a stolen car and submitted to the just newly computerised fingerprint records system. Police plastered Ramirez's picture everywhere. Recognised in Tito's Liquor Store, 819 Towne Avenue, he was chased and captured by an angry mob of LA citizens on August 31st, 1985. Tried in 1989. Sentenced to die in the gas chamber. On October 3rd, 1996, he married freelance magazine editor, Doreen Lioy. She had written some 75 letters to him. He is currently on Death Row in San Quentin State Prison, California.

PRIME SOURCE:
Night Stalker, Clifford L. Linedecker, St. Martin's Paperbacks, New York, 1991.
The Night Stalker, Philip Carlo, Kensington Books, New York, 1996.

Gary Ridgway

The Green Riverman Killer

SERIAL KILLER

MURDERER: Gary Leon Ridgway.

VICTIMS: Wendy Lee Coffield. Debra Lynn Bonner. Cynthia Jean Hinds. Opal Charmaine Mills. Marcia Faye Chapman. Gisellle Lovvorn. Terry Rene Milligan. Mary Bridget Meehan. Debra Lorraine Estes. Denise Darcel Bush. Shawnda Leea Summers. Shirley Marie Sherrill. Colleen Rene Brockman. Rebecca Marrero. Kase Ann Lee. Linda Jane Rule. Alma Ann Smith. Delores La Verne Williams. Sandra Kay Gabbert. Kimi-Kai Pitsor. Gail Lynn Mathews. Andrea M. Childers. Marie Malvar. Martina Theresa Authorlee. Cheryl Lee Wims. Yvonne Shelly Antosh. Constance Elizabeth Naon. Carrie Ann Rois. Tammy Liles. 'Rose'. Keli Kay McGinness. Kelly Marie Ware. Tina Marie Thompson. Carol Ann Christensen. April Dawn Buttram. Debora May Abernathy. Tracy Ann Winston. Maureen Sue Feeney. Mary Sue Bello. Pammy Avent. Patricia Anne Osborn. Delise Louise Plager. Kimberly Nelson. Lisa Lorraine Yates. Cindy Ann Smith. Mary Exzetta West. Patricia Michelle Barczak. Patricia Yellow Robe. Marta Reeves. Roberta Joseph Hayes. Jane Doe C-10. Jane Doe D-16. Jane Doe D-17. Jane Doe B-20.

LOCUS: Mainly in Kent County, Washington State.

DATES: 1982 – 2000.

MEANS: Generally strangulation.

MOTIVE: Sexual gratification.

CRIMEWATCH: November 5th, 2003, was a momentous date in the history of American crime. That was the day that 54-year-old Gary Ridgway put an end to a twenty-year mystery: he confessed that he was the Green River Killer, murderer of 48 women.

The victims were mostly teenage runaways and young prostitutes, many of whom had last been seen on the Pacific Highway's Sea-Tac Strip, the tacky 26-mile stretch of seamy pick-up bars, steamy diners, pay-as-you-go motels, and pay-as-you-come prostitutes, between Seattle and Tacoma.

The saga of horrendous slaughter had all started back in the summer of 1982. It was on July 15th, that two boys bicycling across the Peek Bridge, on Meeker Street, in Kent, Washington, saw below a female corpse, a 'floater' in the brackish shallows of the Green River, that had been washed up against the pilings. Identified by five tattoos on her body,

she was 16-year-old Wendy Lee Coffield, who had worked the Strip as a prostitute. She had been strangled, violently choked with her own panties.

Four weeks later, on the glorious twelfth of August, the Green River yielded up another woman's body. A slaughterman from the PD & J Meat Company, taking a meal break beside the river, about a quarter of a mile from where Wendy Coffield had been discovered, saw what turned out to be the body of Debra Bonner (22). Naked, she was held captive in a net of tree branches and logs. She was identified by her fingerprints, which were on file, her tattoos, and her dental chart. She, too, had worked the Sea-Tac Strip.

And three days after that – August 15th, 1982, – a Seattle man, Robert Ainsworth, rafting on the Green River, came face to face with two partially clothed cadavers, weighed down to the river bed with large rocks on their chests and abdomens, looking up at him with blind eyes through the shallow, hazy water. Detective Dave Reichert, summoned to the scene, suddenly slid on the slippery bank-side grass, and almost stepped on a third female corpse. The two in the river were identified as Marcia Chapman (31) and Cynthia Hinds (17). Both were 'Strippers', both had been strangled, both had had fist-sized, pyramid-shaped stones inserted into their vaginas. The girl on the bank was Opal Mills (16). She, too, had been strangled. But she was not a prostitute.

In November, 1982, came an incident which could have provided a vital breakthrough. Rebecca Quay (19), scrambled into a pick-up truck on the Strip, after its driver had shown her a 20-dollar bill and his ID. In a remote wood, he pushed her face into the earth, and tried to strangle her. She managed to break free. He drove off. Unfortunately, she did not report the incident. His name was Gary Ridgway. By the end of 1982, the Green River Killer's tally of victims had risen to 16.

A family out on a Sunday foray for mushrooms in the woods of Maple Valley, twenty miles south-east of Tacoma Airport, on May 8th, 1983, came upon a dreadful sight. A dead woman, fully clothed, a brown paper bag over her head, was half-lying, half-sitting on the ground. Her hands were folded across her stomach, and they were topped with a small pile of ground sausage meat. Two dead trout, cleaned and gutted, lay vertically along her throat, and an empty Lambrusco bottle had been placed across the lower half of her abdomen.

She had been strangled with a length of bright yellow, braided plastic rope. A small pyramidal stone had been pushed high up in her vagina. Her killer had masturbated and ejaculated over her body, providing evidence which, twenty years later, would link him to his crime. The woman was Carol Ann Christensen (22). She was not a prostitute. The single mother of a little girl of five, on May 3rd, 1983, she had landed a much-needed job as a waitress at the Barn Door Tavern, on the Strip. She had been working only a day or two at her new job when she disappeared. The carefully staged woodland scene was the handiwork of the Green River Killer.

The faceless slayer struck again and again. Over the next seven years, skeletons and bodies kept coming to light. By January, 1990, the remains of 41 women had been discovered. Notwithstanding, it was decided that the Task Force specially remitted to deal with the case should be stood down. The investigation bill had by this time totted up to some 15 million dollars. For much of the 1990s only one detective, Tom Jensen, was assigned full-time to the Green River murders. Then, early in 2001, Dave Reichert, later Sheriff of King County, was authorised to put together a team that was to include forensic scientists as well as police officers.

By September 10th, the scientists were able to tell Reichert that DNA samples recovered from Hinds and Chapman were consistent with that of Gary Ridgway, and that from Christensen proved to be an exact match. On November 30th, 2001, he was arrested. Although born in Salt Lake City, Utah, on February 18th, 1949, Ridgway had spent practically all of his life south of Seattle. His father was a bus driver, whose route was along the Sea-Taco Strip. In his childhood, Gary Ridgway had been given to the committing of impulsive petty crimes. More seriously, at the age of sixteen he had stabbed 6-year-old Jimmy Davis, laying open his liver. There were no witnesses, and he had not been charged.

He graduated from Tyee High with a grade D. After spending over a year in the Navy at San Diego, he returned home and found a job as a journeyman truck painter with a local truck company, remaining in its employ for nearly 30 years. He married three times. Two of his ex-wives testified to his aberrant sexual behaviour. He wanted intercourse several times a day, outdoors as well as in, and would often tie his partner to a stake first.

He also developed signs of religious mania, carrying and reading a Bible wherever he went, and incessantly talking about religion. Convinced that fornication and his strong stirrings of sexual lust were sinful, he visited the blame for their arousal upon the women who incited them. They were the tools of the Devil, and, as such, should be wiped out.

Prostitutes were the epitome of evil.

His sexual drive was powerful, but his performance had grown poor; like the porter in Macbeth, he had the will but no easy way to exercise it. He required preliminary fellatio to attain erection. He would then go into action at his elected victim's rear, anal intercourse providing him with the opportunity to use his crooked forearm to throttle her. If she did not obligingly die at once, he would stand on her neck. Ridgway, quickly realising that a watertight case existed against him, knew that the only way to save his life was to seek a plea bargain. He began to talk. He could not name names, but he did know where he had left each victim's body, and he made it seem that it was his pleasure to take the police to the spots in question. He said that he had killed most of the women at his home, off Military Road South. Others died in the truck, or were strangled al fresco. All were despatched soon after picking them up. Apart from a general animus against prostitutes, he could offer no motive. He made a formal confession on November 5th, 2003, in exchange for a sentence of life instead of death. It would be imprisonment without hope of parole. Meanwhile, investigations continue – to see if Ridgway can be linked to unsolved murders in other jurisdictions, where he may yet face the death penalty which he has thus far adroitly sidestepped.

PRIME SOURCES:
The Search for the Green River Killer. Carlton Smith & Tomas Guillen. The Penguin Group, U.S.A., 1991.
The Riverman. Robert D. Keppel with William J. Birnes. Constable, London, 1995.
Green River, Running Red. Ann Rule. Free Press, U.S.A., 2004.
Chasing the Devil. Sheriff David Reichert. Little, Brown, New York, 2004.

Joel Rifkin

The Prostitute Slayings

SERIAL KILLER

MURDERER: Joel David Rifkin.

VICTIMS: Unknown woman ('Susie'). Julie Blackbird. Barbara Jacobs (31). Mary Ellen De Luca (22). Yun Lee (31). Unidentified Woman. Lorraine Orvieto (28). Mary Ann Holloman (39). Unidentified Woman. Anna Lopez (33). Iris Sanchez (25). Violet O'Neill (21). Mary Katherine Williams (30). Jenny Soto (23). Leah Evens (28). Lauren Marquez (28). Tiffany Bresciani (22).

LOCI: 1492 Garden Street, East Meadow, Long Island. Manhattan. Brooklyn.

DATES: March, 1989 – June, 1993.

MEANS: Bludgeoning. Strangling. Suffocation. Burking.

MOTIVE: Sexual sadism.

CRIMEWATCH: Joel Rifkin was one of life's resentful losers. To be fair, he had ample reason for resentment; not only was he physically unattractive, but his looks and the outmoded clothes in which his parents dressed him were such as to provoke cruel bullying from his playground peers. He stuttered. He stammered. He was dyslexic. He was shy. He was lacking in self-confidence. But he was not unintelligent. He had an IQ of 128. He neither smoked nor drank. He was an inveterate loner.

Born on January 20th, 1959, he was the illegitimate child of two unwed young Jewish students, and had been adopted by Ben and Jeanne Rifkin, who raised him in 'quintessential suburbia, USA,' at No.1492 Garden Street, in the staunchly middle-class neighbourhood of East Meadow, on Long Island. The family was completed when, in 1962, the couple adopted a second child, a daughter, Jan.

At the age of 34, basically unemployed, but describing himself as a 'landscaper', he was still living at home with his widowed mother and sister. Photography and horticulture apart, he had one overriding interest – women. Unfortunately though, his sex appeal quotient was abysmally low. Consequently, he resorted to, and became positively fixated upon, prostitutes. It was an arrangement which, although not perhaps ideal, worked, albeit

somewhat expensively, reasonably well.

That is until, at the age of thirty, when he was suddenly assailed by an irresistible urge – an overwhelming desire to strangle. The blame for this morbid obsession has been attached to Alfred Hitchcock's 1972 film, *Frenzy*, Rifkin's all-time favourite, its powerful strangulation scenes never failing to turn him on.

It was one cold night in early March, 1989, that Rifkin first experienced the compulsion to kill. He picked up a strolling hooker on the streets of Lower East Side Manhattan. She was young, fair-skinned, and the name she used was Susie. That is all that we know of her.

After a swift back-seat coupling in a secluded area of Lower Manhattan, he drove her to Garden Street. His mother and sister were away. He and Susie had sex again in an upstairs bedroom. The girl was sitting smoking in the dining-room when Rifkin translated the fantasy which he had cherished for years into flesh and blood reality.

Creeping down from his bedroom, the Howitzer artillery shell which he had long ago purchased from a flea market gripped fiercely in his hand, he brought it crashing on to Susie's head, again and again and again . . . then strangled her. After that, systematically, he dismembered her; sliced off every one of her fingertips, wrenched out all but two of her teeth, tossing them in a pile on the floor. Thus did he ensure the impossibility of fingerprint or dental chart identification.

Using a box cutter, he amputated her arms and legs and cut off her head. The body parts he stuffed away in four heavy-duty, green plastic garbage bags – all neat, shipshape, ready for ultimate easy distributive disposal. Finally, he scoured the house with necessary obsessional thoroughness.

Joel Rifkin had crossed the great divide. He was a murderer. We know of sixteen further excursions which he made into the territory of serial homicide. Sixteen more women between the ages of 21 and 39 snuffed out by his psychopathy, their spoiled bodies crammed into 55-gallon steel oil drums and steamer trunks, cardboard boxes and plastic bags, and flung into rivers and dumped in the lonely places of woods and glades and rubbish tips.

It couldn't of course go on for ever. And the end came in the early hours of June 28th, 1993. At around 3 o'clock in the morning, he was cruising along the Southern State Parkway when two New York State Troopers spotted that his grey Mazda pick-up truck was lacking a back bumper licence plate; but there was a sticker there which read: 'Sticks and stones may break my bones but whips and chains excite me.'

The Mazda, ignoring the police car's warning flashings and loudspeaker hailings, sped off. There was a chase that ended when the Mazda hit a wooden light pole. Rifkin climbed out as bidden. The Troopers sniffed the air – and sniffed the decomposing corpse of Rifkin's latest victim, 22-year-old Tiffany Bresciani, packaged in blue tarpaulin in the back of his truck.

Later, at police headquarters in Farmingdale, the sandy-haired, rumpled, dishevelled and unkempt-looking man with the gold-rimmed glasses and down-drooping moustache, unburdened himself; in flat, robotic mode, confessing in detail – in inglorious Technicolor, you could say – to the perpetration of 17 horrendous homicides.

Searching his room, a place of utter chaos, brimful like a madman's den of stacks of old newspapers, dried-food-encrusted plates, soiled and unwashed items of clothing, empty soft drink cans and bottles, fragments of stale food, masses of clippings about serial killer Arthur Shawcross, a copy of Carlton Smith and Tomas Guillen's *The Search for the Green River Killer*, and crammed with trophies filched from his victims.

Rifkin attended his trial in dead man's shoes – those of his adoptive father, who had committed suicide. As the trial progressed, he became so relaxed that he actually fell asleep. His indubitable wake-up call came when, on June 8th, 1994, the judge sentenced him to 25 years to life.

PRIME SOURCES:
Garden of Graves. Maria Eftimiades. St. Martin's Press, New York, 1993.
Crossing the Line. Lisa Beth Pulitzer and Joan Swirsky. Berkley Books, New York, 1994.
The Joel Rifkin Story: From the Mouth of the Monster. Robert Mladinich. Pocket Books, New York, 2001.

Dr Buck Ruxton

Human Remains in the Devil's Beef Tub

MURDERER: Dr Buck Ruxton, originally Bukhtyar Rustomji Rantanji Hakim.

VICTIMS: Mrs. Isabella Van Ess (34) common law wife known as Mrs Isabella Ruxton and Mary Jane Rogerson (20): her maid.

LOCUS: 2 Dalton Square, Lancaster, Lancashire.

DATE: September 15th, 1935.

MEANS: Such was the fragmented state of the two bodies that certainty must be absent. Probably strangulation.

MOTIVE: Gross morbid jealousy directed towards the wife, and elimination of the maid as a witness to the killing.

CRIMEWATCH: Dr Ruxton anatomised both bodies to avoid identification and to render them conveniently portable. He drove them by car to a bridge on the Carlisle to Edinburgh road, about two miles north of Moffat. Thence, at the place called the Devil's Beef Tub, he cast them down into the ravine along which runs a stream named Gardenholme Linn. On September 29th, the remains were spotted. Weirdly, a 'Cyclops eye', probably from a lamb, was found amongst the *disjecta membra*. Ruxton, born in 1899, was hanged at Strangeways Prison, Manchester, on May 12th, 1936. The bath used by him in dismembering the bodies is now a horse-trough at Lancashire Constabulary Headquarters, Hutton, Preston.

A popular ditty at the time ran:

> *Red sails in the sunset,*
> *Red stains on the knife,*
> *Oh, Dr Buck Ruxton,*
> *You murdered your wife.*

PRIME SOURCES:

Notable British Trial. Edited by R. H. Blundell & G. Haswell Wilson. William Hodge, Edinburgh, 1937.

Medico-Legal Asperts of the Ruxton Case. John Glaister & James Couper Brash. E. & S. Livingstone, Edinburgh, 1937.

The Deadly Dr Ruxton. T. F. Potter. Carnegie Press, Preston, Lancashire, 1984.

Michael Sams

The Death-Dealing Kidnapper

MURDERER: Michael Benniman Sams.

VICTIM: Julie Anne Dart (18).

LOCUS: Workshop in Swan and Salmon Yard, Newark, Nottinghamshire.

DATE: July 10th, 1991.

MEANS: Blows to the head with a hammer and strangulation.

MOTIVE: Originally to hold for ransom. Then, to preserve his anonymity.

CRIMEWATCH: At 51 years of age, Michael Sams, although three times married, was nonetheless a bred-in-the-gland loner. His grand passion, train-spotting, was an essentially solitary occupation, and his preoccupation with the railway and all pertaining thereto, was a magnificent obsession.

Indeed, his home, Eaves Cottage, in Barrel Hill Road, in the Nottinghamshire village of Sutton-on-Trent, was in the nature of a shrine of Railroadiana, its walls covered with pictures of old engines, their salvaged name-plates, and a bristling forest of lovingly harvested railway artefacts and memorabilia. There was, too, his treasured train set, with which, for long hours, he would potter and play. A deceptive façade. In fact, this shambling, one-legged train-spotter was a most cruelly determined murderer.

On the night of July 9th, 1991, he had picked from a gaggle of prostitutes being disgorged from the White Swan, in Chapeltown, Leeds, an 18-year-old girl, Julie Dart. Actually, she was a novice member of the sisterhood. She did not, as she claimed, work as a medical laboratory assistant, neither was she, as she liked to suggest, just an arm-chancing amateur, out to make the wherewithal to pay off a hefty debt which was a heavy cloud on the otherwise happy horizon of her forthcoming marriage.

She was, in fact, an embryo prostitute, who, as bad luck would have it, happened to be in the wrong place at the wrong time. She was picked up by Sams, cruising in quest of a victim to hold to ransom. Once in his car, threatened at knife-point, she was blindfolded, and driven the

seventy-odd miles to his ramshackle workshop lair, in Swan and Salmon Yard, at Newark, Nottinghamshire.

There, she was forced to strip naked and pushed into the coffin-like wooden box, with air holes drilled in its top, which he had constructed for his victim's confinement. Measuring barely 8 feet by 5 feet, it was suffocatingly cramping, and she lay in it manacled by one ankle to a heavy chain bolted into the floor. Leaving the panicking girl there, Sams went home and clambered insouciantly into his bed. His innocent slumber was suddenly shattered by a harsh ringing. He had wired his captive's box to a burglar alarm, linked to his telephone.

He was out of bed in a flash, driving back to the workshop, where he found that Julie had smashed her way out of the box. He made up his mind there and then that she must be killed, and, later that day, without further ado, he brought two savage blows with a ball-pein hammer down upon her head, and, just to make sure, strangled her. He put her body into a plastic wheely bin for the time being, later transferring it to the boot of his car, and driving with it to Lincolnshire.

Nine days later, a farmer, Robert Skelton, found the body in one of his fields at Easton, five miles south of Grantham. The letter Sams had made Julie write to her fiancé, telling him to get in touch with the police, and the one which he himself had written to the police, demanding the payment of £140,000, or 'the hostage will never be seen again', had lost their potency.

With Julie dead, Sams' get-rich-quick scheme had failed. He looked around for another victim. He found her in the shape of Stephanie Slater, a 25-year-old Birmingham estate agent. Giving the name of Bob Southwall, he arranged to meet her on January 22nd, 1992, at one of the houses that her firm, Shipways, had for sale at 153 Turnberry Road, in the Great Barr district of Birmingham. They were inspecting the somewhat dilapidated bathroom when the client suddenly asked, 'What's that up there?' Then, as she was glancing up at the right-hand wall above the bath, in a much harsher voice he said, 'All right'. She spun round and saw that he was holding a knife or chisel pointing at her. Rapidly, he tied her wrists and put a pair of dark glasses over her eyes. He steered her gently but firmly to his car, and blindfolded and gagged, she was driven off to Newark, and captivity.

Stephanie Slater was to remain a prisoner there, in and out of the box, for eight days. The first thing he did was to rape her, and it did not take her long to realise that her only hope of staying alive was to play up to him, and, at all costs, avoid irritating him. It was a plan that succeeded well; so well that it seems more than likely that he fell in love with her. In any event, unlike Julie, she survived.

Sams had devised a very complicated series of instructions which, over a period of several days, the courier bringing the £175,000 ransom money – Kevin Watts, her manager at Shipways – had to follow. The trail ended eventually at a deserted railway bridge in the Pennines, to the west of Barnsley. Watts was instructed to put the cash on a tin tray which he would find balanced on the parapet of the bridge. Then drive off.

Below, in the darkness of the January night, shrouding the old railway cuttings, Sams , who had travelled along the disused railway line on a moped – he had left his car back at the village of Oxspring – tugged at the rope attached to the tray, and scooped up the ransom thousands that crashed down at his feet. Then it was off full speed to Oxspring, pack the moped in his car, and away home to Newark.

He arrived at Swan and Salmon Yard at 10.30 p.m. Opening her box, he told Stephanie, 'I've got the money. Here are your clothes. You're going home.' He handed her the garments, which he had washed and ironed for her. As a matter of routine he blindfolded her again, led her to his car, drove her to within a few hundred yards of her home, told her, 'I'm sorry it had to be you', and vanished into the night.

But now things were beginning to close in on Sams. The police had lifted the embargo that they had imposed on the ordeal of Stephanie Slater and the link with the murder of Julie Dart. A car sprayer who lived on the corner of the road adjacent to Stephanie's reported seeing a woman walking away from a vermilion red Mini Metro on the night of Stephanie's return.

On February 20th, the television programme 'Crimewatch' featured a tape of the kidnapper's voice. It was instantly recognised by Susan Oake, who had been Sams' first wife. By an extraordinary coincidence, she had recently spotted him driving a vermilion Metro.

On the morning of February 21st, 1992, Michael Sams was arrested. Found guilty at Nottingham Crown Court on July 8th, 1993, he was sentenced to four life terms. Mr. Justice Judge told him: 'You are an extremely dangerous and evil man. You strangled Julie to death when your kidnapping went wrong because she saw more than she should. You tried to turn her death to your advantage. You were heartless at the grief you caused. It was misplaced pride and callous arrogance.'

PRIME SOURCES:
Murder with Menaces. Rod Chayton. Headline, London, 1993.
Deadly Game. Andrew Sheldon and Chris Kiddey. Yorkshire Television, London, 1993.
Unmasking Mr Kipper. Christopher Berry-Dee. Smith Gryphon, London,1995.
Beyond Fear: My Will to Survive. Stephanie Slater with Pat Lancaster. Fourth Estate, London, 1995.

Charles Howard Schmid

The Deadly Pied Piper

MURDERER: Charles Howard Schmid.

VICTIMS: Norma Aileen Rowe (15). Gretchen Fritz (17). Wendy Fritz (13).

LOCI: Killed and buried in the Arizona desert (Rowe). Killed at Schmid's cottage in Tucson. Bodies left out in the Arizona desert (the Fritz sisters).

DATES: May 31st, 1964, (Rowe). August 16th, 1965 , (the Fritz sisters).

MEANS: Battering to death with a rock (Rowe). Strangling (the Fritz sisters).

MOTIVE: Thrill killing, admixed with jealousy in the case of Gretchen Fritz.

CRIMEWATCH: Born July 8th, 1942. Pampered adopted son of Charles and Katharine Schmid, prosperous proprietors of the Tucson, Arizona, Hillcrest, Nursing Home. Young 'Smitty' had a problem. His height. 5ft 3in. At school, he compensated by becoming a champion gymnast. Later, he became a tall-story-telling guru or Pied Piper for the bored teenagers of Tucson. At his small house opposite the nursing home, gift of his parents, he presided, Manson-like, over his drink and drug-fixed followers, and seduced the young girls. To create a macho image, he deep-tanned his face with pancake make-up, built-up a huge black mole with putty on his left cheek, stuffed his cowboy boots with tin cans and rags to give him inches, and explained his resultant awkward walk as the aftermath of a crippling fight with the Mafia. Bored with mere sex, he turned, aided and abetted by girlfriend, Mary Rae French (19), and John Saunders (18), to murder. Their victim was Aileen Rowe. Smitty killed another girlfriend, Gretchen Fritz, and her sister, Wendy, unaided, but his friend, Richard Bruns (19), helped to bury them. Bruns' nerve broke. He told the police. Schmid is serving two terms of life. Saunders got life. French, 4-5 years.

PRIME SOURCES:
The Pied Piper of Tucson. Don Moser and Jerry Cohen. New American Library, New York, 1967.
The Tucson Murders. John Gilmore. The Dial Press, New York, 1970.

Arthur Shawcross

The Genesee River Killer

SERIAL KILLER

MURDERER: Arthur John Shawcross.

VICTIMS: Jack Blake (10). Karen Hill (8). Dorothy Blackburn (27). Anna Maria Daly Steffen (27). Dorothy Keeler (59). Patricia Ives (25). Maria Welch (22). Frances Brown (22). June Stott (29). Elizabeth Gibson (29). June Cicero (34). Felicia Stephens (20). Darlene Trippi (32).

LOCI: Watertown, New York State. Rochester, New York State.

DATES: 1988 – 1989.

MEANS: Strangulation. Asphyxia. Bludgeoning.

MOTIVE: Sexual. To silence her in the case of Dorothy Keeler.

CRIMEWATCH: For nearly two years a reign of terror had held the New York State town of Rochester (population 241,000) in its grip. In the course of 22 months, the bodies of seven murdered women had been found along or near the gorge of the Genesee River, which flows through Rochester, and a further four were discovered at other places in the area.

But now, just a few days into the New Year, 1990, it looked as if the Rochester killings had come to an end. On Wednesday, January 3rd, around midday, State troopers on helicopter surveillance spotted a body lying under a bridge on the ice of Salmon Creek. And on the bridge, situated on Route 31 through Northampton Park, they saw, parked above where the body lay, a grey Chevrolet car; a man was standing beside it, apparently urinating.

As the helicopter hovered, the man got into the car and headed towards the village of Spencerport, ten miles west of Rochester. The helicopter, following him, radioed a ground patrol. They were on its tail when the Chevrolet pulled up at the Wedgewood Nursing Home. Its driver was in the kitchen with a woman named Clara Neal, who worked there. Asked to produce his driver's licence, the man admitted that he had not held one since 1970. Why not? Because he had been in prison. For what? Manslaughter. And that was when the police knew that they had finally caught their serial killer. His name was Shawcross.

Arthur John Shawcross was born on June 6th, 1945, in Portsmouth, New Hampshire. From his earliest years a loner, he was nicknamed 'Oddie' at General Brown High School, at Brownville, a village four miles north-west of Watertown, in upstate New York, where he was known as a sullen, self-contained boy, who was often seen loping around the woods near his home talking and muttering to himself.

At nineteen, he married Sarah Chatterton. She bore him a son, Michael. But the couple had sexual problems. He suffered from premature ejaculation and inability to maintain an erection. He was also put on probation twice – for burglary and for assault. After two years, Sarah divorced him, and he never saw his son again.

He then married Linda Neary, before being drafted into the army, and serving in Vietnam. He returned to the United States in September, 1968, and was soon experiencing the same sexual difficulties with his second wife. He started drinking heavily and beating her. After having a miscarriage, she left him. Shawcross went berserk, started two fires, and stole 407 dollars from a local petrol station. He was sentenced to two years, and Linda divorced him.

On his release, he got a job at the town dump, in Watertown, and married for the third time, Penny Sherbino. She became pregnant, and they moved to No.233 Cloverdale Apartments.

On the night of May 7th, 1972, a 10-year-old lad, Jack Blake, went missing. Jack's mother, Mrs. Mary Blake, was convinced that a creepy guy called Art, a keen fisherman to whom Jack sometimes sold worms, had something to do with his disappearance. Art lived up at the Cloverdale Apartments, a low-rent public housing project. Arthur Shawcross answered the policeman's knock. Yes, he had seen Jack playing that afternoon, but not since. The police believed him. They tagged Jack as a runaway.

Nearly four months later, September 2nd, 1972, a second child, Karen Hill, aged eight, disappeared. Shortly after 9.30 p.m., the police found a little girl's body wedged face down between a sewage pipe and the railings of the Pearl Street iron bridge over the Black River. It was Karen. She was naked from the waist down, and had been raped, and strangled with her own clothing. Her mouth and throat were full of soot and mud. Her corpse was half-covered with paving slabs.

When she heard of Karen's murder, Mrs. Mary Blake had no doubts as to where the police should be looking. Since Jack's vanishing, Shawcross had been caught indulging in certain questionable activities which could, or could not, be interpreted as child-molesting. Anyway, spurred by Mrs. Blake's certitude, the police brought Shawcross in, and after hours and hours of cross-questioning extracted a partial confession from him.

Meanwhile, following up a sighting by a motel keeper, the police had found the shallow grave in the woods behind the motel where Shawcross had buried Jack's body. A plea bargaining in exchange for a full confession reduced the charges of murdering Jack Blake and Karen Hill to manslaughter, and Shawcross went to prison for 25 years.

The winter of 1988 had been a bitter one in Rochester, and the snow was still on the ground that bone-nipping March day when workmen, clearing Salmon Creek, in Northampton Park, of dumped litter, hooked a silt-covered mannequin from the water. But it wasn't a mannequin. One look at the dead woman's frozen face dispelled that comfortable illusion. What they were actually looking at

were the mortal remains of 27-year-old Dorothy Blackburn, a crack and cocaine-addicted prostitute, and the mother of three.

Close on sixteen years had passed since the child murders in Watertown. Arthur Shawcross, grown fat and middle-aged, his time served, had emerged from Green Haven prison, and there was absolutely no possible reason to connect him with this unhappy find. But the plain truth is that the man who had gone to prison as a paedophile had undergone a sea-change to come out as a serial killer of women. And Dorothy Blackburn was his first known victim.

She bore the terrible tell-tale marks, variations of which were to be his insignia: there were bite marks around her vaginal area and evidence of strangulation. Shawcross, later admitting to her murder, claimed that she bit his penis during oral sex, so he bit her back and strangled her.

On September 9th, 1988, the body of another 27-year-old, cocaine-addicted prostitute, Anna Maria Steffen was found. She was pregnant, and she had been dumped in the Genesee River in a plastic garbage bag. Shawcross said that he had murdered her because she would not keep quiet when some children appeared while they were making love in a field. So he strangled her to avoid a parole violation if he had been found naked near children.

While he was in prison, his third wife, Penny, had divorced him. His fourth wife would be Rose Marie Walley, a nurse's aide who had been writing to him during his prison years. They settled into a ground-floor flat at 241 Alexander Street, Rochester. Ever a sexual philanderer, Shawcross was simultaneously carrying on an affair with Clara Neal, whose car he would frequently borrow for nefarious purposes.

Fishermen found 'a bunch of bones in clothes' on Seth Green Island, on October 21st, 1988. The head was missing. The torso was that of Dorothy Keeler, who had been a cleaner at Shawcross' apartment. He said that he had clubbed her to death after she threatened to reveal their sexual affair to Rose Marie Walley. Just six days later – October 21st – Patricia Ives, a 25-year-old prostitute drug-addict, was found by a boy searching for his baseball in waste ground behind the YMCA. A gold ring which she always wore was missing. Shawcross had made a present of it to Clara Neal, saying that it had belonged to one of his ex-wives.

By now, people were beginning to realise that they had a serial killer on the loose, and around the red light district of Lake and Lyell avenues you could almost smell fear in the air. Another prostitute, Maria Welch disappeared on November 5th. Shawcross would later say that he killed her because she stole his wallet. On November 10th, yet another body was found near the Genesee River. It was identified as that of Frances Brown, a 22-year-old heroin addict.

She was found naked from the waist down and with the words 'Kiss Off' tattooed on her buttocks. She had been asphyxiated. Shawcross said he choked her with his penis during oral sex, because she broke the gear stick on the car he had borrowed from Clara Neal.

The cadaver of June Stotts was found on Thanksgiving Day – November 30th, 1989 – wrapped in a rug near the spot where the Genesee River flows into Lake Ontario. She was lying face down, buttocks raised, right leg bent, in a posture suggestive of anal intercourse. In life she had been a feeble-minded, homeless, harmless woman, twenty-nine years of age, who slept rough, and heard voices. Shawcross' story was that she had told him she was a virgin and asked him to have sex with her. Then she had said she was going to call the police; so he strangled her. He subsequently removed a portion of her genitals, and ate it.

Four days later, December 4th, another corpse. Another prostitute. Elizabeth Gibson (29). Killed because 'she tried to scratch me'. Three more deaths to go before Shawcross was netted.

June Cicero, a 34-year-old street walker vanished from her beat. Hers was the body that the helicopter team had spotted on January 3rd, 1990. Her face was frozen to the snow. She had been obscenely posed with raised buttocks, and her genitals had been removed. Shawcross had killed her because, he said, she had called him a faggot.

On New Year's Eve, a pair of jeans belonging to another missing prostitute, Felicia Stephens, were found in Northampton Park. She was discovered on January 4th, 1990, lying among some foundation rubble at the edge of Northampton Park. It was only after Shawcross' capture and confession that the locations of the bodies of Maria Welch and Darlene Trippi were revealed, when he led the police to them.

Maria Welch lay in a shallow grave in woods near the town of Greece. Darlene Trippi, a 32-year-old prostitute missing since December 15th, had been strangled because, so said Shawcross, she had questioned his manhood. He had left her naked body at the side of a remote woodland road, near Clarkson.

When, in the summer of 1990, Shawcross came up for trial in the teak-panelled courtroom of the County Public Safety Building, Rochester, since he had already confessed, he pleaded guilty, and the issue was simply as to whether he would be adjudged sane or insane. 'Sane', said the jury, and, on February 1st, 1991, Judge Donald J. Wisner sentenced him to ten consecutive life terms – a well-earned 250 years behind bars.

PRIME SOURCES:
Murder Update. Brian Lane. Carroll & Graf, London, 1991.
Arthur Shawcross: The Genesee River Killer. Dr Joel Norris. Pinnacle Books, New York, 1992.
The Killer Next Door. Joel Norris. Arrow Books, London, 1993.

Dr Samuel Sheppard

Was it the Bushy-Haired Stranger?

MURDERER: Dr Samuel Holmes Sheppard.

VICTIM: Marilyn Reese Sheppard (31): wife.

LOCUS: 28924 Lake Road, Bay Village, Ohio.

DATE: July 4th, 1954.

MEANS: Thirty-five blows to the head.

MOTIVE: According to the Prosecution, a marital quarrel. Sheppard had not been faithful, and he admitted that Marilyn knew so.

CRIMEWATCH: According to the Accused (surgeon, aged 30), the murderer was a bushy-haired intruder, who knocked him unconscious. Sheppard did, indeed, suffer a fractured cervical vertebra and concussion. Tried in Cleveland, Ohio, he was found guilty on December 21st, 1954, of murder in the second degree. Tragedy clung to the case. One juror committed suicide; Dr Sheppard's mother shot herself; eleven days later, his father died of gastric ulcer; Marilyn's father shot himself. Celebrated trial lawyer, F. Lee Bailey, took an interest. After re-trial, Sheppard was, on November 16th, 1966, acquitted. Released, he married Ariane Tebbenjohanns, but four-and-a-half years later she divorced him, claiming extreme cruelty. He took up professional wrestling for charity, and married the 19-year-old daughter of his wrestling manager. On April 6th, 1970, he died of liver failure.

PRIME SOURCES:

The Sheppard Murder Case. Paul Holmes. Cassell, London, 1962.

Endure and Conquer. Dr Sam Sheppard. The World Publishing Company, Cleveland, Ohio, 1966.

Dr Sam: An American Tragedy. Jack Harrison Pollack. Henry Regnery Company, Chicago, 1972.

Dr Harold Shipman

The Murderous GP

MURDERER: Dr Harold Frederick Shipman.

VICTIMS: The most prolific serial killer in British criminal history. He stood trial for the murder of 15 women. Kathleen Grundy (81). Joan Melia (73). Winifred Mellor (73). Bianka Pomfret (49). Marie Quinn (67). Ivy Lomas (63). Irene Turner (67). Jean Lilley (58). Muriel Grimshaw (76). Marie West (81). Kathleen Wagstaff (81). Pamela Hillier (68). Norah Nuttall (65). Elizabeth Adams (77). Maureen Ward (57). Nobody knows for certain how many he killed.

LOCI: Todmorden, West Yorkshire. 21 Market Street, Hyde, Greater Manchester. The acts of murder also took place in a multitude of patients' private homes in both Todmorden and Hyde.

DATES: 1974 – 1998.

MEANS: Lethal injections of diamorphine.

MOTIVE: Much disputed. It was not about greed, jealousy, or revenge; all those normal motives. Psychologists talked about power and essaying to be a God-like figure. Some psychiatrists saw him as a classic necrophiliac, deriving a sexual thrill from inducing death. These are deep waters, and murky. There seems, indeed, to be no rational explanation for his conduct, but could it, one wonders, have been that his pethidine habit triggered chemicals in his brain which set up the aberration known as serial killing? Our knowledge of the chemistry of madness is scant. Some stolen items of jewellery and other articles of modest value which had belonged to deceased patients, and which would seem to have been in the nature of serial killer's 'trophies' were found at Shipman's home.

CRIMEWATCH: To the 3,100 patients on his list the diminutive Dr Harold Frederick Shipman was the beloved physician, the old-fashioned, caring family doctor, to whom nothing was too much trouble. But, unbelievably, this mild, kindly, colourless little man had been giving a vast number of the elders of his therapeutic flock the needle, the lethal needle, for nearly a quarter of a century.

Born into a humble, working-class home, at 163 Longmead Drive, Edwards Lane Council Estate, Nottingham, on January 14th, 1946, Fred, as he was always called, was the son of Frederick Harold Shipman, a lorry driver, and his wife, Vera. Studious rather than bright, overseen by his ambitious mother, Fred managed to win a scholarship to Nottingham's High Pavement Grammar School.

On June 21st, 1963, after a long and painful lingering, Vera Shipman died of lung cancer. Her 17-year-old son, keeping lengthy, after-school vigils at her bedside, had watched the doctor inject her with pain-killing morphine. Perhaps that was when he decided to become a doctor. Perhaps that was when his twin obsessions with death and morphine took root.

He was accepted into Leeds University Medical School in 1965. The following year, he met a 16-year-old trainee window-dresser, Primrose Mary Oxtoby, on a bus. To the mortification of her strict Primitive Methodist parents, she became pregnant, and Shipman married her in November, 1966. She bore him a daughter, and three sons.

Dame Janet Smith, the High Court judge who, in July, 2002, chaired the Shipman Inquiry, found that the doctor had murdered at least 215 patients while running his single-doctor practice in Hyde between 1975 and 1998, and subsequently expressed her overall conclusion that, extending the period of his active medical practise back to 1971, there was "real suspicion" that the figure was closer to 250, or could indeed, according to her own calculations, be as high as 284.

It is now believed that Shipman began his killings three years earlier than was previously thought. Dame Janet Smith's Sixth Inquiry Report suggests that in March, 1971, while Shipman was still a pre-registration junior house officer at Pontefract General Infirmary, in the West Riding of Yorkshire, Margaret Thompson, a 67-year-old stroke patient from Knottingley, was his first victim. He did not qualify until August 5th, 1971, and in the three and a half years of his residency at the hospital he is said to have been criminally responsible for between 10 and 15 deaths.

One of his early victims is likely to have been 54-year-old Thomas Collumbine, a lorry driver, who was admitted in April, 1972, with serious breathing difficulties. While gravely ill with bronchitis, he came under Shipman's care. Observing that, despite his poorly condition, he was constantly looking for cigarettes, Shipman took a dislike to him. On April 12th, when visited by his son, Collumbine seemed reasonably well. Hours later, he was dead, after being given an injection of morphine.

Shipman may also, it is thought, have been responsible for the demise of John Brewer, aged 84, and Thomas Rhodes, 71. All three deaths occurred in April and May, 1972. On October 11th, 1972, 4-year-old Susie Garfitt, a severely disabled quadraplegic suffering from cerebral palsy, was desperately ill with pneumonia. Her mother pleaded with young Dr Shipman to be kind to her little girl. Just ten minutes later, the child was dead. Dame Janet Smith concluded that there was 'a significant degree of suspicion' that Shipman had administered a lethal injection.

In 1974, he joined a group practice, the Abraham Ormerod Medical Centre, at Todmorden, in West Yorkshire. And it is there that, in March, 1975, another death is thought to have been the new doctor's handiwork It was during the time of his service as a GP at Todmorden that he became addicted to pethidine. He started having blackouts. His addiction was discovered. His resignation from the practice was demanded, and he went into The Retreat, at York, for treatment, emerging six months later to plead guilty at Halifax Magistrates' Court to charges of forging prescriptions and stealing drugs. He was fined £600.

The General Medical Council did not strike him off, and in 1977 he joined the Donneybrook House Group Practice, at Hyde. Restored to a position of medical dignity and responsibility, he seemed all set fair to make a new start. But there were those, non-medical surgery staff, who found him bad-tempered and a bully. He was a control freak and ruled his home with a rod of iron. Once, when Primrose rang the surgery to say that the family were just about to sit down to dinner, Shipman snapped: 'Nobody eats until I get there.'

He remained with the Donneybrook practice for 15 years, before deciding, in 1992, to go solo, setting up a one-man practice at 21 Market Street, Hyde. And now the killings began in earnest. Towards the end, he was averaging a murder a week. He continued targeting, in the main, lone, elderly patients, mostly women. Sometimes he would despatch his elected in the surgery; more usually he did it at the patient's own home, while a relative sat in the next room. As they held out their arms, his victims' last words are likely to have been, 'Thank you, Doctor'.

It was a combination of the acuities of a 28-year-old undertaker, Deborah Bambroffe, a town chemist, and a fellow doctor, that aroused the suspicion that was to bring about Shipman's arrest in September, 1998. That, and the fact that, after two decades of materially motiveless killing, he suddenly perpetrated a purposeful one, clumsily forging, with himself as sole beneficiary, the £385,000 will of Mrs. Kathleen Grundy, a previous mayoress of Hyde. Her daughter, Mrs. Angela Woodruff, a solicitor, called in the police. Dr Shipman's 24-year killing spree was over. His trial at Preston lasted 57 days. He was jailed for life. He consistently refused to acknowledge his guilt. In the dawn hours of January 13th, 2004, the eve of his fifty-eighth birthday, Prisoner CJ8189 took the sheet from his bed in Cell 36, D Wing, Wakefield Prison, tore it into strips, made a noosed rope of it, tied it to the window bars, stepped up on to a heating pipe some two feet above the floor, and, before jumping off, pulled the orange and green curtains around him as a precaution against anyone looking in and saving him. This bore all the symptoms of a final act of altruism, for the good doctor well knew that if he died before he turned sixty his wife would get a widow's pension and a lump sum. Harold Frederick Shipman was certified dead by the prison doctor at 8.10 a.m.

PRIME SOURCES:
Prescription For Murder. Brian Whittle and Jean Ritchie. Warner Books, London, 2000.
Addicted to Murder. Mikaela Sitford. Virgin, London, 2000.
Harold Shipman's Clinical Practice 1974 – 1988. A Review Commissioned by the Chief Medical Officer. Department of Health, Her Majesty's Stationary Office, 2001.
The Good Doctor. Wensley Clarkson. John Blake, London, 2001.
Harold Shipman: Mind Set on Murder. Carole Peters. Carlton Books, London, 2005.

Oscar Slater

The Glasgow Locked Flat Mystery

ACCUSED: Oscar Slater or Oscar Leschziner.

VICTIM: Marion Gilchrist (82).

LOCUS: 15 Queen's Terrace, 49 West Princes Street, Glasgow.

DATE: December 21st, 1908.

MEANS: Battered to death. No weapon found. Possibility suggested that the leg of a chair might have inflicted the injuries.

MOTIVE: No clear motive ever advanced. One possibility punted was that of interrupted robbery.

CRIMEWATCH: In the absence of the maid, Helen Lambie, between 7 and 7.15 p.m., someone succeeded in gaining entrance to the normally hyper-secured flat and felled the old lady. No forced entry. No robbery. Some ransacking. One small diamond crescent brooch said to be missing. Never found. Although Slater served eighteen and a half years in prison for this murder before being grudgingly released on licence in 1927, the true culprit has never been identified. A Secret Inquiry held in 1914 merely confounded the confusion and brought another, totally blameless, man, Dr Francis Charteris, under suspicion as bogus as that attaching to the Great Suspect, Slater. Strange 'evidence' provided by Glasgow detective, Lieutenant John Thomson Trench, backed up by Glasgow solicitor, David Cook, and later widely disseminated by Glasgow crusading journalist, William Park, drew Sir Arthur Conan Doyle and Edinburgh's lawyer and crime chronicler, William Roughead, into a final battle to clear Slater's name, which, with the valiant aid and oratory of the great advocate,

Craigie Aitchison, they succeeded in doing. Despite attempts, variously respectable, wildly imaginative, and downright disreputable, to name the 'real killer', the whole affair remains a complete mystery. Slater died, aged 76, on January 31st, 1948, but his cause goes marching on.

PRIME SOURCES:
Notable Scottish Trial Edited by William Roughead. William Hodge, Edinburgh, 1910. Revised editions as Notable British Trial, 1915, 1925, 1929, 1949.
The Case of Oscar Slater. Arthur Conan Doyle. Hodder & Stoughton, London, 1912.
The Truth About Oscar Slater. William Park. The Psychic Press, London, 1927.
Oscar Slater: The Great Suspect. Peter Hunt. Carroll & Nicholson, London, 1951.
Oscar Slater: The Mystery Solved. Thomas Toughill. Canongate Press, Edinburgh, 1993.
The Oscar Slater Murder Story. Richard Whittington-Egan. Neil Wilson Publishing, Glasgow, 2001.

Dr Thomas Smethurst

A Lucky Medic

ACCUSED: Dr Thomas Smethurst.

VICTIM: Isabella Bankes (43): bigamous wife.

LOCUS: 10 Alma Villas, Richmond, Surrey.

DATE: May 3rd, 1859.

MEANS: Irritant poison.

MOTIVE: Financial gain: there was a will in Dr Smethurst's favour.

CRIMEWATCH: Dr Smethurst got off. A jury did convict him, but the medical evidence was conflicting and unsatisfactory. The great forensic scientist and toxicologist, Professor Alfred Swaine Taylor, made an error when using the Reinsch test for arsenic in this case, which set his own career, and the whole of medical jurisprudence, back for years. Arsenic was found in an evacuation, but not in Isabella Bankes' body. Small quantities of antimony were found in the corpse, but various medicines had been administered. Isabella Bankes was some seven weeks pregnant, and it was argued that she had died of dysentery in pregnancy. Smethurst (aged 54) was reprieved and pardoned. Tried and convicted of bigamy, he was, even so, successful in proving Isabella's will in his favour.

PRIME SOURCES:

The Case of Thomas Smethurst, M.D. A. Newton, Routledge. Warne, & Routledge, London, 1859. *Notable British Trial.* Edited by Leonard A. Parry. William Hodge, Edinburgh, 1931.

George Joseph Smith

The Brides in the Bath Case

MASS MURDERER

MURDERER: George Joseph Smith.

VICTIMS: Beatrice Constance Annie Mundy (35). Alice Burnham(25). Margaret Elizabeth Lofty (38).

LOCI: 80 High Street, Herne Bay, Kent (Mundy). 16 Regent Road, Blackpool (Burnham). 14 Bismarck Road, Highgate Hill, London (Lofty).

DATES: July 13th, 1912 (Mundy). December 12th, 1913 (Burnham). December 18th, 1914 (Lofty).

MEANS: Drowning in bath.

MOTIVE: Financial gain from life insurance policies and wills.

CRIMEWATCH: Beside the seaside was a fine and private place for G.J. Smith to up-end his brides in the bath. Blue in the face, covered in goose-flesh, poor Bessie Mundy lay surprised, with a piece of Castile soap clutched in her hand. A large lump of hair was left behind in plumpy Alice Burnham's bath. But drowning Margaret Lofty in London was a mistake. The *News of the World* reported the tragedy, and people made connections. And at Smith's Old Bailey trial for the murder of Beatrice Mundy, similar fact evidence regarding the other two murders was allowed, by the law that such evidence may be introduced to show a course of conduct. Smith kept interrupting Mr. Justice Scrutton's summing-up. Example: 'I am not a murderer, though I may be a bit peculiar'. He had a good,Cockney, turn of phrase – 'When they're dead they're dead,' and a sharp line in sarcasm: asked by suspicious relatives to account for himself, he replied, 'My mother was a bus horse, my father a cab-driver, my sister a roughrider over the Arctic regions. My brothers were all gallant sailors on a steam-roller'. He valued women not at all. After Margaret Lofty's murder, he told his landlady that he was going on a cycling tour. As the same victim wilted, newly drowned, upstairs, he played on the harmonium in the sitting-room. No evidence that he played 'Nearer My Lord to Thee.' Born in Bethnal Green, East London, on January 11th, 1872, Smith was hanged at Maidstone Prison on August 13th, 1915.

PRIME SOURCES:
Notable British Trial. Edited by Eric R. Watson, William Hodge, Edinburgh, 1922.
George Joseph Smith. Frederick J. Lyons. Duckworth, London, 1935.
The Life and Death of a Ladykiller. Arthur La Berne. Leslie Frewin, London, 1967.

Madeleine Smith

A Lover's Cup of Cocoa

ACCUSED: Madeleine Hamilton Smith.

VICTIM: Pierre Emile L' Angelier (33).

LOCUS: 7 Blythswood Square, Glasgow.

DATE: March 23rd, 1857.

MEANS: Arsenic.

MOTIVE: Elimination of secret lover no longer desired in order to enter into a convenable marriage.

CRIMEWATCH: One of the four classic Glasgow murder cases – the others are those of Jessie M'Lachlan, Dr Pritchard, and Oscar Slater.. Mimi L'Angelier (as she styled herself in her love-letters), aged 21, had the benefit of Not Proven. There is no denying that she did pass a cup of cocoa (warming, or perhaps permanently cooling) to her importunate lover through the bars of her basement window. This was the hazarded means of administration of arsenic. L' Angelier died in agony at his lodgings, 11 Franklin Place. Madeleine Smith married twice, and died in America on April 12th, 1928, at the age of 93. Buried Mount Hope Cemetery, Westchester, New York, (Section 74, Lot 240, Grave 232), as Lena Sheehy.

PRIME SOURCES:

Report of the Trial of Madeleine Smith. Alexander Forbes Irvine. T. & T. Clark, Edinburgh, 1857

A Complete Report of the Trial of Miss Madeleine Smith. John Morison. William P. Nimmo, Edinburgh, 1857.

The Story of Mimi L'Angelier or Madeleine Hamilton Smith. Anonymous. Myles MacPhail, Edinburgh, 1857.

Notable Scottish Trial. Edited by A. Duncan Smith. William Hodge, Edinburgh, 1905.

Notable British Trial. Edited by F. Tennyson Jesse. William Hodge, Edinburgh, 1927.

The Madeleine Smith Affair. Peter Hunt. Carroll & Nicholson, London, 1950.

That Nice Miss Smith. Nigel Morland. Frederick Muller, London, 1957.

Madeleine Smith. Henry Blyth. Duckworth, London, 1975.

Richard Speck

Frenzy of Slaughter in the Nurses' Home

SERIAL KILLER

MURDERER: Richard Franklin Speck.

VICTIMS: Gloria Davy (22). Suzanne Farris (21). Merlita Garguilo(22). Mary Ann Jordan (20).Patricia Matusek (20). Valentina Pasion (23). Nina Schmale (24). Pamela Wilkening (20).

LOCUS: 2319 East 100th Street, Chicago.

DATE: July 14th, 1966.

MEANS: Strangling and stabbing.

MOTIVE: Sadistic pleasure.

CRIMEWATCH: Tattooed with the presignatory emblem, 'Born to Raise Hell', tall, gangling, pockmarked Speck, born December 6th, 1941, none too bright, obsessive-compulsive, gave a history of repeated head injuries. Electroencephalogram showed no major abnormality. Drink and drugs perhaps more significant. Claimed amnesia for his unparalleled sequence of killings. Entering, armed, a residence for nurses, ostensibly to rob, he tied up nine nurses and led each in turn to another room to slaughter them, at intervals of 20-30 minutes. One nurse only, Corazon Amurao, escaped. Only one of his victims, the last, Gloria Davy, was sexually molested. He stripped and sodomised her. She reminded Speck of his estranged wife. His defence, which was run on alibi, not on his mixed psychopathology, failed, and, on June 6th, 1969, he was sentenced to die in the electric chair. Later, his sentence was commuted to a term of 400 to 1,200 years imprisonment at the Stateville Penitentiary, Joliet. He enjoyed oil painting. On December 5th, 1991, he suffered a fatal heart attack.

PRIME SOURCES:

Born to Raise Hell. Jack Altman and Martin Ziporyn, M.D., Grove Press, New York, 1967.
The Chicago Nurse Murders. George Capozi. Banner Books, New York, 1967.
The Crime of the Century. Dennis L. Breo and William J. Martin. Bantam Books, New York, 1967.

Charles Starkweather & Caril Fugate
The Thrill Killers

MURDERER: Charles Raymond Starkweather & Caril Ann Fugate.

VICTIMS: Robert Colvert (21). Marion Bartlett (57). Velda Bartlett (*c.* 38). Betty Jean Bartlett (21/2). August Meyer (70). Robert Jensen (17). Carol King (16). C. Lauer Ward (47). Clara Ward (46). Lillian Fencl (51). Merle Collison (37).

LOCI: Superior Street, a dirt road, just outside Nebraska City limits (Colvert). 924 Belmont Avenue, Lincoln (the Bartlett family). Farm 2 miles east of Bennet, *c.* 20 miles from Lincoln (Meyer). Storm cellar of demolished schoolhouse near Meyer's farm, outside Bennet Uensen, King). 2843 24th Street, Lincoln (the Wards and Fencl). On Highway 87, between Casper and Douglas, Wyoming (Collison).

DATES: December 1st, 1957 (Colvert).January 21st, 1958 (the Bartlett family). January 27th, 1958(Meyer, Jensen, King).January 28th, 1958 (the Wards and Fencl).January 29th, 1958 (Collison).

MEANS: Shooting, battering and stabbing.

MOTIVE: Violent expression of hatred of the world, admixed with convenient acquisition of property by robbery.

CRIMEWATCH: Born – November 24th, 1938 – on the wrong side of the Lincoln, Nebraska, tracks, Starkweather resented his family's low estate. Sensitivity high, I.Q. 110, small. Bow-legged, unprepossessing, he grew up envious, embittered, and enraged. His job as a garbage-man did not help his self-esteem. Taking filmic teenage rebel, James Dean, as his model, he grabbed himself a 14-year-old girlfriend, Caril Ann Fugate. Starkweather had killed before – Robert Colvert, of the Crest Service Station, Cornhusker Highway, just north of Lincoln – for money. He killed Caril's family, the Bartletts, out of hatred. (Caril was the child of a previous marriage.) Then he and his girl went on a three-day murder spree, killing farmer August Meyer, Robert Jensen, his fiancée, Carol King, and the millionaire Ward couple and their maid, Lillian Fencl. Travelling shoe-salesman, Merle Collison, was killed for his Buick. Starkweather was arrested, after a car chase, on January 29th, 1958. He and Caril were both charged with murder. Caril, maintaining her innocence, claimed that 'Chuck' had taken her as a hostage on the murder rampage. She was sentenced to life. Paroled 1976. Starkweather died in the electric chair, Nebraska State Penitentiary, shortly after midnight, June 25th, 1959. Asked if he would donate his eyes for transplant after death, he said: 'Hell, no! No one ever did anything for me!'

PRIME SOURCES:
The Murderous Trail of Charles Starkweather. James Melvin Reinhardt. Springfield, Ohio, 1960.
Caril. Ninette Beaver. B. K. Ripley and Patrick Trese, J. B. Lippincott, Philadelphia, 1974.
Starkweather: The Story of a Mass Murderer. William Allen. Houghton Miffiin, Boston, 1976.

Peter Sutcliffe

The Yorkshire Ripper

SERIAL KILLER

MURDERER: Peter William Sutcliffe.

VICTIMS: Wilomena (Wilma) McCann (26 or 28). Emily Monica Jackson (42). Irene Richardson (28). Patricia (Tina) Atkinson (32). Jayne Michelle MacDonald (16). Jean Bernadette Jordan (21). Yvonne Ann Pearson (22). Helen Rytka (18). Vera Millward (41). Josephine Anne Whitaker (19). Barbara Leach (20). Marguerite Walls (47).Jacqueline Hill (20).

LOCI: Prince Philip Playing Fields, off Scott Hall Road, Chapeltown, Leeds (McCann). Manor Street, Leeds 7 (Jackson). Soldiers Field, Roundhay, Leeds 8 (Richardson). Flat 3, 9 Oak Avenue, Manningham, Bradford (Atkinson). Adventure Playground, between Reginald Terrace and Reginald Street, Chapeltown, Leeds (MacDonald). Land beside Southern Cemetery, Chorlton, Manchester (Jordan). Wasteland, Arthington Street, Bradford (Pearson). Garrard's timber-yard, Great Northern Street, Huddersfield (Rytka). Car park, Manchester Royal Infirmary (Millward). Savile Park, Bell Hall, Halifax (Whitaker). Ash Grove, Little Horton, Bradford (Leach). Grounds of Claremont House, New Street, Farnsley, Leeds (Walls). Alma Road, Headingley, Leeds (Hill).

DATES: October 30th, 1975 (McCann). January 20th, 1976 (Jackson). February 5th-6th, 1977 (Richardson). April 23rd, 1977 (Atkinson). June 26th, 1977 (MacDonald). October 1st, 1977 (Jordan). January 21st, 1978 (Pearson). January 31st, 1978 (Rytka). May 16th, 1978 (Millward). April 4th, 1979 (Whitaker). September 2nd, 1979 (Leach). August 21st, 1980 (Walls). November 17th, 1980 (Hill).

MEANS: Swift blows to the head usually with a hammer, often, but not always, of ball-pein type, followed sometimes by strangulation, and attended by deep, eviscerating knife-attack, or gouging with a weapon such as a sharpened screwdriver.

MOTIVE: The perverted thrill of killing and despoiling a woman. Not all were prostitutes. Actual sexual contact with the victim was not, usually, a part of the pleasure. The death at his hands was what he wanted, and the slashing at the erogenous zones.

CRIMEWATCH: Sutcliffe – born June 2nd, 1946 – was also convicted of seven similar very severe attempted murders over the five-year period: Dr Upaehya Banbara, Marcella Claxton, Maureen Long, Marilyn Moore, Anna Rogulskj, Olive Smelt, Theresa Sykes. At the trial at the Old Bailey in 1981, Mr Justice Boreham, repudiating plea bargaining, unexpectedly insisted that a jury should decide if Sutcliffe (who had confessed) was of diminished responsibility by reason of paranoid schizophrenia.

Sutcliffe appeared to the team of defence psychiatrists to have experienced a classic 'primary delusion', followed by an 'encapsulated system', when, he claimed, he heard the voice of God at the grave of one Bronislaw Zapolski. But the jury would not accept manslaughter, and Sutcliffe was put away in Parkhurst to serve life as a murderer. He might have successfully pleaded Diminished Responsibility by reason of personality disorder, but he was stuck with his 'mission' to kill.

Anyway, in March, 1984, he was moved to Broadmoor Special Hospital with some form of mental deterioration. And the sinister sender of the faked 'Geordie tapes', which so misled the police, remain at large.

By 2005, the 58-year-old serial killer had spent

24 years in 'durance vile', and was scheming to manipulate his release. He claimed that he was no longer insane or dangerous. The voices are silenced. They command no more. He has changed his name to Peter Coonan. He is blind in one eye after an attack upon him with a ballpoint pen by another inmate. But now he sees the error of his former ways. He is a keen amateur artist and plans to move to France and have a home where he could paint and, hopefully, sell his pictures. He is not, he says, reclusive, and would like to remarry.

PRIME SOURCES: ·

Deliver Us From Evil, David A. Yallop, Macdonald Futura, London, 1981.

The Yorkshire Ripper Story. John Beattie. Quartet, London, 1981.

The Yorkshire Ripper. Roger Cross. Granada, London, 1981.

'. . . somebody's husband, somebody's son'. Gordon Burn. Heinemann, London, 1984.

The Street Cleaner. Nicole Ward Jouve. Marion Boyars, London, 1986.

Wicked Beyond Belief: The Hunt for the Yorkshire Ripper. Michael Bilton. HarperCollins, London, 2003.

John Tanner

The Student Pretender

MURDERER: John Tanner.

VICTIM: Rachel McLean.

LOCUS: Student house in Argyle Street, Cowley, Oxford.

DATE: April 4th, 1991.

MEANS: Strangulation.

MOTIVE: Sexual jealousy.

CRIMEWATCH: As getting on for a million of the national television viewers watched their screens on the night of April 29th, 1991, they saw a young man and woman in black leather jackets moving purposively around the platforms, waiting and refreshment rooms of Oxford railway station. The young man was John Tanner, a 22-year-old university student. The young woman beside him was not his 19-year-old girlfriend, Rachel McLean.

She was Police Constable Helen Kay, dressed in black ski pants, leather jacket, and ankle boots, clothes identical, according to Tanner, to those that Rachel had been wearing when last seen. In this police reconstruction of the events of the night on April 15th, 1991, the W.P.C. was playing the part of the vanished girl. The object of the exercise was to jog the memory of anyone who might have seen Tanner, Rachel, and the long-haired stranger of whom Tanner spoke, at the railway station that night.

Rachel McLean, who came from Carlton, Blackpool, was in her second year, reading English at St. Hilda's College, Oxford. John Tanner, although born in England, had been brought up in New Zealand. He had gained an entrance to Wellington University, but had elected to try to get into Oxford instead. When he failed to do so, he took a place at Nottingham University, where he was reading classics.

He and Rachel had met in a nightclub in Blackpool during the summer vacation in 1990, and had fallen in love. Love laughs as heartily at distances as at locksmiths, and every weekend in term time they took it in turns to travel, either John to Oxford, or Rachel to Nottingham.

They had spent Christmas, 1990, together at Rachel's parents' house in Blackpool, but by that year's end, Rachel was no longer starry-eyed, no longer sure that she was prepared to tie herself down at so early an age. She wanted to live, have fun, go out with other men. John, however, was keener than ever on making their relationship a permanency. He sensed that she was vacillating, perhaps slipping slowly away from him, and he began to fear that he would lose her.

Their meetings started to be punctuated by arguments, misunderstandings, silences. John took a decision. On St. Valentine's Day, 1991, he asked her to marry him. Hiding her inner hesitation, she said 'yes'. But two days later, she told him that she had changed her mind; she was too young to think of settling down. There were tears, bitter words spoken. Then a patching-up. The intercity visits continued.

The Easter vacation came: Rachel spent it with her parents. Her mother drove her back to Oxford on Friday, April 12th. Rachel had the house in Argyle Street, which she shared with three other students, to herself. They had not yet returned.

On the Sunday – April 14th – John turned up. He had something important to say to her. And she had something important to say to him. They sat together on the bed in her room. He asked her again if she would marry him. She temporised at first, then ... out it came. She had been seeing other men. Had had sex with two of them.

The following day, Monday, April 15th, Rachel failed to appear to sit a scheduled examination. This was disturbing, for succeeding in getting a place at Oxford had been the realisation of a long-cherished dream, and she had thrown herself into the life of the university, academic and social, with great determination and verve. With such effect, indeed, that she had been elected vice-chairman of the Junior Common Room. Not surprisingly, therefore, her non-appearance caused some concern; and as the days passed with still no sign of the missing Rachel, concern gave way to consternation. Fears for her safety began to be entertained, and after the fifth day the college authorities telephoned the police.

John Tanner was anxious, too. He had been telephoning from Nottingham every evening asking if there was any news. A search was mounted. Gardens, garages, sheds, outbuildings, rubbish skips were inspected. The surrounding countryside was combed. Police divers scoured the underwaters of the Cherwell and the Isis. The CID was called in.

Detectives checked Rachel's room. They found it completely intact. Bed made. Clothes either hanging in wardrobes or neatly folded. Even her handbag, containing cheque book, bank card, college passes, and cash, was there. There were also a couple of unopened letters with recent Nottingham postmarks. Detective Superintendent John Bound, who had taken charge of the case, ordered the searching of the entire house in Argyle Street. It yielded no clues.

Bound decided it was time to talk to John Tanner. He said that he and Rachel were very much in love and planning to get married after university. He had last seen her on the Sunday (14th) evening. She had gone to Oxford station with him, to see him off to Nottingham. They had caught a bus from a stop near the end of Argyle Street. They were having a coffee in the station buffet, when a long-haired young man, who appeared to know Rachel, joined them. He had offered to give her a lift back to Argyle Street. When he got on the train, Rachel was still with the long-haired stranger. That was the last time that he had seen or spoken with her.

It was Bound who arranged the televised reconstruction and press conference. He had been convinced all along that Tanner was the killer. Frustrated when no witnesses came forward, on May 2nd he ordered a third search of the house. Take up the floorboards, he said.

It was there they found the body. Under the floor of a cupboard recessed beneath the stairs. She had become partially mummified by warm air coming in through the air bricks. That is why there was no give-away stench. The pathologist, Dr Iain West, found marks of strangulation. He also found that Rachel had torn a tuft of her own hair from her scalp in a desperate attempt to relieve the terrible pressure on her throat. At Christmas, Rachel's present to John had been a red silk, paisley-patterned necktie. He had worn it every day, as a belt to hitch up his jeans. It seems most likely that it was the ligature used to strangle Rachel.

Confronted, Tanner confessed. He had killed her on the Sunday, slept the night with her corpse beside him, buried her under the boards the following day, and then returned to Nottingham. Tried at Birmingham Crown Court in December, 1991, he was jailed for life.

There is a most unusual and very touching sequel. Rachel's parents, Malcolm and Joan McLean, staunch Methodists, expressed their forgiveness for their daughter's murderer. They said that they wanted to help John Tanner to come to terms with what he had done. 'We have to start on the path to forgiveness, otherwise you cannot start to rebuild your life.' 'I do not,' said Joan McLean, 'wish him any harm. We understand that it is not something that he is going to forget, and will have to live with and come to terms with. I do not see any point in a second life being destroyed. Although it is painful, there is a positive side. Every life, no matter how short, is a life completed.'

PRIME SOURCES:
The Murder Yearbook. Brian Lane. Headline, London, 1992.
Contemporary newspapers.

Arthur Thomas

Behind the Macrocarpa Screen

ACCUSED: Arthur Allan Thomas.

VICTIMS: Jeanette Crewe (30) and her husband, Harvey Crewe (30).

LOCUS: The Crewe farmhouse, Pukekawa, New Zealand.

DATE: June 17th, 1970.

MEANS: One .22 bullet in the head, in both cases. Jeanette had also received a heavy blow in the face.

MOTIVE: Unknown.

CRIMEWATCH: Still a great mystery. Who fed baby Rochelle during the five lost days before the farmhouse, behind its screen of macrocarpa trees, was discovered bloodstained and empty, except for the small survivor, marooned in her cot? The bodies of both her parents, wrapped in bedding and wire, surfaced separately in the Waikato River in the August and September of 1970. Farmer Arthur Thomas (32), a rejected suitor of Jeanette Crewe, was, in 1971, convicted of double murder, but on December 17th, 1979, he was pardoned and released, endowed with £400,000 compensation. A Royal Commission said that a cartridge case from Thomas' rifle had been put in an area of the Crewes' garden which had previously been pattern-searched and sieved, 'by the hand of one whose duty was to investigate fairly and honestly, but who fabricated this evidence to procure a conviction of murder.'

PRIME SOURCES:

Bitter Hill: Arthur Thomas, The Case For a Retrial. Terry Bell. Avant-Garde Publishing, Manurewa, New Zealand, 1972.
Beyond Reasonable Doubt. David A. Yallop. Hodder & Stoughton, Auckland, New Zealand, 1978.
The Final Chapter. Chris Birt. Penguin Books, Auckland, New Zealand, 2001.

William Herbert Wallace

The Man from the Pru'

ACCUSED: William Herbert Wallace.

VICTIM: Julia Wallace (69): wife.

LOCUS: 29 Wolverton Street, Anfield, Liverpool.

DATE: January 20th, 1931.

MEANS: Battering to death.

MOTIVE: None discernible.

CRIMEWATCH: Wallace, insurance agent for the Prudential, was summoned by a mythical client – Mr. R. M. Qualtrough - to a non-existent address – 25 Menlove Gardens East, Mossley Hill – by means of a bogus telephone message to Cottle's City Cafe, in North John Street, Liverpool, to be delivered to Wallace when he arrived to play in a chess tournament later in the evening of Monday, January 19th, 1931. The following night, returned home from a fruitless quest, Wallace found his wife brutally murdered in the parlour. He was arrested, tried, found guilty, and sentenced to death. On appeal, the jury decision was, uniquely, reversed, and Wallace was liberated. He died, aged 54, of natural causes on February 26th, 1933. It has since been revealed that the man whom Wallace himself suspected of having committed the murder was a former assistant of his in his insurance work with whom he had had trouble, and who, Wallace said, bore him a grudge, Richard Gordon Parry.

Then, in 2001, along comes James Murphy to present, in *The Murder of Julia Wallace*, an exceedingly powerful argument for the guilt of her husband, and a massive timetable of the revelatory intricacies of the killer's parleyings and Wallace's travellings. In the course of a total reinvestigation of the case, he has stood many of the previously received 'facts' upon their heads, and additionally uncovered some very persuasive factors, which would appear to militate against the innocent Wallace. To begin with: Julia was not quite what she seemed. Murphy has consulted her birth certificate, and

discovered that she was not 37, as she stated in 1914, when she married the 34-year-old Wallace. She was 53. She was born on April 28th, 1861, and was therefore actually in her seventieth year when she died in 1931. Nor was she, as she claimed, the daughter of a veterinary surgeon. Her father, William George Dennis, was a ruined Yorkshire farmer turned innkeeper of the Railway Hotel, at Romanby, on the outskirts of Northallerton, where he died of drink, aged 40, on February 19th, 1875. Julia was then approaching her 14th birthday. She had lost her mother, Anne, who died giving birth to her seventh child, a son, on April 19th, 1871, just days before Julia's 10th birthday. In Julia's fantasia, her mother, an untutored country housewife was transmogrified into Aimée, a French lady. The story of Julia's owning No. 11 St. Mary's Avenue, Harrogate was also a tale of a tub. Murphy produces witnesses who say that neither of the Wallaces was what on the surface they seemed. The apparently mild-mannered long-suffering, stoical William Herbert was described by Alfred Mather, who worked with him at the Prudential, as 'the most cool, calculating, despondent and soured man' that he had ever met; a man with an evil temper. A Mrs Wilson, who lived with the Wallaces for a period of three weeks in 1923, when she nursed Wallace through a bout of pneumonia, said that the couple's 'attitude to each other appeared to be strained . . . the feeling of sympathy and confidence usually found existing between husband and wife appeared to be entirely absent.' They were not the happy and devoted couple some people thought. Parry is also exhibited in a different light. He did, asserts Murphy, have an alibi for both the time of the telephone call to the City Café and the time of the murder. And Parry's alibi for the night of the murder did not, as has been previously suggested, depend upon the evidence of his friend Miss Lily Lloyd. His alibis were thoroughly checked and verified by the police, and tests carried out on his clothes and car proved negative. He was, therefore, rightly eliminated.

PRIME SOURCES:

The Trial of William Herbert Wallace, W. F., Wyndham-Brown, Collancz, London, 1933.

The Wallace Case, John Rowland, Carroll & Nicholson, London, 1949.

The Wallace Case, F.J. P. Veale, The Merrymeade Publishing Co. Ltd., Brighton, 1950.

The Killing of Julia Wallace, Jonathan Goodman, Harrap, London, 1969.

Murderer Scot-Free, Robert F. Hussey, David & Charles, Newton Abbot, 1972.

Wallace: The Final Verdict, Roger Wilkes, The Bodley Head, London, 1984.

The Murder of Julia Wallace, James Murphy, The Bluecoat Press, Liverpool, 2001.

Kate Webster

The Cook-General who Cooked her Mistress

MURDERER: Kate Webster.

VICTIM: Julia Martha Thomas.

LOCUS: 2 Mayfield Villas, Park Road, Richmond, Surrey.

DATE: March 2nd, 1879.

MEANS: According to legend, an attack with an axe. According to Kate Webster's confession, she threw her victim down the stairs and then choked her accidentally.

MOTIVE: Financial gain – acquisition of all her mistress' worldly goods. An element of resentment and provocation.

CRIMEWATCH: Kate, from Killane, County Wexford, aged 30, quick-tempered, quick-fingered, with 'form' as long as her sinewy arm, was a fatal choice as a cook-general. Mrs. Thomas, widowed, alone, in her fifties, was an epileptic, also quick-tempered, and a notoriously inconsiderate, carping employer. There were altercations. Kate was dismissed. But Kate stayed on. Mrs. Thomas died by her hand on returning from church, and Kate butchered her remains with a razor, a meat saw and a carving-knife. Then she boiled the pieces in the kitchen copper. The head, stowed inside a black American-cloth bag, she threw into the Thames over Hammersmith Bridge. There was a current legend that Kate hawked around Richmond two galipots of meat dripping rendered down from Mrs Thomas' boiled body. She fled to Ireland, but the villa was crammed with clues - charred bones and bloodstains. Tried at the Old Bailey in July 1879, she was convicted of wilful murder and hanged at Wandsworth Prison on July 29th, 1879.

PRIME SOURCE:
Notable British Trial. Edited by Elliot O'Donnell. William Hodge, Edinburgh, 1925.

Frederick & Rosemary West

The Sex Killers of Cromwell Street

SERIAL KILLERS

MURDERERS: Frederick and Rosemary West.

VICTIMS: Anne McFall and her unborn child. Charmaine Carol May West. Catherine 'Rena' West. Lynda Gough. Carol Ann Cooper. Lucy Partington. Thérèse Siegenthaler. Shirley Hubbard. Juanita Mott. Shirley Ann Robinson and her unborn child. Alison Chambers. Heather West. Twelve known victims, but it is believed to be likely that there were many more.

LOCI: At No. 25 Midland Road, Gloucester: Charmaine West, in the coal house under the kitchen. At No. 25 Cromwell Street: Heather West, Alison Chambers and Shirley Ann Robinson, under the patio; Thérèse Siegenthaler, Shirley Hubbard, Lucy Partington, Juanita Mott, and Carol Ann Cooper, in the cellar; Lynda Gough, under the bathroom floor. Buried in Letterbox Field and Fingerpost Field, one and a quarter miles from the village of Much Marcle and 2 miles from Kempley, in Herefordshire, Anne McFall and Catherine 'Rena' West.

DATES: 1967, Anne McFall (18) and her unborn child. 1971, Charmaine Carol May West (8). 1972, Catherine 'Rena' West (28). 1973, Lynda Gough (19). 1973, Carol Ann Cooper (15). 1973, Lucy Partington (21). 1974, Thérèse Siegenthaler (21). 1974, Shirley Hubbard (15). 1975, Juanita Mott (18). 1978, Shirley Ann Robinson (18) and her unborn child. 1979, Alison Chambers (17). 1987, Heather West (16).

MEANS: Not possible to identify in all cases, but strangulation is the most likely certainly in the case of Heather West.

MOTIVE: Mainly the gratification of sexual sadism, but in some instances the removal of inconvenient people, or of victims whose survival posed a threat.

CRIMEWATCH: It was as a result of the persistence of Detective Constable Hazel Savage that, in February, 1994, the Gloucestershire police went to an undistinguished, semi-detached, end-of-terrace house, No.25 Cromwell Street, to look into the disappearance of Heather, the 16-year-old daughter of Fred West (52), a jobbing builder, and his second wife, Rosemary (41).

Of Heather there was at first no sign. What they stumbled upon, was evidence of serial murder - ten bodies of young girls, decapitated and dismembered, dumped in the garden, under the bathroom, in the cellar, and under the patio. At least seven of the bodies bore evidence to the fact that their last moments on earth had been as objects of torture and sexual depravity.

Lynda Gough had had her head covered with stout, brown adhesive tape. To Lucy Partington's corpse were attached fragments of rope and a mask made of tape, similar to that which was found on Lynda Gough. Shirley Hubbard, a 15-year-old schoolgirl, had been made to wear a thick tape mask with a three-inch piece of tubing inserted in it for her to breathe through. She had obviously been kept trussed up but alive 'for use' over an unknown period of time.

Lucy Partington, spirited away from a bus stop in Cheltenham on the night of December 27th, 1973, was the novelist Martin Amis' cousin. In his memoir, *Experience* (Hyperion, New York, 2000), Amis states that, in a number of arrant lies, West claimed that he had had a relationship with Lucy, and that in all the books about the case this utter falsehood has never been refuted, and he wishes to set the record straight.

In common with many over-sexed and jaded men, West could only be stimulated by sadism or voyeurism. He encouraged Rosemary – not that she needed much encouragement – to work as a prostitute, entertaining black men, her favourite kind of clients, often two at the same time, while he watched through a peep-hole.

Interviewed at Gloucester Police Station, West admitted his guilt. His wife, questioned in nearby Cheltenham, was in denial. Then, on New Year's Day, 1995, in his cell at Winson Green Prison, Birmingham, he hanged himself, tying torn strips of bedding into a ligature, which he attached to an air-vent above the cell door.

Rosemary West, still in strenuous denial, was put on trial at Winchester, found guilty, and sentenced to life. In Durham Prison she was reported as dividing her time between cooking and knitting jumpers for her multitude of grandchildren.

No.25 Cromwell Street no longer exists. It was razed to the ground and flowers planted on its site in an act of communal repulsion.

PRIME SOURCES:
Fred and Rose. Howard Sounes. Warner Books, London, 1995.
Inside 25 Cromwell Street. Stephen and Mae West. Peter Grose, London, 1995.
Out of the Shadows. Anne Marie West with Virginia Hill. Simon & Schuster, London, 1995.
'She Must Have Known': The Trial of Rosemary West. Brian Masters. Doubleday, 1996.
An Evil Love: The Life of Frederick West. Geoffrey Wansell. Headline, London, 1996.
Happy Like Murderers. Gordon Burn. Faber, London, 1998.
The Corpse Garden: The Crimes of Fred and Rose West. Colin Wilson. True Crime Library, Forum Press, London, 1998.
The Lost Girl. Caroline Roberts. Metro Publishing, London, 2004.

Tracey Wigginton

The Lesbian Vampire Killer

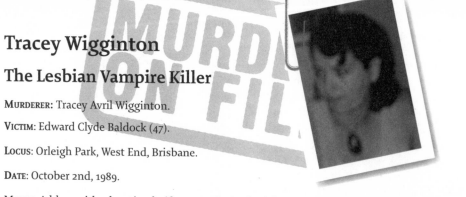

MURDERER: Tracey Avril Wigginton.

VICTIM: Edward Clyde Baldock (47).

LOCUS: Orleigh Park, West End, Brisbane.

DATE: October 2nd, 1989.

MEANS: A blow with a hunting knife across the back of the neck, nearly severing the spinal cord.

MOTIVE: Obscure. Probably some kind of group thrill killing, with occult undertones.

CRIMEWATCH: This senseless killing soon became known as the Australian Lesbian Vampire Murder. There is a ring to it, but it scarcely represents the real story. The nearly naked body was first spotted by a rower on the bank of the Brisbane River, close to a sailing club. The detective called to the scene at 6 am noted five stab wounds to the neck, in addition to the first devastating blow.

The back of the neck was hacked open, leaving a gaping wound, with heavy blood loss. Eight puncture wounds on the upper back and shoulders seemed to have been inflicted by a smaller weapon. After death, the throat had been cut. Three more strong knife blows to the hilt went into the body, and by now all the blood had been drained away. Strange streaks and finger marks in the caked blood on the neck and back looked suspiciously as if some horrible oral contact had taken place.

This time there was no necessity for an exhaustive search for some kind of serial killer, presumably a strong man. The murderer was a woman and she had left, as if purposefully, a calling card, more explicit and immediate than scientific evidence. Her Commonwealth Bank key card was tucked away in the toe of one of the victim's carefully polished shoes. His clothing was neatly stacked on the grass, lending a sexual emphasis to the carnage, as if a prostitute in mid-transaction had turned on her middle-aged, corpulent client in loathing and self-disgust.

When confronted, at her flat over a shop in Wardell Street, Enoggera, a suburb of Brisbane,

the holder of the key card was not an obvious prostitute. Tracey Wigginton, aged 24, who was plausible and soft-spoken, looked like a powerful mannish lesbian, 5ft 11in, weighing 18 stone, with very short black hair. She said that she had lost the card while in the park fooling around with two friends, Kim Jervis and Tracey Waugh.

There was a bloodstained towel in the boot of her car. At interview, she told some lies, but gave in when a fourth woman, Lisa Ptaschinski, her lover, confessed her role in the murder, and thoroughly implicated Wigginton. Cold and detached, she now submitted to a video-taped interview, giving no reason for the murder. They had picked up the man, she said, and taken him down to the sailing club. The other three had stayed in the car and she alone had enticed him down to the river bank. It had started off as a joke. 'All I wanted to do was turn him on, and just leave him. Nobody else was involved. He had his back to me. He was having a cigarette and I killed him. I stabbed him in the back of the neck and continuously stabbed him, and then I sat there and watched him die.'

And the key card? When she took off her blouse to excite Baldock, it fell out of the pocket. 'I then picked up my key card, placed it somewhere, and I cannot remember where I placed it.' There had to be psychological implications, or was it a robbery that had gone wrong? Baldock was obviously a careful individual, because he had pushed his wallet, containing $35 under the aluminium roller-doors of the yacht club.

The other three women, arrested, soon began to voice a unique defence: Tracey Wigginton, they said, had committed the murder because she needed to feed her blood-lust. She was a vampire, hated sunlight, went out mostly at night, wore dark glasses, and eschewed mirrors. Pig's blood came from the butcher's for her to drink, and she cut Lisa Ptaschinski's hand to satisfy her craving. Still she needed more blood, and that was why all four planned to take a victim at random and drain him for Tracey's pleasure. Wigginton denied all this, and just wanted to plead guilty.

The Queensland Public Defender's Office ordered a psychiatric assessment, and Dr Jim Quinn found no evidence of insanity, but came up with the unusual diagnosis of Multiple Personality Disorder. Although rejected as an entity by some psychiatrists, it is regarded as a rare dissociative state of hysteria, a neurotic rather than a psychotic manifestation. The individual has amnesia for the discordant other selves. The precipitating factor may be unbearable stress.

Dr Quinn decided to call in Dr Chris Clarke, an expert in hypnotic techniques, and 27 hours of video-taped material were obtained. 'Bobby' was the female personality who admitted to the murder, because she was 'angry'. 'Little Tracey' told how she was sexually abused. In all there were at least five personalities. Not everyone was convinced: some people thought it was a performance of clever acts.

Although there was a chance of pleading not fit to be tried, Tracey Wigginton insisted on her guilty plea, and in 1991 was sentenced to life imprisonment at Boggo Road Prison, Brisbane. It turned out that she had been brought up by her appallingly violent grandmother, and had been forced to witness outright torture inflicted on her less favoured, informally 'adopted' sister, Michelle, who was sexually abused. Tracey had cold-bloodedly wrung the neck of her own cat. It was Kim Jervis, not Tracey, who was obsessed with vampires. Tracey was, however, very involved in cult witchcraft, in satanic ceremonies.

Ron Hicks traced a strange woman living in a tin shack near the River Dee, turned lime-green by a mineral mine, who said that the grandmother, Avril Wigginton, was herself involved in black magic, and had gained absolute control over Tracey from childhood.

Ron Hicks suggests that the murder was a ritual killing, that it was Kim Jervis, armed with a second, smaller, black knife – the satanic *athame* – who was supposed to perform the sacrifice. When she chickened out, Tracey did the deed – plying first her own hunting knife and then the *athame*. The date was significant: October 21st, computed by the old Julian Calendar used by witches, is the true Halloween.

Tracey had said that she had committed other murders, and had talked about baby sacrifices. In June, 2004, she was transferred to the open custody Numinbah Correction Centre. She was eligible to apply for parole after 14 years, but did not do so. Time will tell.

PRIME SOURCES:
The Vampire Killer: A Journey into the Mind of Tracey Wigginton. Ron Hicks, Bantam Books, 1992.
Contemporary Newspapers.

Christopher Wilder

Playboy Slayer of

Beautiful Playmates

SERIAL KILLER

MURDERER: Christopher Bernard Wilder.

VICTIMS: Theresa Ferguson (21). Terry Dianne Walden (23). Suzanne Wendy Logan (21). Beth S. Dodge (33). Missing, no bodies found: Rosario Gonzales (20). Elizabeth Kenyon (23). Sheryl Bonaventure (18). Michelle Korfman (17).

LOCI: Disappeared attending Miami Grand Prix motor races (Gonzales). Disappeared from Coral Gables, Florida (Kenyon). Disappeared from shopping mall, Merritt Island, Florida. Body found near Lake Alfred, Florida. (Ferguson). Disappeared from shopping mall, Beaumont, Texas. Body found in canal on outskirts of Beaumont (Walden). Disappeared while shopping in Oklahoma City. Body found on reservoir bank outside Junction City, Kansas (Logan). Disappeared from shopping centre, Grand Junction, Colorado (Bonaventure). Disappeared from shopping mall, Las Vegas, California (Korfman). Corpse discovered in a gravel-pit outside Victor, New York (Dodge).

DATES: The dead: March 18th, 1984 (Ferguson). March 23rd, 1984 (Walden). March 25th, 1984 (Logan). April 12th, 1984 (Dodge). The missing: February 26th, 1984 (Gonzales). March 3rd, 1984 (Kenyon). March 29th, 1984 (Bonaventure). April 1st, 1984 (Korfman).

MEANS: Beating and stabbing (Ferguson, Walden, Logan). Shooting (Dodge).

MOTIVE: Rape and torture.

CRIMEWATCH: Arrived in Florida from Australia in 1970, the 39-year-old millionaire playboy soon became well known, not only as a race-car driving ace, but as one of Miami's most eligible bachelors. His wealth, earned from building contracting and invested in real estate, allowed him to indulge a taste for sleek cars, powerful speedboats, luxury homes, and stunning playmates. Not bad looking, superbly tailored, renowned animal lover, energetic, amiable, always ready with a smile, Chris seemed to have it all going for him. But he was fatally flawed. He had a hidden, and murderous, cruel streak. He liked to insert an electric prod into his victims, and glued one girl's eyelids with Superglue. His tricks had got him arrested for raping two teenage girls in Palm Springs in 1980. He had used a camera as his passport to sexual favours, claiming to be able to turn them into cover girls if they became uncover girls for him. Using the ploy, he went on a trans-American slay ride that left at least eight beautiful girls dead and missing presumed dead. Challenged, on April 13th, 1984, by two New Hampshire state troopers, near Colebrook, pushing the Canada border, he started a scuffle and a bullet from Wilder's own .357 Magnum found its way – either accidentally or suicidally, but lethally – into his heart.

PRIME SOURCE:
The Beauty Queen Killer. Bruce Gibney. Pinnacle Books, New York, 1984.

Identity Unknown

The Wimbledon Common Stabbing

MURDERER: Identity unknown

VICTIM: Rachel Nickell (23).

LOCUS: Wimbledon Common, London.

DATE: July 15th, 1992.

MEANS: Frenzied attack with a knife – 49 wounds. Throat cut first.

MOTIVE: The rage and urge to kill and mutilate of an extreme sexual deviant.

Rachel Nickell (victim)

CRIMEWATCH: The peaceful atmosphere of Wimbledon Common was ruined in that summer of 1992. Rachel had thought it was a safer place for a walk than the commons of Tooting Bec and Clapham, where she had been pestered by men. She was very attractive, like a model, blonde and slim, and full of life.

There was another side to her, though. She had been a little depressed and once said that she could not see a future for herself. Sometimes she had nightmares of being attacked by a man. The family video of her, which was repeatedly shown on television, made the investigation more poignant. She laughed and capered by a tree-trunk, carefree and secure from all harm. It was a surprise when it was revealed that 100 known sex-offenders lived within one mile of the common.

The murder took place between 10.20 and 10.35 in the morning, when 500 people were already up there for various recreational purposes. The hazy greenery of the coppicing which softened the open spaces and sandy tracks was in full splendour. It was a retired architect, Michael Murray, walking his Samoyed dog, who found the body of Rachael, under a silver birch tree which has since died. Dreadful to relate, her two-year-old son, Alex, scarcely harmed physically, was clinging to her bloodied body and his fingers had to be prised away. 'Get up Mummy. Get my Mummy,' he was saying. Their black and white puppy, too small to have helped, was still forlornly at the scene.

The killer was of the type that likes to leave a 'display': the buttocks were raised and anal penetration at time of death or shortly afterwards had taken place. A smooth instrument, perhaps the handle of the knife, had been used. Vaginal rape was not noted and no genetic material for DNA analysis *of any kind* was found at that time. The case was baffling, the investigation massive and dedicated. Thirty suspects were interrogated. Psychological profiling was becoming all the rage, and on July 28th, the police called in Paul Britton, the forensic psychologist.

He prepared an offender profile and an analysis of the killer's fantasies: he would have poor social skills and would be likely to suffer from 'some form of sexual dysfunction'. Violent pornography would be a feature. He would be single, and isolated, with solitary hobbies and interests. He would live near Wimbledon Common and know it well. He had probably not murdered before, but there was a 50 per cent probability that he had a history of sexual offences. He was very likely to kill again.

Robert Ressler of the FBI's Quantico also contributed a profile, in which he stated that 'The degree of mutilation on Rachel leads me to believe the killer suffers from some full-blown mental illness, possibly a split personality'. Paul Britton at this stage was more cautious, seeing the unknown killer as having a 'deviant-based personality disturbance.'

On September 17th, 'Crimewatch UK' presented the Rachel Nickell case and showed two videofit pictures of suspects seen by witnesses on the common. One related to a man spotted washing his hands in a stream near the murder site. More than 300 calls came in, and four people named Colin Stagg, aged 29, who lived alone in his flat at 16 Ibsley Gardens, on the Alton Estate at Roehampton, less than one mile from Wimbledon Common.

He described himself as a loner, but he was not a recluse and had some social contacts. A great animal lover, he was in and out all day taking his old dog, Brandy, up to the Common. Although he had no settled employment, he delivered newspapers and did some gardening. He was perceived on the estate as different, but he kept himself to himself and was perhaps as happy as Larry with his dog, his garden, his neat maisonette, and the sun on his back on the common. His worst problem was that he had never had a real girlfriend, and was frustrated. He had no form for sexual offending.

It is not clear if he recognised the impact on other people of the words on his front-door, 'Christians keep away, a pagan dwells here,' together with a painted image of two blue eyes. *Of course* his neighbours thought him odd. His own explanation, a little vague, and dismissive, was that the warning kept away 'bible bashers.' And indeed, the interior of the flat revealed his deeply held beliefs in the old Wicca religion, which is not violent. The police became experts on the subject. Surely though, any detective was likely to say *Eureka* on first seeing the decorated front-door and then proceeding cautiously into what could have been an archetypal Red Dragon's lair, containing a 'black room' with black walls, decorated with chalk drawings of horned gods and a 'pentagram' marked on the carpet.

There were some swords and knives and a black cloak. More Dennis Wheatley, perhaps. It is somehow symptomatic of the case that the police viewed a 'pile' of pigeon feathers as sinister, while Stagg thought them a nuisance, blown in with twigs and other detritus which he had not got round to cleaning up. There was a spot of pornography, but it was just 'girlie' magazines and, however deep they dug the garden and searched the house and examined his clothing, nothing of an incriminating nature was found.

They were looking in particular for a black bag, or a black 'bum bag' as seen by witnesses on the common, or a knife of the correct dimensions. Nonetheless, Stagg was arrested on suspicion. He said that he had been up on the common, but earlier than the relevant time, and had gone home early because he had a bad headache, and slept until the police helicopters woke him. He never, never confessed. There was a matter of indecent assault to which he decided to plead guilty on the advice of his solicitor: some days after the murder he was doing his nude sunbathing on the common and a woman passing by did not like what she saw. He absolutely denied that he had offended, but did not want the stress of a long drawn out fight. The affair obviously did him no good. After three days he was released on bail, and there began a campaign of vilification against him on the Alton Estate.

Inspector Keith Pedder decided that an undercover operation might either lead Stagg to confess, or totally eliminate him. He approached Paul Britton again, and, with the full permission of the Crown Prosecution Service, a police officer, 'Lizzie James,' was coached to form a relationship with Stagg. He seemed to have fallen for it, (although a friend doubted the genuineness of the approach and told him so), and was ever hopeful of finding sexual fulfilment at last. Frankly, that was the powerful bait. Paul Britton insisted that the operation required 'a suspect to actively climb a series of ladders whereby he either eliminates or implicates himself by his own choices.'

It now seems extraordinary, bizarre and unsavoury, *ab extra*, and with hindsight, if you wish, that 'Lizzie James' was encouraged to tell Stagg that, when younger, she had been inveigled into a witchcraft group where she had been an active accomplice in the sexual murder of a young woman. As a result, she said, she believed she could only have a satisfactory sexual relationship with a man who had had similar experiences.

To please her, Stagg invented a murder which he had committed in the New Forest. The investigators quickly found that there had been no such murder. Even so, Colin Stagg was arrested on August 17th, 1992, and his trial for the murder of Rachel Nickell began on September 5th, 1994. He had spent 13 months in custody, consumed with anxiety about his dog, Brandy.

The trial never got off the ground, because Mr Justice Ognall threw out the undercover operation and all its evidence, letters and tapes as inadmissible: it amounted to a breach of the rules against entrapment. He complained about 'an excess of zeal' and 'a blatant attempt to incriminate a suspect by positive and deceptive conduct of the grossest kind.' Thus, cut to the heart, the case was not strong enough to be proceeded with, and Stagg walked free.

In 2004/5 the press reported the most startling news. Advances in DNA techniques had led to the discovery of microscopic DNA material on Rachel Nickell's clothing. The nature of the material was not revealed. A link was found to a convicted killer, Robert Clive Napper, aged 38, detained indefinitely at Broadmoor, and it was stated that a trial was possible in the summer of 2005.

Unlike Stagg, to whom he bore a strong facial resemblance, he was described as a paranoid schizophrenic, and, again unlike Stagg, had a long history of sexual offences. The psychosis often comes on slowly and sexual offending can occur first, and later co-exist.

Robert Napper was a South East, not a South West London man, and his common was Winns Common, Plumstead. He began his crimes on August 10th, 1989, and became known as the Green Chain Rapist, from a series of footpaths, where he lurked. He grew increasingly violent, threatened with a knife, and took risks in broad daylight. His victims reported that he had difficulty in sustaining an erection. Then in July, 1992, there was the murder of Rachel Nickell.

On October 29th, 1992, Napper was convicted of firearms offences and sentenced to two months' imprisonment. A psychiatric report said that he was 'without doubt both an immediate threat to himself and the public.' Notes found in his room showed paranoid thinking.

In July, 1993, police questioned him after he was caught in Peeping Tom activities. On November 3rd, 1993, while Colin Stagg was still in custody awaiting trial, Napper perpetrated the murder of Samantha Bissett and her four-year-old daughter, Jazmine. This was an indoor attack, which gave him full rein. He had been watching her from outside, and climbed over the balcony into the ground-floor flat at 1a Heathfield Terrace, Plumstead.

Samantha resembled Rachel. He stabbed her eight times in the neck – where Rachel's first blows had silenced her – severing her spinal cord. When she was dead, he cut her open from throat to pubic bone, like an amateur anatomical specimen, just as Jack the Ripper operated unrestrained in Mary Kelly's room. Moving on to the daughter, he raped her and smothered her in her bed.

A display was left; dragging Samantha's lifeless body from the hall to the living-room, he stretched the arms above the head and raised the lower body on a large cushion. Then he rifled the kitchen for assorted cloths and wrapped them around what he had done, before bearing away with him a portion of the abdominal wall.

Not too long afterwards, in May, 1994, he was caught by fingerprint evidence. His prints were already on file and matched some found on a bedpost and the balcony. It turned out that he had been questioned as a suspect for the Green Chain Rapes in August, 1992 – one month after Rachel Nickell's murder – but at 6ft 2in he was 'too tall,' had no convictions for sexual offences, and volunteered to take a DNA test. He failed to turn up twice, but was not a strong suspect, and slipped through the net.

The similarity between the Nickell case and the Bissett case was noted at the beginning of the Bissett investigation, but was not proceeded with. At the Old Bailey, on October 9th, 1995, Robert Napper pleaded not guilty to the murder of Samantha and Jazmine Bissett, but guilty of manslaughter on the grounds of diminished responsibility. Paranoid schizophrenia was by now confidently diagnosed, and when the police wanted to interview Napper in Broadmoor about the Nickell case he was pronounced too disturbed.

So the matter rested until the summer of 2002, the 10th anniversary of Rachel's death, when Scotland Yard launched a review leading to the DNA breakthrough. If there are lies, damn lies, and statistics, then we should consider the proposition that the probability of two young men, look-alikes, one with murder in his heart, being on Wimbledon Common on the same day, is (to use a Paul Britton phrase) vanishingly small.

PRIME SOURCES:

Killer on the Loose. Mike Fielder. Blake, 1994.

The Last Thursday in July. Andre Hanscombe. Century Books, 1996.

The Jigsaw Man. Paul Britton. Bantam Press, 1997.

Who Really Killed Rachel. Colin Stagg. David Kessler, Aspire Publishing, 1999.

Picking Up The Pieces. Paul Britton. Bantam Press, 2000.

The Murder of Rachel Nickell. Mike Fielder. Blake, 2000.

The Rachel Files. Keith Pedder. John Blake, 2001.

Contemporary newspapers.

Wayne Williams

The Atlanta Child Murders

MURDERER: Wayne Bertram Williams. Convicted of two murders.

VICTIMS: Jimmy Ray Payne (21). Nathaniel Cater (27).

LOCUS: Atlanta, Georgia.

DATES: Between April 22nd and April 27th, 1981 (Payne). *c.* May 21st, 1981 (Cater).

MEANS: Probably asphyxia.

MOTIVE: Presumably sexual gratification.

CRIMEWATCH: Young Blacks kept disappearing in Atlanta. They were mostly male. There were whispers of Ku Klux Klan. In the early hours of May 22nd, 1981, a police recruit in a patrol car on a bridge over the Chattahoochee River heard a splash. Williams, 23, black, an aspiring music entrepreneur, was stopped in his car on the bridge. On May 24th, the body of Nathaniel Cater was found, nude, in the Chattahoochee. At the trial, in 1982, at the Fulton County Courthouse, Williams was tried for only two murders, but evidence relating to ten others was permitted to show 'pattern'. The evidence was circumstantial. There were fibres. The unusually closely-argued Dettlinger/Prugh book made the case disputatious. The fact that the killings ceased on Williams' arrest had been thought to be powerfully evidential, but the Dettlinger study attacks the sanctity of the official list of 28 murders (plus one added by the Prosecution) and names other victims before and after. Williams was sentenced to two consecutive life sentences.

PRIME SOURCES:
The List. Chet Dettlinger with Jeff Prugh. Philmay Enterprises, Atlanta, 1983.
Evidence of Things Not Seen. James Baldwin. Michael Joseph, London, 1986.

Randall Woodfield

The I-5 Highway Killer

Serial Killer

MURDERER: Randall Brent Woodfield.

VICTIMS: Conviction secured only in the one case of Shari Hull (20). Donna Lee Eckard (37) and her daughter, Janell Jarvis (14). Julie Ann Reitz (18).

LOCI: Trans-America Title Building, River Road, Salem, Oregon (Hull). Holiday Road, Mountain Gate, California (Eckard and Jarvis). S. W. Cherryhill Drive, Beaverton, Oregon (Reitz).

DATES: January 18th, 1981 (Hull). February 3rd, 1981 (Eckard and Jarvis). February 15th, 1981 (Reitz).

MEANS: .32 calibre bullets to the brain (Hull, Eckard, Jarvis). .38 bullet to the brain (Reitz).

MOTIVE: Polymorphous sexual activity, preferably oral, with sodomy.

CRIMEWATCH: Randy Woodfield, the Interstate Highway 5 killer, born December 26th, 1950, star athlete, drafted for the famous Green Bay Packers football team, was also a chronic indecent exposer, or 'flasher'. Apparently, he had felt jealous of his two elder sisters. On one occasion, although he had seemed to be an achiever, his I.Q. tested out as only 100. He had plenty of sexual experience, and herpes, which he passed on to several of his victims. Like Bundy, he favoured a Volkswagen. He often used a .32 silver revolver. As disguise, he stuck Band-Aid over his nose. Up and down the I-5 highway through California, Oregon, and Washington he cruised, raping and robbing, inevitably escalating to random killing. His great mistake was that Julie Reitz was someone he knew. There was strong identification evidence against him, particularly from Beth Wilmot, whom he had left for dead, shot beside Shari Hull. There was very strong ballistics evidence, including one rare .32 bullet found in Woodfield's racquetball bag where he lodged at 3622 South E Street, Springfield, Oregon. He was suspected of a number of other unsolved murders. Put away for life plus 125 years in the Oregon State Penitentiary, some of his cases still lying on the books, untried.

PRIME SOURCE:
The I-5 Killer. Andy Stack (Ann Rule). Signet Books, New York, 1984.

Aileen Wuornos

The Pistol Packing Hooker

MURDERER: Aileen Carol (Lee) Wuornos.

VICTIMS: Richard Mallory (51). David Spears (43). Peter Siems (65). Troy Burress (50). Charles Richard (Dick) Humphreys (56). Charles Carskaddon (41). Walter Gino Antonio (60).

Loci: Florida Highways and By-ways.

DATES: December 1989 – July 1990.

MEANS: High Standard 'Double Nine' – nine-shot .22 calibre revolver, loaded with hollowpoint bullets.

MOTIVE: Lesbian prostitute's revenge on men. Alcoholic rage in a grossly disordered personality. Some kind of repetitive, even cumulative, mental pleasure in elimination of her prey. Substantial gain in making off with men's personal possessions, cars and stashes of cash.

CRIMEWATCH: They called her the world's first female serial killer, but she was not. Any satisfaction came from lust for killing, not from sexual gratification – rather the reverse. Aileen Wuornos, born in Rochester, Michigan, on 29th February, 1956, was a blonde, 'thirty dollar hooker' plying her fleshly wares along the dangerous open highways of central Florida, got up as an ordinary hitchhiker.

She carried a gun for self-protection in case things turned nasty, and favoured middle-aged men, less likely, she reasoned, to turn on her. At home, waiting for her, was her sturdy lesbian lover, Tyria Moore (27), not implicated in the crimes although she did come to some knowledge after the act.

What was the trigger that, after fifteen hellish years, made her suddenly shoot and batter Richard Mallory, who had taken her into his Cadillac? Self-defence against the threat of violent rape, sodomy and even murder, Wuornos herself claimed. Christopher Berry Dee tells us that Mallory had an appalling sexual history, and had served an almost-eleven-year term in Maryland State Mental Institution for attempted rape. This did not come out at the trial. If that had been an isolated incident, perhaps so,

but seven deadly threats against her within the space of half a year pushes belief. There is no reason to suspect premeditation the first time.

Certainly there was a very strong element of gain; she did not scruple to bear away all available pickings, not trophies, from the scene of the crime, usually thus separating the car from the sometimes naked body. She overkilled the men with her full quiver of bullets, finding that one bullet to the body did not kill outright the targets who kept moving on their feet, as if it were a horror film. 'Old fat sonofabitches,' she called them, with a prostitute's loathing. At one time, she had been married to a man fifty years her senior.

We have to believe that, once she had made that first attack – and she was always of a violent disposition, the recipient of abuse and deprivation from a very early age – all her anger, cosmic, some might say, precipitated her, when drunk, into repeat performances which gave her some mental as well as material satisfaction. They said she had a 'border-line personality disorder.'

Her heredity was poor: her father, Leo Pittman, whom she never knew, was sentenced to life imprisonment in 1965 for raping a 7-year-old girl in Kansas, but hanged himself in his cell. Her mother abandoned Aileen and her brother when she was four, and her maternal grandparents, Lauri and Britta Wuornos, brought her up. Wuornos is a Finnish name. It was all a failure.

This was a hot case in America. Women's rights were involved, and there was a perception that the tables had been turned. The execution of a woman was controversial. Aileen was captured by means of composite sketches built up by a forensic artist from good eye-witness descriptions. With Tyria Moore in the passenger seat, she drove too fast and crashed the Pontiac which she had appropriated after killing Peter Siems. People rushed up to help, but of course, the pair of women left the scene as soon as they could, knowing they had been seen in broad daylight. Shown on television, the sketches led to Aileen's arrest on 9th January, 1991, at 'The Last Resort' biker bar, at Port Orange.

Aileen confessed to six killings, always claiming self-defence. At her trial, she was indicted only for the first murder, of Richard Mallory, but the other cases were allowed under the rules of Similar Fact evidence, known in Florida as the Williams Rules. She was sentenced to death by unanimous recommendation of the jury to the judge, and spent 10 years on Florida's Death Row.

Finally, on 9th October, 2002, she was executed by lethal injection. Film footage, near the end, of her strange expressions, rolling eyes, labile mood, and perplexed mien suggested that an insane women might well have been put to death. Her last words were curious: 'I'd just like to say I'm sailing with the Rock and I'll be back like Independence Day with Jesus, June 6, like the movie, big mothership and all. I'll be back.'

PRIME SOURCES:
Damsel Of Death. Sue Russell. True Crime, Virgin Publishing, 1992.
Monster: My True Story. Aileen Wuornos with Christopher Berry Dee. Blake, 2004.

Graham Young

The Thallium Poisoner

Mass Murderer

Murderer: Graham Frederick Young.

Victims: Molly Young (38): stepmother. Bob Egle (59). Fred Biggs (60).

Loci: 768 North Circular Road, Neasden, West London (Young).Hadland's Photographic Instrument Firm, Bovingdon, Hertfordshire (Egle,Biggs).

Dates: April 21st, 1962 (Young). July 7th, 1971 (Egle). November 19th, 1971 (Biggs).

Means: Poisoning with thallium.

Motive: Lust for secret power.

Crimewatch: Born September 7th, 1947, at Neasden. Mother died when he was three months old. Giving the impression of being a neat, clean, well-behaved, intelligent boy, he was actually obsessed with Hitler, Nazism, black magic, poisons, and death. Slow-poisoned his stepmother, Molly Young (38), with antimony and thallium, and attempted to poison his father, Frederick Young (44), sister, Winifred (21), and schoolfriend, Chris Williams (13). Committed to Broadmoor July, 1962. Released February 4th, 1971, on the recommendation of Dr Edgar Udwin. Before leaving told nurse: 'I'm going to kill one person for every year I've spent in this place.' Sent to Government Training Centre at Slough. Poisoned – but not fatally – fellow-trainee storekeeper, Trevor Sparkes (34). May 10th, 1971, secured job as storekeeper at John Hadland Ltd., Bovingdon. Shortly after Young's arrival, a spate of mysterious illnesses broke out. They blamed the 'Bovingdon Bug'.

Storeroom manager, Bob Egle, died. So did Fred Biggs, in charge of stocks and distribution. David Tilson, Jethro Batt (39), Ron Hewitt (41), Peter Buck, and Diane Smart (39) were taken ill with varying degrees of severity after drinking tea or coffee provided by Young. Suspicion came to centre on Young. His background was investigated. On November 21st, 1971, he was arrested. In his pocket was a lethal dose of thallium. Tried at St. Albans in July, 1972, he told the warders that if convicted he would break his own neck on the dock rail. He died in Parkhurst Prison after a heart attack on August 1st, 1990, aged 42.

Prime Sources:

Obsessive Poisoner. Winifred Young. Robert Hale, London, 1973.

The St. Albans Poisoner. Anthony Holden. Hodder & Stoughton, London, 1974.

Index

A6 Killer, The	91
Aberdeen Sack Murder, The	62
Acid Bath Murderer, The	89
Adams, Dr John Bodkin	1
Agra Double Murder, The	74
Allitt, Beverley	3
Armstrong, Major Herbert Rowse	5
Arran Murder, The	114
Atlanta Child Murders, The	204
Australia's Last Woman to Hang	117
Avenger, The	94
Babes in the Wood Mystery, The	17
Backpacker Murders, The	134
Bamber, Jeremy	6
Barber, Susan	8
Barfield, Velma	10
Bartlett, Adelaide	11
Battlecrease House Poison Mystery, The	131
Beast of the Black Forest, The	157
Behind the Macrocarpa Screen	191
Berdella, Robert	12
Berkowitz, David	13
Bianchi, Kenneth & Buono, Angelo	14
Bible John	15
Bishop, Russell	17
Bittaker, Lawrence	19
Black Dahlia Murder, The	20
Black Pad Murderer, The	155
Black Panther, The	142
Black, Robert	21
Bluebeard of Holmes Castle, The	140
Body Parts from the Sky	95
Bogle-Chandler Murders, The	24
Borden, Lizzie	25
Borough Poisoner, The	40
Boston Strangler, The	58
Bradfield, William & Smith, Dr Jay	26
Brady, Ian & Hindley, Myra	27
Bravo Mystery, The	29
Brides in the Bath Case, The	183
Bristolian Lady-Killer, The	35
Brudos, Jerome Henry	30
Bundy, Ted	31
Burke, William & Hare, William	32
Bywaters, Frederick & Thompson, Edith	33
California Torture Duo, The	113
Camb, James	34
Campus Killer, The	31
Cannan, John	35
Cardiff Corpse in a Carpet, The	41
Carraher, Patrick	37
Case of Necrophilia, A	30
Case of the Murdered Rose-Grower, The	79
Chamberlain, Lindy	38
Chantrelle, Eugène Marie	39
Chapman, George	40
Charlton, Alan & Ali, Idris	41
Chikatilo, Andrei	43
Child-Eater of Wisteria Cottage, The	70
Christie, John Reginald Halliday	45
Clark, Douglas	46
Cleveland Butcher, The	47
Co-ed Killer, The	108
Cook-General who Cooked her Mistress	194
Copolino, Dr Carl	48
Corll, Dean	49
Corona, Juan	50
Corpses in Cannock Chase, The	138
Cottingham, Richard	51
Cotton, Mary Ann	52
Cream, Dr Thomas Neill	53
Crippen, Dr Hawley Harvey	54
Dahmer, Jeffrey	55
de Stempel, Baroness Susan	59
Deadly Doctor, The	48
Deadly Pied Piper, The	173
Death Comes to Heath House	59
Death-Dealing Kidnapper, The	171
Deathly Photographer, The	84
DeSalvo, Albert	58
Dingo Baby Case, The	38
Dominant Dominie, The	39
Donald, Jeannie	62
Dougal, Samuel Herbert	63
Downs, Diane	64
Dr X	104
Duffy, John	65
Durrant, Theodore	67
Düsseldorf Monster, The	112
East End Icon Gangsters, The	110
Edinburgh Body Snatchers, The	32
Ellis, Ruth	68
Fahmy, Marie Marguerite	69
Fall River Axe Murders, The	25

Family Man, The	129	Killer by Numbers	19
Fatal Doses of Curare	104	Killer Clown, The	75
Feil	76	Killing Caretaker, The	96
Fiendish Housemaids of Le Mans, The	152	Killing of Janie Shepherd, The	115
Fish, Albert	70	Kray, Ronald and Reginald	110
Flynn, Billy	71	Kürten, Peter	112
Fox, Sidney	73	Lady of the Lake, The	153
Frenzy of Slaughter in the Nurses' Home	185	Lake, Leonard & Ng, Charles	113
Fullam, Augusta & Clark, Henry	74	Lashley, David	114
Gacy, John Wayne	75	Last British Woman to Hang, The	68
Gallego, Gerald Armond	76	Laurie, John	116
Gardiner, William	77	Lee, Jean	117
Gein, Theodore	78	Lesbian Vampire Killer, The	197
Genesee River Killer, The	174	Lethal Candy Man, The	49
George, Andrew	79	Lethal Psychopathy	128
George, Barry	81	Light, Ronald	120
Girl in the Belfry Murder, The	67	Lonely Necrophile, The	145
Glasgow Locked Flat Mystery, The	181	Long, Bobby Joe	121
Glatman, Harvey	84	Lover's Cup of Cocoa, A	184
Glover, John	85	Lucan, Lord	122
Granny Killer, The	85	Lucas, Henry Lee	124
Green Bicycle Case, The	120	Lucky Medic, A	182
Green Riverman Killer, The	165	Lupo, Michele de Marco	125
Guilty or Not Guilty?	127	M'Lachlan, Jessie	137
Haigh, John George	89	MacDonald, Dr Jeffrey	127
Hall, Archibald	90	Mackay, Patrick	128
Hammersmith Nudes Murders, The	103	Madman with a Machete	50
Hanratty, James	91	Main Line Murders, The	26
Hay Poisoner, The	5	Man from the 'Pru, The	192
Heath, Neville	92	Manson, Charles	129
Heidnik, Gary	93	Manuel, Peter	130
Hillside Stranglers, The	14	Margate Matricide, The	73
Homan, Elbert	94	Matricide and Uxorcide	132
Horror at Hilldrop Crescent, The	54	Maybrick, Florence Elizabeth	131
Human Flesh Eater of Milwaukee, The	55	Merciless Angel, A	10
Human Gorilla, The	143	Merret, John Donald	132
Human Remains in the Devil's Beef Tub	170	Merrifield, Louisa	133
Hume, Donald	95	Milat, Ivan	134
Huntley, Ian	96	Moat Farm Murder, The	63
Hypocritic Oath, The	160	Monster Butler, The	90
I-5 Highway Killer, The	205	Monster of Florence, The	146
Ireland, Colin	99	Moors Murders, The	27
Jack the Ripper	102	Morris, Raymond	138
Jack the Stripper	103	Mudgett, Herman Webster	140
Jascalevich, Dr Mario	104	Mullin, Herbert William	141
Jill Dando Murder, The	81	Münchausen's Killer Nurse, The	3
Jones, Arthur Albert	105	Murder for Pleasure	130
Kearney, Patrick	107	Murder for the Teacher, A	71
Kemper, Edmund	108	Murder Most Aristocratic	122
Kent, Constance	109	Neilson, Donald	142

Nelson, Earle	143	Sex Maniac Murders, The	121
New York Hotel Murders, The	51	Sex Slave Cellar of Horror, The	93
Night Prowler, The	164	Sex Slave Murders, The	76
Nilsen, Dennis	145	Shawcross, Arthur	174
Original of Hitchcock's Psycho, The	78	Sheppard, Dr Samuel	177
Pacciani, Pietro	146	Shipman, Dr Harold	178
Pageant Beauty Queen Murderer	149	Slater, Oscar	181
Papin, Christine & Léa	152	Smethurst, Dr Thomas	182
Paraquat Poison Pie, The	8	Smith, George Joseph	183
Park, Gordon	153	Smith, Madeleine	184
Passing Easer, The	1	Son of Sam	13
Peasenhall Murder, The	77	Speck, Richard	185
Pimlico Mystery, The	11	Stabber from the Gorbals, The	37
Pink Pills for Pale Prostitutes	53	Stabbing of Percy Thompson, The	33
Pistol Packin' Momma	64	Starkweather, Charles & Fugate, Caril	186
Pistol Packing Hooker, The	206	Strangler Wore Silk, The	125
Pitchfork, Colin	155	Strangling of Little Brenda Nash, The	105
Playboy Slayer of Beautiful Playmates	199	Student Pretender, The	189
Pommerencke, Heinrich	157	Sunset Slayer, The	46
Porthole Murder, The	34	Sutcliffe, Peter	187
Pritchard, Dr Edward William	160	Tanner, John	189
Prostitute Slayings, The	168	Texas Multicide, The	124
Puente, Dorothea	161	Thallium Poisoner, The	208
Railway Rape Murders, The	65	Thomas, Arthur	191
Ramirez, Richard	164	Thrill Killers, The	186
Rampaging Child Killer, The	21	Torture Man of Bob's Bizarre, The	12
Rat Poison in a Blackpool Bungalow	133	Trash Bag Murders, The	107
Rest Home Murders, The	161	Voices Said 'Kill', The	141
Ridgway, Gary	165	Wallace, William Herbert	193
Rifkin, Joel	168	Was it the Bushy-Haired Stranger?	177
Rillington Place Strangler, The	45	Webster, Kate	194
Road Hill House Murderess, The	109	West Auckland Bogey-Woman, The	52
Russian Ripper, The	43	West, Frederick & Rosemary	195
Ruxton, Dr Buck	170	White House Farm Massacre, The	6
Sadist of Notting Hill, The	92	Wigginton, Tracey	197
Sams, Michael	171	Wilder, Christoper Bernard	199
Sandyford Mystery, The	137	Williams, Wayne	204
Savoy Hotel Murder, The	69	Wimbledon Common Stabbing, The	200
Schmid, Charles Howard	173	Woodfield, Randall	205
Self-Made Serial Killer, The	99	Wuornos, Aileen	206
Severin Klowsowski	40	Yorkshire Ripper, The	187
Sex Killers of Cornwell Street, The	195	Young, Graham	208